# REBUILDING AMERICA

A PRESCRIPTION
FOR CREATING
STRONG FAMILIES,
BUILDING THE WEALTH
OF WORKING PEOPLE,
AND ENDING WELFARE

## JOHN KENNETH BLACKWELL
and **JEROME R. CORSI**

WND BOOKS
AN IMPRINT OF CUMBERLAND HOUSE PUBLISHING, INC.
NASHVILLE, TENNESSEE

REBUILDING AMERICA
A WND BOOK
PUBLISHED BY CUMBERLAND HOUSE PUBLISHING, INC.
431 Harding Industrial Drive
Nashville, Tennessee 37211

Cover design by Gore Studio, Nashville, Tennessee

**Library of Congress Cataloging-in-Publication Data**

Blackwell, John Kenneth, 1948–
    Rebuilding America : a prescription for creating strong families, building the wealth
  of working people and ending welfare / John Kenneth Blackwell and Jerome R. Corsi.
        p.  cm.
    Includes bibliographical references and index.
    ISBN-13: 978-1-58182-501-5 (hardcover : alk. paper)
    ISBN-10: 1-58182-501-3 (hardcover : alk. paper)
1. Public welfare—United States.  2. Family policy—United States.  3. Urban policy—
United States.  I. Corsi, Jerome R.  II. Title.
HV95.B587  2006
362.973—dc22

                                                                      2006007542

Printed in the United States of America

1 2 3 4 5 6 7 8 9 10—10 09 08 07 06

To my wife, Rosa, and my children,
Kimberly, Rashshann, and Kristin,
for their unconditional love and inspiration.
And to our parents,
Dana and George Blackwell
and Bernice and Robert Smith,
for their Christian witness, their commitment to family,
and their powerful example of the American work ethic.
*John Kenneth Blackwell*

For my sister, Joan Marie Tischler,
who has brought keen insight and great joy into our lives
*Jerome R. Corsi*

# CONTENTS

# PREFACE

OHIO SECRETARY OF STATE Ken Blackwell is running as a Republican candidate for governor of Ohio in the 2006 election. Ken is a native of Ohio, born in the projects of Cincinnati to a father who was a meat-packer and raised in a family where he was read the Bible every night. Jesuit-educated, Ken attended Xavier University where he received bachelor of science and master of education degrees and was a football star. His history of distinguished public service includes terms as mayor of Cincinnati, as an undersecretary at the U.S. Department of Housing and Urban Development, and as U.S. ambassador to the United Nations Human Rights Commission. In 1994 he became the first African American elected to a statewide executive office in Ohio when he was elected treasurer of the state. His international activities have taken him to fifty-three countries and strengthened his understanding of emerging international markets and the growth of democracy worldwide. Blackwell has held the nation's highest security clearance, and he has twice received the U.S. Department of State's superior honor award from the administrations of Presidents George H. W. Bush and Bill Clinton for his work in the field of human rights.

Jerome Corsi, also a native of Ohio, was born in East Cleveland. Like his coauthor, Jerry Corsi also has a Jesuit education, having graduated from St. Ignatius High School in Cleveland. While he was an undergraduate at Case Western Reserve University in Cleveland, Corsi coauthored with political science professor Louis H. Masotti a report entitled *Shoot-Out in Cleveland,* about a gun battle that raged in Glenville between black militants and police on July 23, 1968.[1] The report, known as the Masotti Report, became a task force report to the Eisenhower Commission, formally known as the National Commission on the Causes and Prevention of Violence. While getting his Ph.D. at Harvard, Corsi continued to study racial violence and political violence under the direction of Drs. John Spiegel and Ralph Lewis at the Lemberg Center for the Study of Violence at Brandeis University.

In 2004 Corsi coauthored with John O'Neill *Unfit for Command: Swift Boat Veterans Speak Out Against John Kerry.*[2] Shortly after the 2004 election, Blackwell and Corsi met, discussed their mutual roots in Ohio, and decided to work together. This book reflects the interest both Ken Blackwell and Jerry Corsi have to applying conservative solutions to America's continuing social and economic problems. Both are very committed to racial justice and equality in America. This book reflects a concrete plan that Blackwell intends to implement should the voters of Ohio honor him with election in 2006 to be Ohio's next governor.

Together, we believe America has the opportunity to advance into an era where poverty is dramatically reduced, possibly even eliminated, and where our inner cities are revitalized as economically rewarding places to do business as well as productive places to own homes and raise families. We share common values in the importance of families and the education of our children as necessary commitments we must all make to secure the bright future we know America can have in the years to come.

# REBUILDING AMERICA

# PART 1

## The Problem

# 1

## Lives Lost to Poverty

Welfare reform must also, whenever possible, encourage the commitments of family. Not every child has two devoted parents at home—I understand that. And not every marriage can, or should be saved. But the evidence shows that strong marriages are good for children.

—President George W. Bush, April 30, 2002

POVERTY IN AMERICA DOES not lend itself to a quick fix. The poor are poor not because they have fallen on hard times or are experiencing an unexpected run of bad luck. The poor in America, particularly after the successes and failures of Lyndon Johnson's Great Society programs, are poor because they are chronically poor. A poverty culture reinforces itself: racial minorities who are poor live in depressed areas that attract precious little productive economic activity. Men abandon pregnant women; single-parent mothers who are saddled with child-care responsibilities find it hard, if not impossible, to find work that is sufficiently rewarding economically. Children who are born into these disadvantaged circumstances suffer inadequate education, which in turn leaves them ill equipped to pursue competitive employment opportunities. This pattern of poverty in America has perpetuated itself over four decades despite the best efforts of the Great Society and the War on Poverty. Chronic poverty has been resistant to change because the welfare state does not attack the fundamental cause of poverty. The legacy

15

of the welfare system is a dependency upon the state from which these poor do not emerge. Yet even today the political Left still refuses to accept the fundamental dynamics of poverty in America, dynamics that have not changed for forty years. People with minimal work skills who live in areas that are economically depressed are more likely to be poor. And that likelihood is increased if the person was raised in a single-parent household headed by an unwed woman.

America and the world were shocked by the images after Hurricane Katrina struck New Orleans in August 2005. The severe economic plight of the African Americans living in the depressed areas around the Crescent City was never before seen by so many middle-class Americans. In the United States and around the world, millions gasped in horror while watching on television these predominately African American poor people who lived in what amounted to run-down homes and shanties. Viewers were shocked that many of these black poor had no automobiles, that virtually all of these people were desperately poor and lacked the resources to subsist during a crisis, let alone a storm of this magnitude. To poverty experts watching the disaster, this was not news. The African American poor in New Orleans are typical of the poor who live in urban ghettos throughout America as well as in concentrated counties of rural poverty. Major areas of America have virtually been abandoned to minority poverty.

President Bush was blamed for not responding quickly enough to the victims of Hurricane Katrina; he was accused of racism and his administration was perceived as indifferent to the plight of these storm-oppressed poor people. The truth is that every administration since Lyndon B. Johnson first launched the War on Poverty forty years ago has known that these conditions continue to exist in America. No administration has been able to solve the problem, despite the wide variety of government programs that have thrown trillions of dollars into the effort. The Bush administration actually had increased the financial resources thrown at the problem by the welfare system with no better results than have been achieved by any previous administration since 1965.

Four factors continue to define poverty in America. First, the majority of the poor in the United States are African American, Hispanic, or Native Indian. Second, poverty in America concentrates in urban ghettos and certain economically depressed rural counties. Third, poverty tends to result from a chronic complex of social and economic factors from which people have a hard time escaping, not from temporary conditions such as the loss of a job or separation from a spouse. Fourth, poverty in America is defined by the tragedy of illegitimate births to unwed mothers.

No other single factor explains or defines poverty in America as well as this: single families headed by unmarried women are a national economic disaster from which few emerge. The authors of this book maintain that poverty in America is a problem government itself will never be able to solve, no matter how often we change the poverty program rules, no matter how large or well trained a bureaucracy we create, no matter how many trillions of dollars we throw at the problem. Until we realize this, concentrations of minority poverty will continue to coexist in a majority America that is characterized by middle-class affluence and substantial economic opportunity.

## YESTERDAY'S DARK GHETTO AND
## TODAY'S BLACK URBAN UNDERCLASS

In 1965 African American psychologist Kenneth B. Clark published an important study entitled *Dark Ghetto*.[1] Clark's work brought to national attention the degree to which African Americans had become concentrated in urban ghettos. He documented census tract areas that were 90 percent or more African American in major cities, including Baltimore, Chicago, Cleveland, Los Angeles, New Orleans, New York, St. Louis, and Washington DC. In every instance, the black ghetto was established where whites had lived before; whites had moved out as African Americans moved in. The black ghetto was characterized by "congestion, deterioration, dirt, and ugliness."[2] The economic condition of the dark ghetto was defined by poverty, the psychological dimension by despair:

> The symptoms of lower-class society afflict the dark ghettos of America—low aspiration, poor education, family instability, illegitimacy, unemployment, crime, drug addiction and alcoholism,

17

frequent illness and early death. But because Negroes begin with the primary affliction of inferior racial status, the burdens of despair and hatred are more pervasive. Even initiative usually goes unrewarded as relatively few Negroes succeed in moving beyond menial jobs, and those who do find racial discrimination everywhere they go.[3]

The ghetto, as Clark described it, is in physical disrepair and filthy with neglect; stores are closed and houses are left vacant. Store walls are "unpainted, windows are unwashed, service is poor, supplies are meager." The ghetto lacks for museums, churches, even schools that can deal with the daily reality of poverty and despair. The streets are filled with idle people, everywhere "there are signs of fantasy, decay, abandonment, and defeat."[4]

As a social psychologist, Clark understood that the inadequate and deteriorating housing in the ghetto, the lack of adequate health services, and the availability of only menial jobs resulted in a social pathology that produced "dependency, disease, and crime."[5] This depressed condition led to unemployment, despair, and family instability. Clark found, for instance, that only about half the children under age eighteen living in Harlem were living with both parents, a statistic that has since deteriorated in black communities throughout the nation. He noted, "The child without a secure family life is often forced either into aggression and delinquency or into apathy and despair."[6] African Americans in the ghetto who managed to get education and good jobs, as a result of economic successes since the 1960s, tended to advance to the middle class beyond the ghetto, a flight from center-city poverty that only served to intensify the plight of those left behind. Clark typified the dark ghetto as a "chronic, self-perpetuating pathology."

Not only is the pathology of the ghetto self-perpetuating, but one kind of pathology breeds another. The child born into the ghetto is more likely to come into a world of broken homes and illegitimacy; and this family and social instability is conducive to delinquency, drug addiction, and criminal violence. Neither instability nor crime can be controlled by police vigilance or by reliance on the alleged deterring forces of legal punishment, for the individual crimes are to be understood more as symptoms of the contagious sickness of the community itself than as the result of inherent criminal or deliberate viciousness.[7]

Ghetto schools were separate and unequal, deteriorating institutions that "have lost faith in the ability of their students to learn" as the ghetto itself "has lost faith in the ability of the schools to lead."[8] Qualified teachers quickly left ghettos for better opportunities elsewhere; ghetto students suffered from overcrowded classrooms, inadequate facilities, and substandard instruction. Second-class education was a sure formula to be "a chief contributor to the perpetuation of the 'social dynamite' which is the cumulative pathology of the ghetto."[9]

In the forty years since Kenneth Clark published *Dark Ghetto,* the United States has gone from a population of just under 180 million people to just under 294 million. Still, black ghettos remain within our major cities. Over the last four decades we have experienced significant "white flight" from our major cities. Theodore White in his classic *Making of the President 1960* observed the postwar expansion of our cities into the newly developed suburbs being occupied by new families of returning soldiers who were giving birth to the "baby boom."[10] The construction of the interstate highway system that began during the Eisenhower administration made accessible areas adjacent to major metropolitan areas that were in the early 1950s considered far away from the central business district. Inner-belt highway bands built in concentric rings around major downtown areas further expanded the reach of the city. What in the 1950s would have been a distant hour's drive through rural and city streets to reach downtown could be driven in fifteen or twenty minutes by the end of the 1990s, simply by traveling along a network of interlocking limited-access highways. As the 1960s were beginning, America's major cities were actually losing population as whites began the process of abandoning the cities to the urban poor minorities.

Racial developments over the last forty years contributed to white flight from major metropolitan areas. The riots in the 1960s burned out major sections of cities across America; many burned-out homes and businesses were boarded up and abandoned instead of being rebuilt. Lower-middle-class ethnic neighborhoods that in the 1950s were predominately white became the new expansion areas as blacks were displaced from riot zones and forced to find new residential areas. Court decisions that mandated busing to desegregate inner-city schools caused more whites to abandon the cities for the suburbs. As new towns emerged outside the original 1950s ring of suburbs, major cities began developing multiple business districts, generally to the detriment of the original downtown central business districts that, by comparison, were decaying and in need of rebuilding. Today, many downtowns are depressed, sometimes nearly abandoned, lower-class problem zones inhabited primarily by minorities. Cities that are shells of their former selves bear little resemblance to their 1950s appeal as hubs of business activity.

Kenneth Clark in 1965 identified eleven major cities with two hundred thousand or more African American residents (see Table 1 on the page 21). He argued: "In every one of these cities, Negroes are compelled to live in concentrated ghettos where there must be a continuous struggle to prevent decadence from winning over the remaining islands of middle-class society."[11] Looking at these same cities today, we can see that all except one have experienced increases in the percentage of African American residents since 1965.

Even here, the numbers are deceptive. Many of these cities today have to be examined as major metropolitan areas that include several cities within their definition. Cleveland, for instance, includes East Cleveland, which is 94 percent African American, adding another nearly 20,000 African Americans to the total African American population living in the Cleveland metropolitan area. The racial pattern of Cleveland remains basically the same as it was in the 1950s. The Cuyahoga River divides the Cleveland metropolitan area, with the East Side remaining predominately African American and the West Side remaining predominately white. The black population of Cleveland has spread beyond the 1950s confines of Hough. After the Hough riots in 1965, the black population moved into Glenville. After the Glenville riots in 1968, the migration of the black population into East Cleveland picked up speed. Cleveland's population in 1960 was 876,050, ranked as the eighth largest

| | % AFRICAN AMERICAN IN 1960 | % AFRICAN AMERICAN IN 2000 | % CHANGE |
|---|---|---|---|
| **CITIES WITH 200,000 OR MORE AFRICAN AMERICANS IN 1960** | | | |
| Washington DC | 53.9% | 60.0% | 11.3% |
| New Orleans, LA | 37.2% | 67.3% | 80.9% |
| Baltimore, MD | 34.7% | 64.3% | 85.3% |
| Detroit, MI | 28.9% | 81.6% | 182.4% |
| Cleveland, OH | 28.6% | 41.5% | 45.1% |
| St. Louis, MO | 28.6% | 51.2% | 79.0% |
| Philadelphia, PA | 26.4% | 43.2% | 63.6% |
| Chicago, IL | 22.9% | 36.8% | 60.7% |
| Houston, TX | 22.9% | 25.3% | 10.5% |
| New York, NY | 14.0% | 26.6% | 90.0% |
| Los Angeles, CA | 13.5% | 11.2% | -17.0% |
| **SAMPLE CITIES, 1960** | | | |
| Kansas City, MO | 17.5% | 31.2% | 78.3% |
| Pittsburgh, PA | 16.7% | 27.1% | 62.3% |
| Boston, MA | 9.1% | 25.3% | 178.0% |
| Rochester, NY | 7.4% | 38.5% | 420.3% |
| Minneapolis, MN | 2.4% | 18.0% | 650.0% |

**TABLE 1**[12]

city in the United States; in 2004 the population of Cleveland had fallen to 458,684 and its rank to thirty-sixth.[13]

A similar story can be told for Detroit and Wayne County. In 1960 Detroit was the fifth largest city in the United States, with a population of 1,670,144; in 2004 Detroit was ranked as the seventh largest city, with a population reduced to 900,198 residents. Wayne County is plagued with some 12,000 abandoned homes despite an aggressive program to bring litigation against deadbeat property owners and to demolish abandoned properties. For the past twenty-five years, Detroit has leveled some 2,000 abandoned properties annually without solving a problem that is defined as "a source of blight and neighborhood shame," with vacant houses serving only to attract crime and discourage business development.[14] Detroit has never recovered from the riots that burned much of the city in 1967. As is clear from the preceding table, Detroit has moved to an extreme point where more than 80 percent of its population is now African American. The pattern we saw in

Cleveland has also played out in Detroit—over the past forty years, the more affluent whites have moved farther and farther away from the original downtown, driving on limited-access highways to multiple business hubs in adjoining newly developed, more-distant suburbs, and abandoning the city's inner core to poorer African Americans. The dark ghetto that in 1960 constituted less that 30 percent of Detroit's population has expanded to the point where Detroit itself has become a dark ghetto distinguished by depressed economic activity, vacant lots, and abandoned properties.

Boston, Chicago, and New York are exceptions to this pattern in that these cities have each developed upscale apartment and condominium complexes in their original central business districts. These high-priced properties attract young white singles and older, more-affluent white couples who want to enjoy the dining, entertainment, and sports still vibrant in these cities. For the last forty years most central business districts have been abandoned in the evenings and on the weekends as white employees and business executives leave the downtown corporate headquarter offices and drive to their outlying white residences. Boston, Chicago, and New York all still retain active downtown public transit systems and a network of taxicabs that make moving about the city relatively easy and safe at night and during weekends. The cities have maintained an active downtown lifestyle enjoyed by an upscale white crowd. Other cities, such as Philadelphia and Pittsburgh, have tried to replicate the pattern, but with much less success.

Los Angeles remains a sprawling connection of towns with multiple foci, including Beverly Hills, Burbank, and Hollywood, to name just a few. The segregation that remains in LA is more evident when we examine the complex of census tracts and towns that remain 90 percent African American, areas that include Compton, Inglewood, Ladera Heights, Valley Park–Windsor Hills, and Willowbrook. The black ghettos of Houston and New Orleans demonstrate that the problem is a problem of metropolitan areas, not simply a problem of Northern cities. The percentage of African Americans concentrated in Baltimore and Washington DC make it clear that even the white bureaucrats and elected government officials who have been so supportive of poverty programs over the past four decades still ride the Metro and get in their cars to commute home to predominately white suburbs, not just the traditional close-in suburbs of Bethesda and Chevy Chase, but to the more distant suburbs of Silver Spring and Falls Church.

For the past forty years, social scientists have been documenting the same harsh reality detailed by Kenneth Clark as discussion of the "dark ghetto" has transformed into the discussion of the "ghetto underclass." University of North Carolina sociologist John Kasarda's summary of the situation shows little fundamental change in the situation of urban blacks despite forty years of massive changes in our society, in our economy, and in our metropolitan areas. Kasarda's insight was succinct:

> Major U.S. cities have transformed industrially from centers of goods processing to centers of information processing. Concurrently, the demand for poorly educated labor has declined markedly and the demand for labor with higher education has increased substantially. Urban blacks have been caught in this change. Despite improvements in their overall educational attainment, a great majority still have very little schooling and therefore have been unable to gain significant access to new urban growth industries. Underclass blacks, with exceptionally high rates of school drop-out, are especially handicapped. Whereas jobs requiring only limited education have been rapidly increasing in the suburbs, poorly educated blacks remain residentially constrained in inner-city housing. Within underclass neighborhoods, few households have private vehicles, which are shown to be increasingly necessary for employment in dispersing metropolitan economies.[15]

If we map poverty numbers onto black ghetto numbers, the pattern becomes immediately obvious. Poverty in our major cities remains largely a black ghetto phenomenon. That fundamental reality has remained unchanged since Kenneth Clark wrote *Dark Ghetto*.

Gunnar Myrdal, author of the 1944 classic *The American Dilemma*, wrote the foreword to *Dark Ghetto*. In that foreword, Myrdal expressed his hope that Johnson's Great Society programs would solve the problem of African American segregation in depressed urban areas:

> Obliterating in America the Negro ghetto and all other pockets of subhuman existence, involving even more non-Negroes than Negroes, is a necessary condition for President Johnson's Great Society. As long as they are permitted to exist, they constitute a drag on American prosperity generally. Even leaving aside the moral issue of justice and the more perfect realization of the American ideals of liberty and equality of opportunity, and speaking in cold financial terms, eradicating the rural and urban slums and giving the youth there an education for productive employment are the most profitable investments that can be made in America today.[16]

Kenneth Clark himself shared Myrdal's optimism that the Great Society would succeed, even if all that drove white society to the task was a form of enlightened self-interest. He wrote, "The great tragedy—but possibly the great salvation, too—of the Negro and white in America is that neither one can be free of the other."[17] Yet what enthusiasts of the War on Poverty had underestimated was how intractable the problem of African American poverty is. Sociologists, psychologists, political scientists, and lawyers have written hundreds of volumes on the problem over the last forty years. Nearly all have persisted in the generally unchallenged assumption that a redefinition of laws, well-designed government programs, and the good-hearted spending of trillions of dollars would in some combination be the formula required to accomplish the task.

What we are saying here is that now is the time to abandon that approach. No redefinition of laws, no matter how equitable; no government program, regardless of how brilliantly it can be designed; and no expenditure of funds, even if we spend trillions more, will ever solve the problem of black poverty in America. Forty years ago Kenneth Clark was writing brilliantly about the "dark ghetto," and today we still have with us the segregated black urban underclass. Nothing has fundamentally changed for the black poor in the ghettos; if anything, the problem is more entrenched and more difficult to solve. This is a hard conclusion that many will find impossible to embrace. Still, four decades of trying is enough time to declare the elimination of poverty by the welfare state a complete failure.

## RURAL POVERTY REMAINS GEOGRAPHICALLY CONCENTRATED

RURAL POVERTY is concentrated geographically, with minorities suffering disproportionately from the economic hardship.

African American rural poverty is concentrated in some 210 counties that stretch across the southern states of Alabama, Arkansas, Florida, Georgia, Louisiana, and Mississippi, reaching as far north as North Carolina, South Carolina, and Virginia, and as far west as Texas. Some five million African Americans live in these counties that are characterized as the old plantation belt of the southern Coastal Plain, especially from southern North Carolina through Louisiana. Approximately 39 percent of the African Americans living in these rural southern counties are poor, which is well above the percentage of blacks in metropolitan areas that are poor (approximately 24 percent).

Again, this poverty is characterized by female-headed families with children but no husband. Black single-mother families in rural areas have a poverty incidence of 42 percent, compared nationwide with only 10 percent for all other households with minor children. In looking at the data, the Economic Research Service of the U.S. Department of Agriculture stated unequivocally: "It is difficult for female-headed families to attain adequate income, unless they receive child support, given the lower average wages of women and the lack of other wage earners in such a family." Black high-poverty counties also face the additional disadvantage of having a high percentage of households without a motor vehicle (12.5 percent). And this limited access "can inhibit access to employment and essential services in rural and small-town communities that have little or no transportation."[18]

The second tier of poverty also has a racial characteristic. Some seventy-four Hispanic high-poverty rural counties are concentrated in the Southwest, especially Texas and New Mexico. The pattern suggests that Mexican immigrants are entering the country with minimal job skills, little education, and virtually no English skills. These newly arrived immigrants may settle in New Mexico or Texas when they first arrive, but their ultimate goal may be to join families scattered throughout the country. And the pattern holds that those Hispanics who settle in New Mexico and Texas appear to improve their economic condition over time.

A third belt of racially identified rural poverty is associated with Native Americans. The high-poverty counties occupied by Native Americans fall into a geographical pattern that reflects tribal settlements and reservations. A total of forty rural high-poverty counties inhabited by Native Americans include the Four Corners area of Arizona, Colorado, New Mexico, and Utah, as well as the northern states of Montana, North Dakota, and South Dakota, plus a few isolated counties in Oklahoma. A stretch of these high-poverty counties in Alaska is occupied by Alaskan Natives. The high-poverty rural counties occupied by Native Americans not only have a higher incidence of poverty, they also have an unusually high incidence of deep poverty. One out of five Native Americans in these forty high-poverty rural counties live in households with incomes below 75 percent of the poverty line.

White areas of rural poverty are concentrated in the backwater rural areas that have been occupied for generations by non-Hispanic white poor, an area that is broadly described as the Southern Highlands. Most of ninety-one high-poverty counties occupied by poor non-Hispanic whites are found in the Allegheny and Cumberland Plateau country of Kentucky and West Virginia, with a few scattered counties found west of the Mississippi River, in the Ozark Plateau and the Ouachita Mountains. The states involved in these pockets of highly concentrated white rural poverty are Arkansas, Kentucky, West Virginia, and to a lesser extent Missouri, Oklahoma, Tennessee, and Virginia. The Southern Highlands high-poverty counties are characterized by a topology that offers limited potential for commercial farming. Few urban centers have developed in the Southern Highlands, and the area is characterized by lagging education, with the overall employment picture plagued by a boom-and-bust pattern typical of the area's logging and mining industries. The Southern Highlands continue to have a high ratio of high-school dropouts, and many of the young people who advance in education leave the area to pursue greater opportunities for economic achievement elsewhere.

These rural concentrations of poverty reflect old patterns that are hard to break. The black high-poverty rural counties lie in the southern belt that recalls plantation estates that were followed by share-crop farming. The Hispanic high-poverty areas of the West clearly reflect the huge wave of immigration, legal and illegal, coming through Mexico. The Native American concentrations of rural poverty remind us that Indian reservations were economically depressed from virtually the first days they were opened. The white poverty concentrations in the back-country rural mountains of the East call to mind images of Appalachian poverty that we first saw in the Farm Security Administration photographs of the Great Depression era.

These pockets of rural poverty have been resilient to change over decades and generations, reminding us once again that poverty, at its core, perhaps even more than an economic problem, is a social problem involving family structure and the education of children. We will have to wait another decade or so to see if the pattern of Hispanic rural poverty in the Southwest is a passing phenomenon as new immigrants and their children gain English-language skills and assimilate into the population, or whether the problem is of a more permanent nature.

Only twenty-seven high-poverty counties lie outside these classifications. In other words, about 95 percent of all rural high-poverty counties are defined by a disproportionate segment belonging to racial classifications—African American, Hispanic, Native Americans, or non-Hispanic whites. Slightly less than half of all these counties are defined by disproportionately high concentrations of African Americans. The twenty-seven high-poverty counties that do not fall into the racial classifications are thinly settled among the farming areas in the northern Great Plains, mostly across the states of Montana, Oklahoma, North Dakota, and South Dakota. Income in these states varies widely from year to year, depending largely upon cattle and wheat prices. There are only two counties (in this last group of twenty-seven) where Asians are more than half the poor. While there is some Asian poverty in America, Asians rarely show up proportionately in poverty statistics.

## THE "WORKING POOR"

In 2004 David Shipler wrote *The Working Poor: Invisible in America.*[19] With this book, he tried to accomplish what Michael Harrington accomplished in 1962 by writing *The Other America.*[20] Harrington challenged the 1950s postwar complacency that all America was typified by the middle-class white affluence that was the popular image projected by advertising, movie, and television images of the time. Harrington wanted to bring attention to the "other America," one less affluent but nonetheless pervasive, a poor America that was typically absent from the public consciousness and neglected by public policy. Harrington's poor included the old and the sick as well as America's largest minority in need, the African American poor. Harrington's writing influenced the Kennedy administration and led to the development of Johnson's Great Society. Shipler hoped to have the same impact on the national awareness by bringing attention to a group rarely identified—the working poor—those with jobs whose lifestyle was precariously positioned just marginally above poverty definitions.

Both writers intended to challenge traditional assumptions that the poor were poor because they were lazy or somehow morally deficient. Their shared contention was that the poor are poor because of circumstances: they were born to the wrong family, they lived too long, or they simply lacked the education and skills needed to compete in a society that was advancing technologically at a very rapid pace. The contention is that poverty is "structural," embedded into the fabric of a complex industrial society. According to this logic, the less economically fortunate among us are "shut out," excluded from economic advancement because the nature of highly compensated employment within society demands access to opportunities they lack. Many were acknowledged to lack the mental capacity or to be handicapped. Still, these disadvantages were not seen as anything that could reasonably be attributed to individual responsibility or a pattern of personal choices made by the people suffering the condition. Both writers wanted America to see the people they were identifying as the "invisible poor" as being among us.

Shipler devoted years to getting to know the working poor personally. He interviewed many people over time so he could understand their predicament and convey their stories with a sensitivity that reflected understanding. His writing, as much as the writing of Michael Harrington, conveys a first-person directness that is captivating and compelling. As Shipler explained, "My purpose was to look into their lives as thoroughly as they would allow, to unravel the tangled strands of cause and effect that led to their individual predicaments."[21] The first two paragraphs of his book identify whom he has in mind as the working poor:

> The man who washes cars does not own one. The clerk who files cancelled checks at the bank has $2.02 in her own account. The woman who copy-edits medical textbooks has not been to a dentist in a decade.
>
> This is the forgotten America. At the bottom of its working world, millions live in the shadow of prosperity, in the twilight between poverty and well-being. Whether you're rich, poor, or middle-class, you encounter them every day. They serve you Big Macs and help you find merchandise at Wal-Mart. They harvest your food, clean your offices, and sew your clothes. In a California factory, they package lights for your kids' bikes. In a New Hampshire plant, they assemble books of wallpaper samples to help you redecorate.[22]

Shipler acknowledges the many hardships the working poor face. Some are struggling to come off drugs, others are doing everything they can to leave welfare; some are homeless, others live in broken-down housing. Their families may have been torn apart by divorce, some were sexually abused. His stories of the children are heartbreaking—many suffer from malnutrition or inadequate medical care. The parents, often single women without husbands, worry about taking care of the children whom they leave unsupervised during working hours. How will the children be fed? clothed? He documents the depression and hopelessness felt by the working poor, and he acknowledges honestly that many times the desperate circumstances result from poor decisions or the all-too-human inability to surmount what look like overwhelming obstacles.

The solution to the plight of the working poor is as complex as the problem, so Shipler argues:

> A job alone is not enough. Medical insurance alone is not enough. Good housing alone is not enough. Reliable transportation, careful family budgeting, effective parenting, effective schooling are not enough when each is achieved in isolation from the rest. There is no single variable that can be altered to help working people move away from the edge of poverty. Only where the full array of factors is attacked can America fulfill its promise.[23]

The working poor have advanced from unemployment into inadequate employment, yet always the risk is present that they will slide back. When it comes to proposing solutions, Shipler reverts to a comfortable liberalism, relying on the government to solve the problem. He argues that the poor and working poor should band together to mobilize politically. By voting their class interests, the poor and working poor could make their economic and social needs heard simply by the threat that their votes may be the swing votes sufficient to determine close elections. His clear bias is against conservative Republicans, whom he feels are perhaps even more callous to the needs of the working poor than they are to the poor. He argues that the minimum wage should be increased, not concerned that more marginally employed workers in relatively menial jobs might lose their employment as a result of the higher cost. Shipler does not call directly for a guaranteed minimum living income for everyone, regardless whether they work or not. Still, his suggestions rely heavily on pouring more government money on a problem whose definition he has expanded beyond the poor who are unemployed or those who have dropped out of the labor market to include the working poor.

Shipler's comfortable reliance on the government programs and federal spending typically championed by the political Left are surprisingly simplistic, especially after the subtlety with which he has described the problem of the working poor. Yet, before passing on the question of the working poor, we want to pose a couple of arguments to consider in this context. First, as we move into the twenty-first century, we are going to experience a tremendous increase in jobs that require advanced information-processing skills and specialized, often highly technical knowledge. Ironically, job expansion will also occur at the exact opposite end of the spectrum. Scores of menial jobs are going to increase, jobs that require lower-end skills and minimal education, if any at all. Many employers providing lower-end jobs will probably not care if the employees hired to do these jobs speak English or not, just so the job is done correctly, promptly, and politely. Nor will age or race be important to employment, just the ability to show up on time with the energy and dedication needed to accomplish whatever physical effort is involved.

The Bureau of Labor Statistics projects that of the thirty occupations with the largest job growth potential between 2002 and 2012, two-thirds will not have any educational requirement, except for moderate or short-term, on-the-job training. These jobs include retail salespersons, food-preparation workers (including fast-food workers), janitors, waitresses, receptionists, security guards, truck drivers, delivery assistants, and land-scaping or groundskeepers.[24] None of these jobs are expected to be high paying. To fill these jobs, there will not even be a requirement to have passed grade school, let alone hold a high-school diploma. Many will have no English-language requirement at all, or, if there is an English-language expectation, successful applicants may not be required to read English as long as they can speak and understand minimal English.

Hispanic workers have responded favorably to lower-end jobs. Although Hispanics make up only about 13 percent of total U.S. employment, Hispanics took nearly half of all new jobs created in 2004.[25] Why? Hispanics were more willing than other workers to accept low-paying jobs. This is especially true for newly arrived Hispanic immigrants. Hispanics who arrived in the United States between 2000 and 2004 took more than one million new jobs created in 2004, and only a quarter of that number of new jobs were taken by U.S.-born Hispanics.[26] While Hispanics are listed among the ranks of both the poor and the working poor, some important dynamics within the immigrant Hispanic community make it possible for Hispanics to take lower-paying jobs without necessarily suffering the full extent of hardships most low-paid workers have no choice but to suffer.

The driving reason most Hispanic immigrants come to the United States is to get work. Immigration from Latin American countries is not

In reducing or eliminating poverty, we cannot underestimate the importance of the need to strengthen two-parent families, families in which a husband and wife stay together to raise the children.

In today's world of cultural relativism, many on the political Left attack families, arguing (as in earlier decades true socialists or communists did) that families are simply historical human structures that came into existence to socialize children into the class ideology of a bourgeois capitalist economic structure. Today the political Left still attacks traditional families, though generally without specifically articulating the above argument. The current challenge from the Left is that virtually all "family" structures are equal: families headed by two gay men or two lesbians or single parents or anyone.

We strongly reject this relativism regarding the family. The history of welfare programs in the United States suggests what conservatives such as us believe: family structures headed by the natural father and the natural mother are determined by our human nature to be the ideal social structure in which to raise children in a setting essential for cultivating the moral values that are needed to live productive lives, including the pursuit of economic advancement and education. "Families" headed by unwed mothers run an unfortunate risk of dysfunction, with the result that children are raised in a subculture of poverty that sets up a downward spiral that the children perpetuate and repeat in their adult lives.

Seeing unwed mothers and illegitimate births as the primary cause of poverty is central to the conservative vision. The 1994 *Contract with America,* authored by Newt Gingrich and Dick Armey and advanced by conservative Republicans in the House of Representatives, expressed this point directly:

> Currently, the federal government provides young girls the following deal: Have an illegitimate baby and taxpayers will guarantee you cash, food stamps, and medical care, plus a host of other benefits. As long as you stay single and don't work, we'll continue giving you benefits worth a minimum of $12,000 per year ($3,000 more than a full-time job paying a minimum wage). It's time to change the incentives and make responsible parenthood the norm and not the exception.[28]

The *Contract with America* strongly influenced the design of the 1996 welfare reform bill signed by President Bill Clinton. The House Republicans had attacked welfare provided to unwed mothers, especially if the mothers involved were teenagers. They insisted that fatherhood needed to be established for unwed mothers to receive welfare and that deadbeat fathers needed to be pursued to make good on all required child-support payments. The House Republicans were determined to make the pursuit of employment a condition for obtaining welfare payments. The *Contract with America* declared, as we do here, that Lyndon Johnson's War on Poverty was an "unqualified failure." Despite spending trillions of dollars, the War on Poverty had "the unintended consequence of making welfare more attractive than work to many families, and once welfare recipients become dependent on public assistance, they are caught in the now-familiar welfare trap."[29]

The 1996 Personal Responsibility and Work Opportunity Reconciliation Act (PRWORA) has nearly cut in half the number of families on welfare. More single mothers have found employment, and welfare caseloads have been dramatically reduced.[30] Equally clear is that poverty is nowhere closer to being eliminated. On the contrary, the number of poor the United States increased in 2004. Unmarried births continue at alarmingly high levels. Nearly 70 percent of all African American births are to unmarried mothers; white births to unmarried mothers are approaching 30 percent (the level where unmarried births to blacks were at the start of the War on Poverty).

Nor has the welfare-to-work shift, evidenced by the first ten years under PRWORA, been tested by a serious, long-term recession. With the exception of the business downturn experienced after the 9/11 terrorist attacks, we have had nearly ten years of steady, strong economic growth since 1996. With energy prices increasing dramatically in 2004, the strength of the U.S. economy may well be tested. Critics like Charles Murray take some encouragement that PRWORA has moved welfare mothers into the workplace, yet they continue to stress that we will make no dent on our ultimate goals as long as we continue to believe that government programs can be made to work if only they are properly aimed and adjusted. As recently as 1996 Murray republished his appeal to at least test the impact of closing down PRWORA, even on an experimental basis with a small group of welfare recipients.[31]

Under PRWORA, the administration of welfare is more complex and bureaucratic. A whole new series of forms and computer programs to automate the forms had to be developed by social workers in each of the fifty states. The new rules and regulations focused everyone away from handouts, but the new work orientation of the program made the job of welfare professionals more burdensome. A whole new set of questions had to be asked, new information collected, and new programs implemented. Many of the welfare mothers who left the program did so, not because they no longer needed assistance, but because they were no longer "entitled" to benefits unless they jumped through all the new work-oriented requirements imposed by PRWORA. Welfare recipients, for example, can be "sanctioned" if they do not follow the rules. Perhaps recipients leave a job for no "good reason," or they are fired because of something they did wrong. According to the new rules, these behaviors might trigger their being sanctioned, a condition that translates into a stoppage or reduction of welfare benefits. While sanctioned, the "clock" on receiving benefits for a maximum of five years continues to tick.

Let's return to sociologist Sharon Hays for her observations on how all this plays out:

> Most of the sanctioned welfare mothers I encountered were surprised and angered by being sanctioned. As many as half, I would estimate, didn't fully understand the reason for the sanction when it occurred. Even though these mothers received "official" notification of the requirements in advance and received written notice of the sanction when it occurred, the system of participation and reporting requirements they face is extraordinarily complex. Welfare caseworkers contend with these rules day in and day out, and most still have a hard time remembering them all. I was therefore not surprised that a good number of welfare clients were uncertain as to which rule they had broken.[32]

Any welfare mother who can receive benefits under PRWORA might be poor, but she is unlikely to be stupid. The welfare bureaucracy today is complicated by fifty different programs, each with its own system of encouraging people to seek work and form families, plus a demanding set of requirements that require form filling, question asking, and information gathering on a wide variety of questions ranging from paternity issues to child-care requirements to job training and vocational education questions. The end result is that, under PRWORA, the welfare system hands out fewer checks to a diminishing group of "clients." Successful welfare recipients are forced to learn a new set of rules and behaviors that involve more effort to prove they do care about work, even if they do not believe they can work for long or very successfully. In the end, the welfare mothers under the new program know that their benefits will not last forever, and in the end they may still face the problem of how to find a job, even if it is menial and low paying, how to find child care so they can go to work, and how to raise children while they still have no husbands or extended families to help them.

Critics like Charles Murray could well rejoinder that we are headed in the right direction as long as the caseloads continue to reduce and welfare mothers are chased from the program. At the extreme, these results might even encourage critics to complicate the rules even more in order to push more welfare recipients off the public dole. If the rules become sufficiently complex and onerous to administer, maybe government welfare social workers will quit altogether to seek easier, more lucrative work. A welfare system with fewer, less-well-trained workers may make the process of getting benefits even harder on applicants, a result those who want to see welfare come to a complete end could embrace.

In the final analysis, we have to ask: if PRWORA can demonstrate no result in reducing poverty in the United States, or in reducing the incidence of single mothers and illegitimate births, then why should anyone fight to keep PRWORA? No government program designed to fight poverty has worked to solve the problems in the last forty years. Now, even the conservative design has failed to achieve its stated goals. Should we keep trying for another ten or twenty years while we spend another $10 trillion? What gives any reasonable person confidence to believe that any government program designed and implemented to fight poverty will ever solve the problem?

# 2

## The War on Poverty Fails

The Great Society rests on abundance and liberty for all. It demands an end to poverty and racial injustice, to which we are totally committed in our time.

—President Lyndon Baines Johnson, May 22, 1964

On January 8, 1964, less than two months after John F. Kennedy was assassinated in the streets of Dallas, President Lyndon B. Johnson delivered his first State of the Union address to a joint session of Congress. With a rousing call to action, he declared an "all-out war on human poverty," asserting that this session of Congress would do more for civil rights "than the last hundred sessions combined." Using language generally reserved for America's resolve to defeat foreign enemies, President Johnson dedicated the nation to combating the internal enemy of poverty: "This administration today, here and now, declares unconditional war on poverty in America. I urge this Congress and all Americans to join me in that effort."[1] Franklin D. Roosevelt, a mentor of Johnson, had created the New Deal. For a man of Johnson's imagination and ambition, that goal, lofty as it was, was still not aimed high enough. Johnson proposed more than a new deal, he proposed a "great society," one that would bring the opportunity for peace, health, and economic security to all Americans, regardless of age, sex, or race.

39

Nearly a quarter century later, in January 1988, President Ronald Reagan delivered a State of the Union address in which he declared that the War on Poverty had failed: "My friends, some years ago, the Federal Government declared war on poverty, and poverty won." The remark brought laughter from the joint session of Congress that Reagan addressed. Yet President Reagan meant what he said that night:

> Today the Federal Government has 59 major welfare programs and spends more than $100 billion a year on them. What has all this money done? Well, too often it has only made poverty harder to escape. Federal welfare programs have created a massive social problem. With the best of intentions, government created a poverty trap that wreaks havoc on the very support system the poor need most to lift themselves out of poverty: the family. Dependency has become the one enduring heirloom, passed from one generation to the next, of too many fragmented families.[2]

That night President Reagan issued a direct conservative challenge to the heart of the liberal political agenda that had dominated the American Left since the 1930s. The government had failed to devise a program that could eradicate poverty in America. After spending trillions of dollars and creating a massive federal bureaucracy, Reagan returned to a simple but critically important theme: without strong families, the poor would never emerge from poverty. Even more damaging, Reagan directly stated that federal antipoverty programs actually functioned to destroy poor families, thereby perpetuating the culture of poverty they were trying to eliminate. Federal antipoverty programs, in Reagan's analysis, had become part of the problem, not the solution.

## POVERTY IN AMERICA PERSISTS

WHAT EVIDENCE is there to support President Reagan's contention that we lost the War on Poverty? If we take a careful look at the statistical data compiled by the U.S. Census Bureau, we find ample evidence that the incidence of poverty remains disturbingly large, both as a percentage of the population and in absolute numbers. To document the point, we will have to struggle through a few paragraphs of statistical data, but the numbers are important if we are to state the case correctly.

The Census Bureau reported in August 2005 that the poverty rate in 2004 had actually increased since 2003, up to 12.7 percent in 2004 from 12.5 percent in 2003.[3] This translated into an additional 1.1 million people in poverty, with some 37 million Americans living in poverty in 2004. The progress eliminating poverty in the forty years since Lyndon Johnson declared war on poverty is negligible. In 1964 the Census Bureau estimated that 19 percent of the U.S. population lived in poverty, approximately 36 million people. In that forty-year interval, poverty never measured less than 11 percent of the population. In 1983, under President Reagan, poverty registered 15.2 percent; in 1993, at the beginning of Bill Clinton's presidency, poverty was measured at 13.7 percent of the population. In 2004, under George W. Bush, a president often accused by the political Left as not caring about the poor, the poverty rate declined to 12.7 percent. Still, some 37 million Americans remain poor.

Putting the best possible face on the War on Poverty, we should note that in 1959 and 1960, before the War on Poverty began, poverty was measured at approximately 22 percent of the population, some 39 million Americans. We can argue that a reduction from 22 percent in 1959 to 12.7 percent in 2004 means that the incidence of poverty has been reduced by roughly half over the last forty-five years. Yet some 39 million Americans were counted as poor in 1959, nearly the same number as the nearly 37 million Americans counted as poor in 2004. Despite all the money and effort expended by government, a core group of poor persists, resistant to any and all efforts to remove them from the poverty rolls. It is this core group of "underclass" Americans that the War on Poverty and the political Left has failed. If the War on Poverty was meant to eliminate poverty, rather than merely reduce poverty, then a new strategy is needed.

In addition, attributing causal effects is very difficult in social science. How can one prove that the reduction in the incidence of poverty since 1959–60 is a direct result of the Great Society's War on Poverty programs? A reasonable alternative explanation is that the U.S. economy has experienced a world-historic expansion since 1958–60, a time when the country was emerging from an economic recession. In 2004 the World Bank measured the U.S. gross domestic product (GDP) at $11.7 trillion, up from $9.8 trillion in 2000.[4] A historical database maintained by the U.S. Department of Commerce shows the dramatic straight-line rise of the GDP from $526 billion in 1960 to $10.9 trillion in 2003 and $11.7 trillion in 2004.[5] The U.S. economy remains the largest in the world. U.S. job growth has also more than doubled since 1960. The U.S. Bureau of Labor Statistics reports total nonfarm employment at 54 million jobs in 1960, a number that has expanded to an estimated 131 million jobs in 2005.[6] This dramatic economic expansion, plus an aggressive federal War on Poverty, should have eliminated poverty, that is, if eliminating poverty through government programs alone were possible. Still, in 2004 we have 37 million poor Americans among us.

The War on Poverty has spanned the terms of eight different Democratic and Republican presidents: Lyndon B. Johnson (D, 1964–69), Richard M. Nixon (R, 1969–74), Gerald R. Ford (R, 1974–77), Jimmy Carter (D, 1977–81), Ronald Reagan (R, 1981–89), George H. W. Bush (R, 1989–93), Bill Clinton (D, 1993–2001), and George W. Bush (R, 2001–present). These presidents seriously took on the hard question of poverty; their administrations did their utmost to apply techniques they honestly believed to be politically sound methodologies designed to eliminate poverty. We have tried both conservative and liberal solutions to the problem, all without realizing success. If anyone could have eliminated poverty, these gentlemen should have accomplished the task, especially since they commanded the full resources and authority of the U.S. government and were backed by multiple Congresses willing to pass countless antipoverty laws.

On August 22, 1996, President Clinton signed the Personal Responsibility and Work Opportunity Reconciliation Act, announcing that he had fulfilled his promise to "end welfare as we know it." Looking critically at the legislation, we could see that a liberal Democrat was trying to take ground that had traditionally been the preserve of conservative Republicans. Clinton was trying to change *welfare* into *work-fare*, devising a plan to get welfare recipients off the public dole and onto the private sector's payroll. Perhaps by 1996 the political Left had come to the conclusion that the American public was so tired of funding antipoverty programs that the only way to save the governmental welfare programs was to redefine them as work programs. Welfare bureaucrats were being redirected to get welfare recipients into the private workforce or lose their welfare jobs. Clinton legitimately considered this a major redirection of the poverty program. Still, poverty persisted. Thus, even a Democrat president willing to embrace proposals that were typically advanced by conservative Republicans could not solve the problem.

Nor is the problem that we have failed to spend money generously. The public expenditure on the variety of governmental schemes devised in the last forty years to eliminate poverty has been extraordinary. Since 1964 we have spent $8–10 trillion on antipoverty programs. In 1996, at the midpoint in the Clinton administration, the federal government expended $191 billion on poverty programs, fully 12.2 percent of the federal budget. President George W. Bush actually increased the effort. The 2006 budget, at the midpoint of Bush's administration, calls for a massive increase in poverty programs, increasing the expenditure $368 billion to 14.6 percent of the federal budget.[7] The Bush administration oversees a host of continuing poverty programs that includes Medicaid, food stamps, supplementary security income, temporary assistance to needy families, child day-care payments, child nutrition payments, foster care, adoption assistance, and health insurance for children.

The conclusion is virtually inescapable: if the availability of nearly an unlimited amount of money and the determination of countless government bureaucracies were the necessary and sufficient conditions to eliminate poverty, then in 2004 we should not still have more than 12 percent of the U.S. population—nearly 37 million people—in poverty.

Even though the political Left wants to make all biblical references suspect, we are led to affirm the admonition of Jesus in the New Testament: "For ye have the poor always with you" (Matthew 26:11). Some two thousand years ago, one of the wisest teachers suggested that the problem of poverty was truly intractable. Is there any governmental poverty program left that we have not implemented one way or another in the literally hundreds of antipoverty laws Congress has passed since 1964? Maybe we should just take another $10 trillion and hand it out as a lump-sum payment to the 37 million Americans who are poor. The expenditure might be cheap if a one-time massive payment would make poverty disappear. Apparently, there are dimensions of poverty that money alone cannot solve. That is our first important conclusion.

Yet there is a more subtle point that we will want to consider. As we noted, President Johnson followed the liberal tradition of Democratic Party politics founded by his mentor, Franklin D. Roosevelt. Central to Roosevelt's New Deal thinking was the assumption that massive governmental intervention in what before had been considered a largely private economy was needed to solve the problems of the Great Depression. When Johnson initiated the Great Society, he almost intuitively reasoned that governmental action would be required if we were to end poverty. Alternatives to government intervention and spending were never seriously considered by his administration. Conservative opponents, who at the time opposed the creation of a massive new government bureaucracy, were a minority whose views seemed out of step if not downright dangerous. Even today, the political Left is hard pressed to consider that we have no choice but to persist and fine-tune government antipoverty programs. How many more years of failure will it take before the political Left is finally willing to admit that the approach to eliminate poverty through massive government programs has fundamentally failed to meet the originally stated goal of the Great Society?

Do we have to wait another ten years before we declare the War on Poverty a failure? Should we keep trying until the year 2064, when we will have wasted one hundred years on an effort that was doomed to fail from the start? President Reagan believed a quarter of a century was enough. In 1988 he declared that poverty had won. We doubt that the political Left will ever admit that the War on Poverty has failed. It's much more likely that the political Left will simply argue that the Great Society's original stated purpose of eliminating poverty was never meant to be taken literally, but was rather a lofty goal, a metaphoric statement of intent. Moreover, the Left will claim any reduction of poverty has resulted from governmental action, not from the historic expansion of the U.S. economy that we have experienced since the 1960s.

Our charge is different. We maintain that massive government spending will never eliminate poverty. After another forty years of governmental effort and the expenditure of another $10 trillion in public funds, what confidence can the political Left give us that we will be able to reduce the incidence of poverty by half once again, to only 6 percent of the population? Even then, if the U.S. population continues to grow at the same rate we are experiencing today, we could still be left with more than 30 million Americans in poverty.

From the moment the Great Society conceived of the War on Poverty, it was a bad idea to believe that we could eliminate poverty by allowing a government bureaucracy to distribute massive amounts of public money to the poor. In the antipoverty efforts of the last four decades, we have witnessed one of the largest income redistributions from the taxpayers to the poor that the world has ever seen. Still, we have not eliminated poverty. Why should we believe that continued or expanded, new, and "improved" government programs, spending more trillions of dollars, will ever achieve more?

Maybe money could have solved the problem of poverty, but only if the money had not been distributed through a government bureaucracy. Perhaps we would have achieved greater results if a different solution had been considered, a solution that relied predominately upon the private economy to produce the desired results of eliminating poverty. Whatever made us think that a huge government bureaucracy with nearly unlimited funding could eliminate poverty? Perhaps President Reagan was right—if we do not reinforce family structures, we will never eliminate poverty. Maybe he was also right in arguing that government welfare programs actually destroy the family structures of those Americans remaining in poverty since the start of the Great Society. Reagan's vision was that no amount of dependence upon government bureaucracy could ever substitute for the fundamental values only a family can instill in a person. This is a vision religious leaders would understand. Considering the degree to which the political Left has become radicalized in a secular direction, we expect this message will fall on deaf ears in that corner of the political spectrum. Nonetheless, we intend to advance the theme in the pages that follow.

## POVERTY CONTINUES TO HAVE AN AFRICAN AMERICAN FACE

WHEN LYNDON JOHNSON talked about eliminating poverty, he always seemed to mention eliminating racial injustice. Why? The answer is simple. When poverty in America is mentioned, the thought of racial discrimination is never far behind. Yes, there always have been pockets of white poverty, the rural "backwater" poverty typical of the remote areas of the Appalachian Mountains or isolated rural communities typical of West Virginia. African American poverty is different in nature, a phenomenon considered inherent to the fundamental situation of second-class citizenship that blacks have had in the United States since the days when slavery was tolerated in this country. The assumption that poverty is largely a "black problem" has been a generally unspoken understanding when Americans ponder why we have a persistent poverty problem. Our understanding of racial discrimination against African Americans translates almost unconsciously into an understanding that racial inequality stretches across all dimensions of life, including economic, and always to the disadvantage of African Americans. Again, we will have to examine a few paragraphs of dense numbers to make the case that poverty in America has been disproportionately an African American problem.

In 2004 the U.S. Census Bureau further reported that the poverty rate for African Americans (24.7 percent) was nearly three times the poverty rate for non-Hispanic whites (8.6 percent). The poverty rate for Hispanics (21.9 percent) was not far behind that of African Americans. In a population numbering more than 290 million people, African Americans make up only approximately 13 percent of the total; non-Hispanic whites are by far the largest group, approximately 67 percent. Yet when we look at poverty, African Americans and Hispanics make up a larger percentage of the poor than their numbers in the population would suggest. Put more bluntly: the poor are disproportionately African American or Hispanic. Some 25 percent of the poor are African American, another 25 percent are Hispanic, and only about 46 percent are non-Hispanic whites, even though non-Hispanic whites constitute about 67 percent of the total population. Put even more bluntly: in 2004, after a forty-year effort to remove the legal barriers of racial discrimination, poverty in the United States still impacts America's racial minorities more deeply than it affects America's white majority.

Over the four decades of the War on Poverty, progress has been made on the percentage of African American families that are poor. In

1959, before the War on Poverty, more than 55 percent of all African Americans were poor. The percentage of African Americans who were classified as poor held at approximately 30 to 35 percent from 1968 through 1994, when a reduction is evident, down to the present level of about 25 percent. In this same time, the percentage of whites classified as poor remained reasonably constant at around 10 percent. The dramatic growth of the U.S. economy, as we argued earlier, is the most likely reason poverty among African Americans has improved since 1959. Also, numerous Supreme Court decisions have attacked a legal structure that permitted racial discrimination, a subject we will cover more extensively later. Still, African Americans continue to suffer twice the incidence of poverty as whites. On this the data are clear. Finding the cause and answering the question "Why?" are much more difficult problems. To address these questions, we need to examine some of the key arguments of the past decades that have undergirded the intellectual basis for understanding the complex question of racial discrimination and poverty.

First, we want to make a few comments on the question of Hispanic poverty. In 1964 the percentage of Hispanics in the United States was so small that the U.S. Census Bureau made no effort to track this group separately. Today, after decades of "multicultural" thinking impressed upon America by the political Left, the Census Bureau contends with many categories of racial distinction. Today the Census Bureau distinguishes American non-Hispanic whites from Hispanics, from African Americans, from American Indians, from Alaskan Natives, from Asians, from Native Hawaiians, and from Other Pacific Islanders. Other tables distinguish white alone and black or African American alone from those of "two or more races." "Melting pot" characteristics that have distinguished America since the first European immigrants hit these shores. Forty years from now we may have difficulty making racial distinctions at all. Today, the Census Bureau makes no attempt to identify people based on whether their grandparents or great-grandparents came from Italy, Ireland, or dozens of other countries. Sorting out ethnic distinctions among the U.S. population has already become nearly impossible as subsequent generations intermarry and mix together.

The wave of immigration from the Spanish-speaking countries within the Western Hemisphere has grown to such a level that Hispanics threaten to overtake African Americans as the country's largest minority group. Current poverty reports issued by the U.S. Census Bureau document that the incidence of poverty among Hispanics is about the same proportion as the incidence of poverty among African Americans. While the Census Bureau aims to be good at counting, very little effort is put forth into the more politically difficult area of explanation. The Census Bureau data do not explore whether the nature of Hispanic poverty is the same as African American poverty, or whether the causes and direction of the observed poverty among the two groups are different. But we will return to this subject later in this chapter.

The point here is that while the Census Bureau is documenting an incidence of poverty among Hispanics roughly equivalent to that of African Americans, the phenomenon of a statistically large and growing Hispanic population in America is yet relatively new. Historically, the discussion that there is a racial dimension to American poverty has focused on African Americans and the racial injustice blacks have experienced in America. Before taking up the question of Hispanic poverty, however, we want to examine African American poverty more closely. What are the intellectual arguments that have been forwarded to understand black poverty in America? What direction has public policy taken as a result of that intellectual debate? These are our next key questions.

## GUNNAR MYRDAL AND *AN AMERICAN DILEMMA*

IN 1937 the Carnegie Corporation of New York organized "a comprehensive study of the Negro in the United States, to be undertaken in a wholly objective and dispassionate way as a social phenomenon."[8] The decision was made to recruit a foreign scholar to bring to the study a "fresh mind, uninfluenced by traditional attitudes or by earlier conclusions."[9] The nod to organize the study went to Swedish social economist Gunnar Myrdal, a professor at the University of Stockholm and a member of the Swedish senate. He organized a large staff and worked diligently to produce an extensive report that was published in 1944 under the title *An American Dilemma: The Negro Problem and Modern Democracy*. Almost immediately the work was considered a classic, an important statement on an important social issue that has continued to be the center point of the drama on race and social justice that has been playing out since slavery was allowed to continue when the U.S. Constitution was drafted. Reading the book today, much of the language is stilted, and the social references to "Negroes" are dated. Still, Myrdal's analysis remains compelling. Much of the legal and social debate since the book was written has turned on the fundamental moral issues he and his associates brilliantly articulated.

Fundamental to the analysis was the conclusion that poverty and economic equality characterized the situation of African Americans in the United States. Chapter 9, entitled "Economic Inequality," began with a section devoted to "Negro Poverty." The first paragraph clearly states the argument:

> The economic situation of the Negroes in America is pathological. Except for a small minority enjoying upper or middle class status, the masses of American Negroes, in the rural South and in the segregated slum quarters in Southern and Northern cities, are destitute. They own little property; even their household goods are mostly inadequate and dilapidated. Their incomes are not only low but irregular. They thus live from day to day and have scant security for the future. Their entire culture and their individual interests and striving are narrow.[10]

This was a harsh analysis of an economic reality that Myrdal and his team thoroughly documented. Their conclusion was that America was trapped in what amounted to an economic caste system. In this caste system, African Americans were systematically relegated to the lowest class. And their analysis was accurate.

By framing the analysis as a class argument, however, Myrdal set up the basis for arguing that black America constituted an "underclass." Much of his argument was set against the communist class argument that dominated much of the intellectual political debate of the years between World War I and World War II. He argued that the situation of

African Americans did not fit the prescriptions that communist ideology would predict. Still, by identifying the situation of African Americans as a class distinction, Myrdal set up the basis for an argument that would later be used to identify African American communities as dominated by an inferior subculture. And he portrayed black communities, especially in Northern cities, as dominated by a "Negro underworld" made up of "petty thieves and racketeers, prostitutes and pimps, bootleggers, dope addicts, and so on, but also a number of 'big shots' organizing and controlling crime, vice, and racketeering, as well as other more innocent forms of illegal activity such as gambling—particularly the 'policy,' or the 'numbers,' game."[11]

To be fair, Myrdal identified the African American situation as one that arose because of discrimination, not because of an assumed genetic or racial inferiority. This was at the heart of what he defined as the "American dilemma," a conflict between our beliefs in equality and the systematic discrimination African Americans have suffered since slavery was introduced to these shores:

> In so far as Negro poverty is caused by discrimination, the American Creed is challenged in one of its most specific and longest established precepts. Equality of opportunity, fair play, free competition—"independence of race, creed or color"—is deeply imprinted in the nationally sanctioned social morals of America. This value premise must direct every realistic study of the Negroes' economic status in America.[12]

And again:

> In this sense the Negro problem is not only America's greatest failure but also America's incomparably great opportunity for the future. If America should follow its own deepest convictions, its well-being at home would be increased directly. At the same time America's prestige and power abroad would rise immensely. The century-old dream of American patriots, that America should give to the entire world its own freedoms and its faith, would come true. America can demonstrate that justice, equality and cooperation are possible between white and colored people.[13]

This language was especially poignant since Myrdal penned it as World War II was raging. He had a foreigner's perspective, yet he appreciated how America was fighting against the tyrannies of Nazi Germany and Imperial Japan. He was aware that America could only be true to its values internationally if Americans were also true to them at home. This line of analysis set in place the logic that African American poverty resulted from discrimination, a problem that could be addressed legally. As an economist and social scientist, Myrdal also established the contribution his academic disciplines could bring to analyze the problems.

Myrdal's analysis began to play out in 1954 when the Supreme Court decided *Brown v. Board of Education*,[14] a decision that reversed precedent to establish that segregated "separate" schools could not be "equal." The majority of the Court cited Myrdal's work in coming to this conclusion, a conclusion that relied heavily on social science to establish that a legal structure embodying racial discrimination was inconsistent with the basic freedoms that were fundamental to American principles of law and justice—the same conclusion Myrdal himself had reached in his classic work.

Still, the issue of "subclass" or "underclass" persisted in the analysis of race and African American poverty. Even if the cause of black poverty were identified as unacceptable racial discrimination, the solution might not simply be to remove the legal structure that embodied that discrimination. If, as a result of historical and unacceptable racial discrimination, a black underclass is developed and then perpetuates a subclass lifestyle, then merely removing the legal barriers might not be enough to eliminate black poverty. In other words, corrective legal decisions might be a necessary condition to eliminate black poverty, but it might not be a sufficient condition to remove the intractable black poor "underclass" from poverty. Two other barriers remained. Attitudes in the majority community would have to change to allow African Americans to advance, even if more open "equal opportunities" were fully established in law. The other barrier looked back to African Americans themselves. If legal barriers were removed and opportunities opened, would African Americans be themselves equal to the majority whites with whom they would then have to compete?

## THE MOYNIHAN REPORT AND AFRICAN AMERICAN FAMILIES

In March 1965, Daniel Patrick Moynihan, who was then under a presidential appointment as assistant secretary of labor heading the Office of Policy Planning and Research, wrote a report entitled *The Negro Family: The Case for National Action*.[15] Yet the published report did not bear his name. Still, the private circulation of the report within the government prior to its publication carried with the recognition that Moynihan was the author. The huge controversy the report generated once the public read it led to the document being commonly known as the Moynihan Report. The core argument of the report was that the cause of African American poverty was the deterioration of the African American family, not white prejudice and discrimination. Moynihan began chapter 2, "The Negro American Family," with a sentence that left little doubt where his argument was headed: "At the heart of the deterioration of the fabric of Negro society is the deterioration of the Negro family." With that, a firestorm of controversy broke out.

Moynihan argued that the family is the basic structure of society, responsible for shaping the character and behavior of children. His criticism of African American families was direct and sharply stated:

> The white family has achieved a high degree of stability and is maintaining that stability. **By contrast, the family structure of lower class Negroes is highly unstable, and in many urban centers is approaching complete breakdown.**[16]

Drawing heavily from Census Bureau data at the time he was writing, Moynihan documented that nearly a quarter of all urban African American marriages were dissolved, nearly a quarter of all African American births were illegitimate, and females headed almost a quarter of all African American families. He compared these data to statistics for the white population, documenting the relative health of white families.

Moynihan's analysis drove to a damaging conclusion, namely, that the "breakdown of the Negro family has led to a startling increase in welfare dependency."[17] His attention focused on the Aid for Families with Dependent Children (AFDC) program, an original New Deal social assistance program initially created in 1935 for widows with children. Now expanded to include poor families in which the father was absent because of divorce or desertion, the AFDC program had become a centerpiece of welfare assistance to the African American community. Moynihan documented that 14 percent of African American children were receiving AFDC assistance, compared to 2 percent of white children. Moreover, while 56 percent of nonwhite children could be expected at some time to receive AFDC assistance, only 8 percent of white children would ever receive similar assistance. Moynihan argued that this formed a pattern of dependency that in effect paid African American families to remain fatherless. What he saw forming was a vicious downward spiral:

> As with the population as a whole, there is much evidence that children are being born most rapidly in those Negro families with the least financial resources. This is an ancient pattern, but because the needs of children are greater today it is very possible that the education and opportunity gap between the offspring of these families and those of stable middle-class unions is not closing, but is growing wider.
>
> A cycle is at work; too many children too early make it most difficult for the parents to finish school. (In February, 1963, 38 percent of the white girls who dropped out of school did so because of marriage or pregnancy, as against 49 percent of non-white girls.) An Urban League study in New York reported that 44 percent of girl dropouts left school because of pregnancy.
>
> Low education levels in turn produce low income levels, which deprive children of many opportunities, and so the cycle repeats itself.[18]

Critically, Moynihan argued the breakdown of black families resulted in a matriarchy dominating African American society, a condition that further necessitated a host of social and economic problems. The result was "poverty, failure, and isolation among Negro youth," a condition that led to a "disastrous delinquency and crime rate." Life from there led to more poverty and alienation, setting up a pattern destined to become even worse in the next generation. Moynihan typified the situation as "a tangle of pathology," using psychological language to describe the social and economic plight of poor African Americans, language almost identical to Gunnar Myrdal's earlier analysis.[19] If the African American family were not restored, Moynihan saw little hope for restoring the type of child socialization he viewed as essential to ending the cycle of African American poverty:

> In a word, a national effort towards the problems of Negro Americans must be directed toward the question of the family structure. The object should be to strengthen the Negro family so as to enable it to raise and support its members as do other families.[20]

Moynihan was very concerned that the AFDC effort was misdirected. African American families were being rewarded for staying fatherless. AFDC payments were only being made to families without fathers; if the mother reunited with her spouse, or if she married another man, the AFDC payments would stop. With fathers staying outside the family structure, the problem of poverty would not be solved even if employment opportunities in the African American community began to increase. Jobs going to separated fathers would not necessarily benefit children. Moynihan cited data that showed a pattern of AFDC cases in the African American community increasing when black unemployment was decreasing. This pattern was the opposite of what we would expect if new jobs truly benefited families and children.

By arguing that one of the causes of black poverty was the disintegration of the black family, Moynihan's analysis was bound to be controversial. Most analysts on the political Left wanted to argue the causal relation in the exact opposite direction. When the Moynihan Report became public in 1965, liberals were already deeply invested in arguing that the cause of the problem was white prejudice, not the destructive influence of the AFDC program in the African American community itself. Discrimination and denial of equal opportunity resulting from white hatred were the clear culprits blamed by liberals for the problem of African American poverty. To the political Left, African Americans were victims of decades of a white-dominated society that had kept

blacks systematically oppressed. What Moynihan suggested was tanta-
mount to heresy; the Left was not prepared to allow African American
self-reliance to end their poverty plight.

Moreover, Moynihan's argument threatened the political Left's
agenda. For liberals in 1965 the solution to black poverty was to wage
Johnson's War on Poverty; their intention was to create a massive
government bureaucracy aimed at creating new poverty programs. The
goal was to get more money into the hands of poor blacks. But the formula also created a bureaucracy that benefited from keeping some
blacks perpetually poor and underclass. The formula of the political
Left centered on the following three components: a huge increase in
poverty payments, an aggressive civil rights legislative program in Congress, and a prolonged program of litigation in court designed to eliminate the legal structure of unequal justice. These were the action steps
required to eliminate black poverty. Nothing in the agenda of the political Left called for blacks to accept responsibility for themselves. And
that shortcoming helped perpetrate the black underclass still found in
America's cities.

The influence of the Moynihan Report was first seen in a speech by
President Johnson on June 4, 1965, at Howard University. By the time
Moynihan's thinking was translated into the president's rhetoric, the
responsibility for the breakdown in the black family had been placed
right back where the liberals wanted it—solely on white society and
white prejudice:

> Perhaps most important—its influence radiating to every part of
> life—is the breakdown of the Negro family structure. For this,
> most of all, white America must accept responsibility. It flows
> from centuries of oppression and persecution of the Negro man. It
> flows from long years of degradation and discrimination, which
> have attacked his dignity and assaulted his ability to produce for
> his family.[21]

So the hatred of whites was responsible for depriving the black man
of the dignity needed to be a family head—that was the argument
launched to counter Moynihan's basic charge. The political Left would

not be deflected from that core strategy. It had calculated that once the legal structure of prejudice collapsed, the tables could be turned so that racial discrimination itself would become a crime. Then massive amounts of poverty money and an aggressive strategy to provide new opportunities, perhaps even on an advantaged basis, would surely end African American poverty. But Moynihan's analysis was threatening to the political Left because he questioned these premises. Moynihan suggested that the Left would fail; he argued that unless African Americans could form strong family structures, nothing government could do would work to eliminate black poverty. And he was right.

Where the large and growing black middle class continues to grow and prosper, it is because of a causal link of a father with a job being the head of the family. Where there is a breakdown of this core formula—especially of a family with the father gainfully employed—economic failure is virtually a certain result, along with the further consequence of increasing poverty in the black community. Nothing—not even fairer laws along with much more money being given to the poor by a huge government bureaucracy—will solve the problem as long as these African American families remain dysfunctional. Children who are socialized to develop the values needed to advance in education and employment are doomed to a life of economic problems. Moynihan's argument to add a personal responsibility to the Great Society—that is, fathers with jobs—failed. As noted above, the 2006 federal budget calls for spending $368 billion on poverty programs, a massive 14.6 percent of the total federal budget. Over the last forty years, starting with Johnson's War on Poverty, the political Left has succeeded, not in eliminating poverty, but in creating its dream of a state welfare system larger than ever before attempted in human history.

Unfortunately, the trend Moynihan identified in 1965 has only intensified. In 2002 nearly 70 percent of all African American babies were born to unmarried mothers. The data confirm a deterioration of the family structure across all American society. In 2002 more than 28 percent of all white babies were born to unmarried mothers. White births today are where African American births were forty years ago. That seven out of every ten black babies would be born to an unmarried woman would have been shocking to Moynihan when he wrote his report. This was his worst nightmare, that unmarried births would increase and that African American families would continue to deteriorate to the point where families were no longer the central social structure in the black community.

The attack on all American families should alarm us all. There is no clearer predictor of poverty than to have a child born to an unwed mother. Unmarried births not only predict poverty, they predict a host of social and economic dysfunctions, including delinquency, crime, drug use, poorer health, and shorter lives. A society in which unmarried births are increasing is on the path to the exact downward spiral that Moynihan so clearly identified. Consider this conclusion by Robert Rector of the Heritage Foundation, a leading expert in the study of families:

> Children born out of wedlock to never-married women live in poverty 51 percent of the time. By contrast, children born within a marriage that remains intact are poor 7 percent of the time. Thus, the absence of marriage increases the frequency of child poverty by 700 percent. However, marriage after an illegitimate birth is effective, cutting the child poverty [rate] in half.
>
> From the very beginning, children born outside of marriage have life stacked against them. In addition to poverty, children born into illegitimacy are more likely to experience retarded cognitive development (especially verbal development); lower educational achievement; lower job attainment; increased behavioral and emotional problems; lower impulse control; and retarded social development. Such children are far more likely to engage in sexual activity; have children outside of marriage; be on welfare as adults; and engage in criminal activity.[22]

Again, as we have noted, the political Left has been attacking the family since the early days of communism. In the thinking of extreme socialists, the family is an artificial structure, man-made, designed to imprint traditional thoughts of political and social control on the young. For conservatives, the family is a fundamental structure that human beings need to educate and raise children with social and political values that will make their lives productive and satisfying. Extreme socialists tend to attack any idea of God; for conservative thinkers, the institution of marriage is a naturally right structure ordained by God for our growth and advancement. Unfortunately, the social scientific data, as well as the governmental data collected by agencies such as the U.S. Census Bureau, tend to confirm the conservative viewpoint.

Unable to answer Moynihan's argument directly, the political Left resorted to launching an ad hominem attack on Moynihan, a tactic the political Left generally resorts to whenever a critic on the right scores a point that the Left cannot refute. James Farmer, a legendary figure in the civil rights movement and one of the founders of the Congress of Racial Equality (CORE), came forward almost immediately to charge that Moynihan had provided the "fuel for a new racism."

> By laying the primary blame for present-day inequalities on the pathological condition of the Negro family and community, Moynihan has provided a massive academic cop-out for the white conscience and clearly implied that Negroes in this nation will never secure a substantial measure of freedom until we learn to behave ourselves and stop buying Cadillacs instead of bread.[23]

So the counterattack strategy of the political Left was to demonize Moynihan. This was to become a classic response pattern of the Left to its conservative civil rights critics. Anyone who disagreed with the political Left's agenda to create a massive welfare state, anyone who even suggested that the deterioration of the African American family was a core cause of continuing African American poverty was destined to be labeled a racist. The Left aimed to "discredit" its civil rights opponents personally, so their critical arguments could be dismissed without being answered.[24] The problem is that Moynihan was right. Without strong family structures, poverty is the inevitable result, not just for African American communities, but for any community and all societies. No amount of federal antipoverty spending, no army of government bureaucrats, no rewriting of Supreme Court decisions will ever eliminate poverty in a community or a society where families are deteriorating.

The issue Moynihan raised is important. A young, single mother in the African American community is often trapped. Welfare becomes almost a "job."

But the money a single mother can draw from welfare is limited—possibly several thousand dollars a month, but never enough. Without an extended family structure to rely upon, child care is difficult, if not impossible. Working, even part time, is nearly impossible without child care, especially when children are very young. Putting together a few dollars from various sources to supplement welfare is hardly a solution. Children need food, clothes, and ultimately education. All this costs precious dollars. Welfare becomes a dependency trap. Single mothers cannot afford to lose welfare, yet welfare does not provide adequate resources to advance. Then, too, single mothers may lack the required training and skills to hold any but the lowest-paying jobs available. Hours of work away from children do not provide the resources to escape the trap. Moreover, too many documented hours of work may threaten the continuance of welfare itself. All this occurs while the price of housing, food, and gasoline increases every day. Single mothers end up in substandard housing, often without automobiles or the money for gasoline. They struggle to provide a subsistence lifestyle to children who lack parental supervision or the fundamentals required to build within them a culture of learning.

## CHARLES MURRAY AND THE FAILURE OF THE FEDERAL WELFARE STATE

IN 1984 political scientist Charles Murray published *Losing Ground,* a revolutionary book arguing that the social welfare experiment begun by the Great Society's War on Poverty was such a failure that we should scrap all welfare state programs.[25] Murray analyzed poverty statistics going back to the 1950s. He demonstrated that the major drop in poverty that we have experienced began with the post–World War II economic boom of the 1950s. In 1950, U.S. poverty stood at a remarkable 30 percent of the population. From there, poverty dropped to 18 percent in 1964, Lyndon Johnson's first year in office. Poverty continued to fall, from 18 percent in 1964 to 13 percent in 1968. The low point, Murray observed, was in 1973, when poverty was measured at 11 percent. From there the drop in the poverty rate stalled, despite the growing expenditures of the welfare state. He wrote:

A higher proportion of the American population was officially poor in 1980 than at any time since 1967. By then it stood at 13 percent and was heading up. The number of people living in poverty stopped declining just as the public-assistance program budgets and the rate of increase in those budgets were highest. The question is why this should be.[26]

Murray provided an answer. He too focused on the increasing number of poor black households that were headed by single females. "Such families have historically shown high rates of poverty, whether because the single-female head of household is untrained to work at a well-paying job, because of her need to stay home to care for the children, or because of chronic unemployment for other reasons."[27]

Most important, Murray's analysis demonstrated that the structure of welfare payments made rational the decision of a father to abandon his pregnant wife: "Economically, the total package of AFDC and other welfare benefits has become comparable to working." Applying the analysis to a hypothetical couple, he demonstrated that the decision to not get married was reinforced by the economics of the welfare system:

The old-fashioned solution of getting married and living off their earned income has become markedly inferior. Working a full forty-hour week in the dry-cleaning shop will pay Harold $64 ($136 in 1980 dollars) *before* Social Security and taxes are taken out. The bottom line is this: Harold can get married and work forty hours a week in a hot, tiresome job; or he can live with Phyllis and her baby without getting married, not work, and have more disposable income. From an economic point of view, getting married is dumb. From a noneconomic point of view, it involves him in a legal relationship that has no payoff for him. If he thinks he may sometime tire of Phyllis and fatherhood, the 1970 rules thus provide a further incentive for keeping the relationship off the books.[28]

For the hypothetical woman involved, having the baby made economic sense as long as she stayed unwed and did not work. She could draw a variety of benefits: including AFDC payments, food stamps, Medicaid, and possibly even rent subsidies under one or more federal housing programs. Murray wrote: "*The only circumstance under which giving up the baby is rational is if she prefers any sort of job to having and caring for the baby.*"[29]

Murray's analysis was remarkably close to Moynihan's argument: a "poverty culture" was developing, especially in African American communities, where the welfare state itself was actually encouraging the breakup of families by the rules under which welfare payments were available. Murray's analysis and writing made the argument compelling. To make sure he drove home his point, he called for the complete abandonment of the entire welfare system. He would put to an end any and all federal entitlement "transfer payments" to the poor:

> The proposed program, our final and most ambitious thought experiment, consists of scrapping the entire federal welfare and income-support structure for working-aged persons, including AFDC, Medicaid, Food Stamps, Unemployment Insurance, Worker's Compensation, subsidized housing, disability insurance, and the rest. It would leave the working-aged person with no recourse whatsoever except the job market, family members, friends, and public or private locally funded services. It is the Alexandrian solution: cut the knot, for there is no way to untie it.[30]

Murray pointed out that a majority of the population would be unaffected. "A surprising number of the huge American middle and working classes go from birth to grave without using any social welfare benefits until they receive their first Social Security check."[31] His goal was to force mothers to find husbands or other family support to raise their children. He wanted to end the "poverty culture" by eliminating the economic choice to drop out of the employment force and live off welfare. Murray knew that a move this drastic would cause disruption; his calculation, however, was that we could only make more progress in removing poverty if we removed the safety net.

Murray's analysis was dramatic, but he drew national attention for his argument. He believed that eliminating the entire welfare system was the only way to accomplish the goal of ending poverty. His analysis centered on the family and the realization that children must be allowed "to grow up in a system free of the forces that encourage them to remain poor and dependent." As a society, we have not made the decision to take away the safety net, but Charles Murray pushed us further down that line. His book was published during Reagan's first term. Arguably, he began the line of thinking that has led to the job-oriented welfare reforms that the Republican Congress enacted in 1996, with President Clinton leading the charge to get in front of the revolution and claim credit. Still, we plan to spend $368 billion on poverty programs in the 2006 budget, without any assurance we will make a dent in the poverty problem. Maybe Murray is right and it's time to stop pouring more money into efforts that show no measurable impact. As we noted to start, poverty in 2004 actually increased despite our continued massive expenditures.

In frustration, Murray asked why we don't simply give the poor enough money to make them no longer poor. In reading the quotation, note Murray's frustration in exploring the thought:

> Fixing the last 10 percent of a problem is often more difficult than fixing the first 90 percent of it. But poverty as officially defined is a matter of cash in hand from whatever source. The recipient of the benefit does not have to "do" anything—does not have to change behavior or values, does not have to "qualify" in any way except to be a recipient. To eliminate such poverty, all we need to do is mail enough checks with enough money to enough people. In the late sixties, still more in the seventies, the number of checks, the size of the checks, and the number of beneficiaries all increased. Yet, perversely, poverty chose those years to halt a decline that had been underway for decades.[32]

Ironically, Murray concluded, giving away money did not solve poverty. We are reminded of the apocryphal story of the homeless person who wins the lottery; within a short time the money is gone and the person is again homeless. If we are dealing now with a culture of poverty that perpetuates the problem, we will have to deal with the root cause of attitudes, values, and lifestyles before we can make any final progress. To eliminate poverty we have to start with the soundness of the family structure and move to examine the effectiveness of the education experience. From there we have to consider jobs and homeownership. Only when these basics are in place will we no longer need massive government bureaucracies spending billions of dollars while achieving no measurable progress in accomplishing their goal. To many on the political Left, this will sound like conservative nonsense, a fundamentalism that is out of fashion. Rather than attack us personally, however, we invite our critics to refute the argument and prove us wrong.

Moreover, Charles Murray raised the fundamental question of whether a government bureaucracy could ever solve poverty in America. Government in America was envisioned by our Founding Fathers to be a limited government, responsible primarily for defending against foreign enemies and, on the state or local level, for providing the basics of local security, including police and fire protection. Starting with the New Deal, America launched into an enthusiastic enterprise on the premise that government bureaucrats could solve a host of social problems, including unemployment and welfare.

All too often, what has resulted is a complex matrix of obscure regulations that require a blizzard of paperwork to be completed by overworked and undercompensated government employees demanding detailed responses and strict rule compliance from the least-advantaged citizens among us. Government offices are notorious for long lines and short answers. In a society where a person can get an instant response from scores of telephone-order and Internet-driven businesses, with goods delivered reliably to doorsteps perhaps even the next day, patience with a slow-moving and methodical government bureaucracy is thin. This is especially so when the government bureaucracy year after year appears to be making great progress only in compiling reports, not fundamentally solving the social problem for which it was designed.

## AFRICAN AMERICAN POVERTY VERSUS HISPANIC POVERTY

THE CENSUS Bureau documented that the percentage of African Americans in the United States in 2000 (12.7 percent) was nearly identical to the percentage of Hispanics (12.6 percent). But by 2050, the projected

Hispanic population (24.4 percent) will nearly double the percentage of African Americans (14.6 percent).[33] The number of Hispanics is projected to grow from a 2000 total of 35.6 million to a 2050 total of 102.6 million. Since the days of slavery, blacks have been the largest minority in the country, but that situation is about to change. We are experiencing one of the largest migrations ever seen in history. America is being inundated by a wave of immigration from the Spanish-speaking countries to the south, and much of that immigration is illegal. Realizing the magnitude of that influx should be no surprise to anyone who lives in Arizona, California, New Mexico, or Texas, nor should it surprise anyone who lives in any major U.S. city. Spanish has become America's second language whether we recognize it officially or not. Just fly on any airline or go into any public building across America, and you are likely to find instructions and signage in Spanish as well as English. Virtually every cable television network across the country carries one or more Spanish-speaking channels.

As we noted earlier, poverty rates among Hispanics (21.9 percent) are approximately the same as that of African Americans (24.7 percent). Yet the demographic characteristics of the two groups give reason to believe that their poverty situations are different. In July 2005 the Pew Hispanic Center released a study of Hispanic immigration into six southern states: Alabama, Arkansas, Georgia, North Carolina, South Carolina, and Tennessee. All six states experienced very fast rates of Hispanic population growth in the decade 1990–2000. And economic growth in these states was robust during this decade, a factor that drew many Hispanics to settle there. What was at play was a family phenomenon. The strong growth of jobs in these six southern states drew young males who were seeking employment. Many of those settling in these states were unmarried, and many were illegal immigrants. A pattern of settlement was evident here: the unmarried young men arrived to "establish the beachhead," as it were. Once settled, family members joined the young men, families formed and children were born, and grandparents and other family members followed. Observers noted:

> The prospect of work has attracted large numbers of young Hispanics, often unmarried and mobile enough to pick up and move

where the jobs are. Because the Hispanic population in the new settlement areas of the South had been so small prior to the recent surge, the region has seen less immigration due to family reunification than is common in areas of long-established Hispanic settlement. As a result, Latinos in the new settlements of the South are much more likely than those in areas of traditional settlement to have been born abroad, to have arrived recently (particularly from Mexico), to be male, to be unmarried, and to be young. Most have relatively little education, and many do not speak English well.[34]

These Hispanic immigrants came to the United States to look for work. They took lower-paying jobs and benefited from the surge in manufacturing and construction jobs these southern states experienced in the 1990s. Marriage and "family reunification" were followed by the birth of children within family structures as these new Hispanic immigrants, both legal and illegal, settled. Observers suggested:

> Because the large growth in the Hispanic region is so recent, much of the impact of the new wave of immigration is only beginning to make itself felt on the infrastructure of the host communities. But it is already clear that the impact will be dramatic, particularly on the schools. For now, employers in the region are happy to have a dependable source of low-cost labor available to them. As the new immigrants grow older and utilize more health services, and as more wives join their husbands, evening out the gender imbalance and leading to more children, the demands they make on public services will increase but so too may their contributions to the tax bases supporting these services.[35]

The family-building pattern that is evident in this analysis is encouraging. Initially, uneducated Hispanic immigrants, many of whom cannot speak English well or at all, many of whom are illegal, may experience relatively high levels of poverty. Yet the driving motive behind the immigration is the desire to seek better economic opportunities than are currently available in Mexico, Latin America, or many South American countries, including Colombia, Chile, and even Argentina.

Once here, Hispanic immigrants begin working, even if the only work available is lower-paying jobs of relatively low status. As the economic situation of the initial immigrants improve, additional family members emigrate to join them, and new families form. The children enter the schools and learn English. Families stay together. Extended families include grandparents, brothers and sisters, or other relatives—a structure that provides ample opportunities for child support in a family context, even if mothers and fathers are both employed. While unmarried births among Hispanics are still high (43.5 percent in 2002), many of the children are still cared for in the extended family that remains resident with the mother.[36]

Another indication of strong family ties at the center of Hispanic immigration is the growing magnitude of "remittances," money sent back to families in Mexico by immigrants (both legal and illegal). The Federal Reserve Bank of Dallas estimated that Mexico in 2003 received some $13.3 billion in worker's remittances, an increase of almost 22 percent from the 2002 level.[37] Workers' remittances now occupy third place as a foreign-exchange generator for Mexico. The top foreign-exchange generator ($18.4 billion in 2003) continues to be "maquiladoras," the three thousand manufacturing or export assembly plants that have sprung up in northern Mexico after NAFTA to take advantage of relatively cheap Mexican labor to produce parts or products for the U.S. market. The second largest generator of foreign exchange for Mexico is the export of oil ($15 billion in 2003). Clearly, the magnitude of remittances has given an important boost to the overall Mexican economy. For the purposes of the discussion here, the point is that Hispanic workers in this country remain attached to their families back home, with the ultimate goal being to bring more family members to the United States as fast as the economics permit them to emigrate.

Remittance payments are not limited to Mexican immigrants. A study by the Pew Hispanic Center estimated that $30 billion in remittance payments were sent by some 6 million Hispanic immigrants to Latin America and Caribbean countries. The study concluded that the remittance channel from the United States to these countries was the largest remittance channel in the world. Broad sectors of the adult populations in the recipient nations were benefiting from remittance payments—14 percent of the adult populations in Ecuador, 23 percent in Central America, and 18 percent in Mexico. A majority of the remittance payment recipients were women, a conclusion that supported the analysis that remittance payments are family-oriented in nature.[38]

The wave of Hispanic immigration we are experiencing is still too new a phenomenon for us to draw any final conclusions regarding how many of the new immigrants will remain poor in the long term. Many of the older social science studies examine the more traditional "Latino" communities that had settled in the United States prior to 1990; these studies may not be relevant given the massive new wave of job-seeking Spanish-speaking immigrants we have been experiencing since 1990. Much of the available data does support the conclusion that family structures are relatively strong within Hispanic culture. The Population Resource Center reported that in 1999 approximately 63 percent of Hispanic children in America lived with two parents, as contrasted with 35 percent of African American children.[39] Also, about 81 percent of Hispanics in the year 2000 lived in family households, compared to 69 percent of non-Hispanics; Hispanic family households were also larger, with 56 percent having four or more people, while only 32 percent of non-Hispanic households had four or more people.[40]

A massive government program may not be needed to reduce the incidence of poverty in Hispanic communities. Given their strong family structures and the tendency of children to learn English, the likelihood is that Hispanic immigrants will continue to assimilate into the workforce, taking whatever jobs that are available, even if they are lower-paying and lower status. Early indications are that the earnings potential of second-generation Hispanic immigrants quickly eclipse the more limited earnings potential of those who "established the beachhead." Second-generation Hispanic immigrants benefit both from learning English as a primary language and from their years of schooling in America.[41] These trends bode well for a conclusion that current poverty levels measured in the Hispanic community may be disproportionately high because the statistics include a large number of recent immigrants who are struggling to overcome language and education barriers.

Yet, again, we are cautious in these conclusions. If the number of illegal immigrants grows unchecked, America may be taking in social and economic problems that could result in increasing poverty both in the Hispanic and non-Hispanic communities.

## WHAT HAS WELFARE REFORM ACCOMPLISHED?

As we noted earlier, President Clinton in 1996 signed the Personal Responsibility and Work Opportunity Reconciliation Act, a fundamental redefinition of welfare that the president characterized as designed to "end welfare as we know it." The bill ended the "entitlement" nature of the previous AFDC program. No longer were families able to claim benefits simply because they qualified under AFDC definitions of poverty. Instead, the new legislation imposed work requirements on families receiving assistance. Block grants, as had been defined by conservative Republicans in Newt Gingrich's famous 1994 "Contract with America,"[42] were awarded to the states with the requirement that welfare caseloads and certain measures be instituted to encourage job placement as well as marriage and family development. To prevent welfare from becoming a permanent benefit, a cap of five years was placed on benefits. The program was renamed Temporary Assistance for Needy Families (TANF) so as to leave no room for doubt that the goal of the redefined program was to provide only temporary assistance to families in need, not permanent public assistance for single-parent children. With TANF, the AFDC program was declared over and done with.

One result of the program change is clear. The number of families receiving welfare has dropped dramatically. In 1996, the last year of the AFDC program, 4.4 million families were receiving assistance, numbering some 12.3 million people. By 2003 the number of families receiving assistance was reduced by more than half to a total of slightly more than 2 million families, and the number of individuals had been reduced nearly 60 percent to only 4.9 million individual recipients.[43] In an important sense, one of Charles Murray's goals was being accomplished: people were being removed from welfare. What is less clear is whether those who left the AFDC program were truly assisted in their struggle to get out of poverty. Again, the number of poor actually increased in 2004. There are indications that the new bureaucratic complications and massive paperwork required in administering the TANF program simply discouraged applicants from continuing. Other analyses suggest the demand for social workers to reduce caseloads resulted in their pushing aid recipients out of the program.

Even a cursory examination of the mountains of documentation generated on the state and federal level leave no doubt that the TANF program has become exceedingly complex and difficult to understand, even to professional social workers. In effect, TANF is fifty different state programs, not a national program administered under consistent standards. Some observers have concluded that many of the program's supposed requirements, such as the need to encourage marriage and discourage illegitimate births, are guidelines that have largely been ignored by administrators who are overwhelmed by the massive thicket of rules and regulations, or who are not in agreement with the program's political redefinition. Clearly, the initial effort of state welfare programs under TANF has been devoted to implementing a wide variety of work-to-welfare efforts and to reducing caseloads, not to developing programs designed to help families form or strengthen marriages.[44]

A survey by the National Council of Churches in 2000 revealed that pushing people into "workfare" was not a solution to ending poverty:

> A majority of respondents said that adults on TANF are being forced to take any job that is available without regard to their family needs. Often they are pushed into jobs for which they are not qualified and then sanctioned for failing at work. The jobs they get when they lack education and training often don't pay enough to support a family and in many cases they lose Medicaid, food stamps, child care and housing subsidies when they get a job (or the value is sharply reduced). The result may be that they are poorer when they are working than they were on welfare, a fact that also shows up in responses to later questions.[45]

The survey's conclusions reaffirmed Murray's argument that simply ending welfare would force private charities to become more involved:

> Although this is a limited survey that does not cover the entire religious community, it covers a wide enough diversity of opinion for

the compiler to feel confident that the observations indicate some fairly clear trends among the population that has come to the attention of this segment of the religious social service community. Those trends are that more people are working as a result of TANF and a strong U.S. economy than would have been had there not been any 1996 welfare law, but that many of them have not escaped poverty by leaving welfare, and that their care is being shifted away from government agencies to the non-profit sector, which has a limited capacity to meet the need.[46]

Still, welfare caseloads under TANF have been cut virtually in half. Conservative supporters of TANF note an important conclusion, one at the core of Charles Murray's reasoning: the "existence of generous welfare programs for the past several decades" had made "not-working" a reasonable alternative to long-term employment. TANF went a long way to eliminate the option that single-parent families could find permanent subsistence on welfare without being forced to take steps to find employment.[47] If Congress stays the TANF course, substantial caseload reductions should continue as an increasing number of current participants reach their fifth and last year of welfare benefits. But whether the effort will actually reduce poverty remains to be seen. A government program mandating that the poor go to work (TANF) might turn out to be no more effective in eliminating poverty than was the government program that gave money directly to needy families (AFDC).

In summary, brilliant minds have implemented massive federal and state programs with nearly unlimited funding. Perhaps after more than forty years of determined effort, we should finally admit we have failed. The Great Society failed because money turned out not to be the solution to ending poverty. Unless the ultimate goal of TANF is to get government out of the poverty business altogether, we still have not learned the fundamental lesson. What the Great Society should have taught us may be more difficult to accept: government programs, no matter how they are designed, may never succeed in eliminating poverty or even in reducing it beyond the level we have already reached. In the final analysis, poverty is a social and an economic problem. Perhaps we should finally acknowledge that poverty is a problem government alone will never solve.

# 3

## The Politics of Guilt, Rage, and Violence

Prejudice, by clouding the issue, retards a realistic solution to the problem.

—Psychologist Gordon W. Allport, 1954[1]

THE NATIONAL DEBATE ON poverty over the last forty years has played out against the background of the civil rights movement so much so that, when the subject of poverty is discussed, the topic tends to shift to African American poverty. Why should this be so?

Michael Harrington's 1960 book *The Other America* did much to raise the national consciousness on African American poverty, but he also focused attention on poor white rural poverty and on poverty among the aged, most of whom were white. Still, the issues of poverty and race in America have become intertwined in large part because African American poverty directly challenges America's core beliefs that racial discrimination has excluded blacks from fully enjoying the mainstream benefits of the economic success America realized in the post–World War II world.

As Gunnar Myrdal so capably pointed out in his seminal work *An American Dilemma*, racial prejudice remains the lie at the heart of an American dream that proclaims equality for all. Slavery, the fatal flaw in our Constitution, was not the primary reason Abraham Lincoln fought the Civil War—his central goal was to preserve the Union at any cost, a goal for which he too would have compromised over slavery, especially when the war was just beginning. Lincoln is generally credited with freeing the slaves even though the Emancipation Proclamation liberated slaves only in the Rebel states, not in the North. Nor did the Gettysburg Address directly address African Americans, even though Lincoln successfully articulated a changed emphasis for the American experiment by declaring that we were dedicated to the proposition that all are equal. Racial injustices were perpetuated in the Reconstruction era after the Civil War. Many rights, including voting rights, were not fully secured for African Americans until key civil rights legislation was passed during Lyndon B. Johnson's Great Society program. Today we are some 230 years into the American experiment with free government, yet the dilemma of unequal economic success for African Americans remains in front of us as an issue that will stay alive as long as blacks remain disproportionately poor. Truthfully, Lincoln put us on the path of racial equality, a destination we are still trying to reach.

In the 1950s the nation began to see the reality of racial discrimination on the daily television news. Out of that realization a political debate stirred the nation to change. Our national goal today remains to end poverty, even though we have yet to make progress on many of the same problems we faced when Dwight Eisenhower was president. Many problems, especially urban poverty concentrated in black ghettos, may even be worse and more intractable today than ever before.

In this chapter we are going to examine the intellectual and political debate over poverty and race to see if we have made some fundamental mistakes in our thinking. Even in 1996, when we tried to fix the welfare state with more conservative principles, we still failed to reduce poverty. Poverty increased in 2004 despite the welfare reform legislation passed under President Clinton. Why did the thinking behind the Great Society fail? Is conservative thinking about poverty equally doomed to failure? Before we throw in the towel and admit we will never make progress in eliminating poverty in America, let's examine our premises and see if we can detect any important defects.

## THE CIVIL RIGHTS MOVEMENT, 1954–64

THE LANDMARK 1954 Supreme Court decision *Brown v. Board of Education* established that racially segregated schools could not be equal.[2] With this decision the Court started America down a new pathway. Still, establishing racial equality as a de jure legal principle was a long way from establishing de facto economic, political, or social racial equality in reality. A series of dramatic confrontations gave birth to a decade of civil rights activism that stretched from the mid-1950s until the founding of Johnson's Great Society.

- On December 1, 1955, Rosa Parks, an African American seamstress, boarded the Cleveland Avenue bus in downtown Montgomery, Alabama.[3] She sat in the first row of the section reserved for blacks and refused to move to the back of the bus when the bus driver ordered her and three other black passengers to do so.
- In September 1957, Arkansas governor Orval Faubus stood in front of Little Rock's all-white Central High School, surrounded by National Guardsmen, to prevent nine African American children from registering for the fall term.
- On February 1, 1960, four freshmen from the all-black Agricultural and Technical College in Greensboro, North Carolina, entered a Woolworth's department store. They sat at a lunch counter and placed their orders; when refused service, the four students remained peacefully in their seats until the store closed.
- On May 14, 1961, Mother's Day, an angry white mob in Birmingham, Alabama, not stopped by Police Chief Eugene "Bull" Connor, severely beat a group of African American and white "Freedom Riders" who were passengers on a public bus traveling through the city. Earlier that day a group of Freedom Riders on another bus had been firebombed and beaten by an angry white mob in Anniston, Alabama.

These incidents received national press attention, including coverage for the first time on the newly emerging nationally broadcast evening news on the major television networks. Captivating photographs were published in newspapers across the country. Presidents Eisenhower and Kennedy were drawn into the incidents and forced to support a series of Supreme Court decisions that were beginning to uphold the civil rights of African Americans on an equal basis with whites.

Millions of Americans viewed the images of this racial violence with horror and disgust.

Books such as Richard Wright's dramatic 1940 novel *Native Son* had done much to make Americans aware of the racial prejudice and injustice suffered by blacks.[4] Yet the impact reached a new plateau when white Americans could watch these dramatic incidents of racial injustice on television in their living rooms or see photographs in their local newspapers. The images were compelling—a nicely dressed, mature black woman harassed because she refused to move to the back of a bus, vicious white mobs preventing peaceful black children from going to school, polite black youths sitting quietly at lunch counters while being refused service, buses burned and heads broken simply because African Americans wanted to use public transportation to travel the roads of the South. Many white Americans were seeing these images for the first time with their own eyes. Now, viewing the angry, hateful face of racial intolerance, many white Americans awoke with a feeling that they had been complicit in the crime of racial prejudice, a guilt that was compounded by how little they had been aware that a racial problem existed before being confronted visually by the reality.

The reality was impinging upon the White House as well. On September 26, 1962, Mississippi governor Ross Barnett met black student James Meredith with four hundred armed police officers to prevent him from enrolling at the all-white University of Mississippi in Oxford. On September 27 Meredith made his fourth attempt to enter the university, this time accompanied by a convoy of U.S. marshals. Governor Barnett ordered the campus surrounded by hundreds of state troopers, sheriffs, deputies, and local police officers armed with gas masks, clubs, helmets, and trained dogs. Nearly one thousand students stood by and watched as Meredith and the federal officers were turned back. Attorney General Robert F. Kennedy intervened. On September 29, President John F. Kennedy ordered hundreds of U.S. marshals to converge on Oxford, federal troops were alerted for action, and the Mississippi National Guard was federalized.

On September 30, violence erupted after Meredith was escorted onto the Ole Miss campus by the marshals. Order was restored the next morning when sixteen thousand federal troops descended on Oxford, virtually establishing martial law. In the violence, two died and many more were injured. Six weeks later, five hundred armed troops and fifteen U.S. marshals were still stationed in Oxford to maintain order and protect Meredith as he exercised his right to enter the university. James Meredith managed to "integrate" the University of Mississippi some nineteen months after he first applied for admission. Moreover, the nation watched in their living rooms as the drama unfolded on television. The president of the United States and the U.S. Army had to become involved so that one courageous African American student could attend a previously all-white public university.

In 1963 the unfolding civil rights drama returned to Bull Connor and Birmingham, Alabama. Dr. Martin Luther King Jr. and the Southern Christian Leadership Council organized an economic boycott of the city's downtown businesses to protest the city's racial segregation and economic discrimination. The boycott was aggressive, utilizing a variety of tactical actions—sit-ins, rallies, and marches—designed to strictly follow King's principles of confrontational nonviolent protest. On April 19 the city obtained a court injunction forbidding further demonstrations and marches. On Good Friday, King led a march, directly violating the court injunction. With this action, King's principles of nonviolent protest crossed a new frontier, entering a dimension where the decision not to obey the judicial directive required "civil disobedience." He violated the law to demonstrate that the law itself violated higher principles of justice. King was arrested and imprisoned.

Subsequently some twenty-five hundred demonstrators, many of them students, came to Birmingham and poured into the streets. Unable to cope with the seemingly unending flow of young people ready to go to jail, Bull Connor brought out police dogs, shifting tactics from arrest to violent dispersal of the crowds. The photographs of angry police dogs and high-pressure fire hoses used against the black protesters and their white supporters scarred the national consciousness. The images were unforgettable: official violence had been unleashed to suppress the rights of African American citizens who were, by law, equal among us. In the weeks that followed the Birmingham protests, similar confrontations broke out in more than seventy-five Southern cities, resulting in more than ten thousand arrests. What was building was a national resolve that racial injustice had to be addressed head on. Americans had always accepted racial equality in principle, but now it was time to confront the "American Dilemma" by establishing racial equality in fact.

On April 28, 1963, nearly 250,000 Americans, of whom approximately one-third were white, converged on the nation's capital in a "March on Washington." The march culminated in a rally in front of the Lincoln Memorial. Here Martin Luther King Jr. gave the famous "I have a dream" speech that called out the demonstration's lasting message of freedom and racial equality. President Kennedy initially had not fully embraced the March on Washington. Rather, he had viewed King and the civil rights movement as extortionists pressing for the realization of their demands. Moreover, the administration was sensitive to criticism from many civil rights leaders that its efforts were too little, too late. The civil rights movement had played a secondary role in Kennedy's bid for the presidency in 1960. He had campaigned against former Vice President Richard M. Nixon largely on national security issues such as the "missile gap" with Russia and the need to get the nation moving ahead economically after the sluggish years typified by a recession in 1958.

Still, the April 1963 March on Washington was an overwhelming success; at its conclusion President Kennedy met officially with King and other organizers of the march in the Oval Office. Then, on November 22, 1963, only seven months later, Kennedy was assassinated in Dallas; the momentum gained by the civil rights movement came to a halt, uncertain what would happen next. But within Lyndon Johnson's first few months in office, the White House embraced the civil rights movement and declared that the Johnson administration would do everything possible to advance the legislative agenda for racial equality that the Kennedy administration had begun. When the Civil Rights Act was signed into law on July 2, 1964, President Johnson put the cornerstone of the Great Society into place, determined to pass whatever was necessary to make the de jure principle of racial equality articulated by the Supreme Court a de facto economic, political, and social reality.

If Supreme Court decisions and federal laws were all that was needed to establish racial equality, we should have accomplished the task in 1964. But that did not happen. The reality then, as now, is that a disproportionate number of African Americans lived in a condition of poverty that was resistant to change by edict.

The confrontations that gave birth to the civil rights movement since 1955 and the images that emerged from those confrontations placed a judgment of blame on white America for allowing racial inequality to persist in the hundred years since the Civil War had ended. By pursuing a strategy of nonviolence, Martin Luther King Jr. had carried the moral high ground. Blacks were denied entrance to public schools by belligerent white southern governors; angry police were willing to use dogs to restrain peaceful demonstrators; those who protested for racial justice were beaten and arrested. All these incidents contributed to the conclusion that the blame for this injustice rested on white prejudice. And with the blame, guilt followed. White racism was at fault for causing discrimination against blacks. Thus, since 1964, this was a virtually unquestioned truism at the heart of any analysis of civil rights and racial injustice. A great injustice had been done African Americans, so now was the time to atone for this sin committed by white hatred. The legislative agenda of the Great Society can only be understood if we realize that blaming white society and causing white society to feel guilty were central to the analysis and the resulting strategy.

The Johnson administration was determined to wage an economic, social, and political war whose true aim was to break up once and for all the structural barriers of white racism that perpetuated poverty in America. Since blacks were disproportionately poor, everyone was expected to understand that achieving racial equality was essential to winning the War on Poverty. To win this war the president himself would mobilize the executive branch into action. The alphabet agencies of the federal bureaucracy were unleashed in the realms of health, education, and welfare to right the wrongs of racial injustice. The bureaucracy of the welfare state was empowered and funded to end poverty. Here is how the logic of the argument fit together: when racial equality is achieved, then the War on Poverty would be won as a consequence. Nothing could have been more obvious to those whose underlying premise was that generations of determined white prejudice had created a complex network of institutional barriers whose goal was to hold African Americans in their subservient place. The Supreme Court would outlaw the institutionalized structure of racism, and Congress stood ready to enact any laws that were needed. Finally, an aggressive welfare bureaucracy directed from the White House would be given the necessary resources to solve the problems of housing, education, employment, and welfare. If white America were at fault, then government would solve the problem—that was the conventional wisdom at the heart of the civil rights movement begun in the 1950s and continued until the race riots of the mid-1960s.

## THE POLITICS OF VIOLENCE: A TIME TO BURN?

ON JULY 16, 1964, two weeks after the Civil Rights Act was signed into law, racial violence erupted in Harlem. That summer, race riots also broke out in Chicago, Jersey City, Patterson-Elizabeth, Philadelphia, and Rochester. And a common pattern emerged with the riots: a precipitating event triggered the riot, generally a police altercation with a black youth. Next, the African American community responded in anger, with people coming into the streets. Violence against property then broke out in the black community, characterized by burning and looting. After several days of continued disruption, a massive show of law enforcement was required to restore order. The majority of injuries occurred to black residents of the African American urban ghettos where the riots occurred, the properties and businesses damaged were generally owned by blacks. Those who were arrested for disorderly conduct or looting were generally black as well. At the end of the riot, the black communities affected were left poorer and more distressed than ever. Few black communities that experienced racial violence were ever rebuilt or restored.

Social scientists argued that the civil rights movement had set in motion a tide of rising expectations in the African American communities around the nation. When too few new job opportunities were created, those African Americans living in depressed urban ghettos realized that their poverty was not going to be quickly eliminated. Their frustration created a tinderbox environment where confrontations with white police that might otherwise have been considered minor were now out of control. Angry reactions led to a cycle of more violence in the streets. Race riots were in one sense self-destructive, yet the violent outbreak was understandable as an expression of frustration. Fundamental conditions of racial inequality remained even after white racism had been identified as a cause of the poverty. To eliminate racial injustice, a massive federal effort had been unleashed.

On August 6, 1965, President Johnson signed into law the Voting Rights Act, another key piece of Great Society legislation. Five days later a riot broke out in the Watts neighborhood of Los Angeles. The Watts riot became a "signature race riot," one that established a pattern for other riots to follow. After Watts, the civil rights movement shifted. Within the shadow of Martin Luther King's nonviolence strategy, violence became a possible and expected form of protest against racial injustice and poverty. A contemporary analysis emphasized the impact the Watts riot had on America:

> The Watts riot wore on for five days—144 hours. Calm was not restored until some 15,000 national guardsmen and 1,000 policemen occupied the area. The statistics were grim. Thirty-four persons had died and there were 1,032 reported injuries. A total of 3,952 adults and juveniles were arrested—almost three-quarters on charges of burglary and theft. Estimated property damage was 40 million dollars. But these staggering statistics do not begin to measure the impact of the Watts riot. The Governor's Commission on the Los Angeles Riots titled their report, *Violence in the City— An End or a Beginning?* If there was any doubt, the summers which followed answered the rhetorical question.[5]

The pattern of race riots in the black ghettos of America was repeated in the summers 1966 and 1967. Americans watching the nightly television news were impacted by violent images that replaced the nonviolent images of sit-ins and marches that had marked the earlier civil rights movement.

Almost forty years later, in the summer of 2005, when Hurricane Katrina flooded New Orleans, many white Americans were shocked to see poor black communities in distress. Media commentators expressed surprise to find so many poor blacks without automobiles with which to escape the oncoming storm. The world press charged that President Bush was a racist in that he did not respond as fast to the misery of the thousands that were left homeless because they were poor African Americans, not middle-class or rich whites. When looting and violence broke out in the flooded city, the liberal mainstream media acted as if these images of minority poverty had never been seen before. The reality was that similar images had been seen in the mid-1960s, with the national outbreak of race riots that destroyed many inner-city black ghettos. Many American adults today were born after the race riots of the 1960s; if a person is not fifty years old today, he or she may have no firsthand memory of what the riots of the 1960s were like. The violence of the race riots ended once and forever the peaceful era of civil rights protest typified by the civil disobedience that Martin Luther King Jr. championed. Sit-ins and marches were replaced with images of arson, looting, and the National Guard.

The worst riots of 1967 hit during a two-week period in July, first in Newark and then in Detroit. A chain of more than one hundred urban communities across the country were inflamed in similar riots as the nation watched the repeating pattern. In July 1967 President Johnson appointed a national commission to study the riots and to report on what could be done to stop them. Headed by Otto Kerner, governor of Illinois, the National Advisory Commission on Civil Disorders became known as the Kerner Commission. The central conclusion of its report, articulated on its first page, was written to shock the nation: "Our nation is moving toward two societies, one black, one white—separate and unequal."[6]

These words harkened back to the 1954 Supreme Court decision *Brown v. Board of Education* and the ruling that segregated schools could never be construed as equal. Now the Kerner Commission was telling the nation that essentially nothing had been accomplished since 1954. Despite the mandate of the Supreme Court, we remained a racially divided nation such that the African Americans among us continued to suffer economic, social, and political injustice. Again, the culprit was identified as racial discrimination, and the themes of white responsibility and white guilt were fully articulated. White prejudice had caused racial discrimination and segregation. In the words of the commission:

"What white Americans have never fully understood—but what the Negro can never forget—is that white society is deeply implicated in the ghetto. White institutions created it, white institutions maintain it, and white society condones it."[7] The new argument was that the violence would not stop until white America understood the fierce intensity of black rage.

Still, the analysis of the Kerner Commission could easily have come out of the pages of Gunnar Myrdal's 1944 classic, *An American Dilemma*. Again, nothing had changed. The commission documented the patterns that had been known to social scientists for more than two decades: blacks in America's inner cities continued to live in "squalor and deprivation in ghetto neighborhoods."[8] Inner-city ghetto life was profoundly inferior to the expectations of middle-class white America. the unemployment rate for blacks was nearly twice that of whites. Black ghettos were dominated by a cycle of poverty—broken families, single mothers, crime, poor educational systems, and inadequate medical care. The relation between white urban police forces and the black residents of urban ghettos had descended into hostility. Today, the same words could be written to describe race relations in the United States.

The recommendations of the Kerner Commission were almost as familiar as their analysis of the problem. Regardless of what the commission was evaluating—employment, education, welfare, or housing—the recommendation was always for the federal government to do something different. The phrase, "the Commission recommends that the federal government . . . ," was repeated over and over, always followed by directives for new legislation or redirected bureaucratic involvement. The Kerner Commission had analyzed that the problem was attitudinal, namely, white racism. These attitudes had led to structural barriers, a pattern of institutionalizing racial discrimination into the way Americans ran everything from jobs to schools to hospitals. And the Kerner solution was more government involvement. What the commission never seriously considered was the possibility that government could not solve the problem of poverty and racial inequality, no matter how many laws were passed, no matter how many Supreme Court decisions were issued, no matter how many bureaucracies were created.

Kenneth B. Clark, one of the first witnesses to appear before the Kerner Commission, reflected on the déjà vu nature of the nation's reaction to the 1960s race riots. His testimony was quoted in the commission's report summary:

> I read that report . . . of the 1919 riot in Chicago, and it is as if I were reading the report of the investigating committee on the Harlem riot of '35, the report of the investigating committee on the Harlem riot of '43, the report of the McCone Commission on the Watts riot.
>
> I must again in candor say to you members of this Commission—it is a kind of Alice in Wonderland—with the same moving picture re-shown over and over again, the same analysis, the same recommendations, the same inaction.[9]

Clark was right. The analysis and recommendations of many experts and commissions stretching back decades were always the same: poverty and discrimination caused African American inequality. Clark concluded, however, that the previous efforts had failed because of "inaction." But this was not the problem. As we have pointed out, the government's huge welfare state has spent nearly $10 trillion trying to eliminate poverty and solve the problems of racial injustice, and yet in 2004 poverty increased and racial inequality continued. The logic behind the longstanding blame for racial injustice had many white Americans feeling guilty. Still, turning the government loose with a massive bureaucracy and a nearly unlimited budget was not a successful formula to solve the problem. After four decades of a massive War on Poverty, we are exactly where we started—poverty remains in America, many underclass African Americans remain concentrated in pockets of urban and rural disadvantage, and white America is at fault. The rhetoric has not changed, only the intensity of the argument given the violence of the race riots. Today we are no closer to realizing Lyndon B. Johnson's dream of a Great Society than we were in 1964. The images of poor blacks suffering in New Orleans in the aftermath of Hurricane Katrina should have made these conclusions obvious to anyone watching events unfold at the Superdome, the convention center, or in the lower Ninth Ward.

## THE POLITICS OF RAGE: ENTER BLACK POWER

ON JUNE 5, 1966, James Meredith started a solitary "March Against Fear," resolving to walk from Memphis to Jackson, Mississippi, to protest racism. Shortly after starting, he was shot by a sniper. In a show of solidarity, civil rights leaders, including Martin Luther King Jr. and Stokely Carmichael came to Mississippi to continue Meredith's march. Carmichael was born in Trinidad; he moved to the United States and attended high school in New York. In 1961 he was a Freedom Rider; by 1966 he was head of the Student Non-Violent Coordinating Committee (SNCC), a group that was becoming increasingly militant, as was Carmichael.

When the marchers reached Greenwood, Mississippi, Carmichael spoke at a rally and coined a new phrase: "What we need is black power." One of SNCC's more fiery orators jumped on the platform to seize the moment. He began shouting over and over again, "What do you want?" With increasing enthusiasm, the crowd answered, "Black power!" The phrase caught on nationally, together with another phrase coined by radical H. Rap Brown who succeeded Carmichael as the national director of SNCC. "Violence is as American as apple pie," Brown declared; he also stated, "If America don't come around, we're gonna burn it down." With these statements, the nonviolent civil rights movement of King added the possibility of violence if white America failed to enact bureaucratic "reforms" to realize "equality."

The slogan "black power" and the radicalism of the Black Panthers came together through the Stokely Carmichael connection. In October 1966, radicals Bobby Seale and Huey Newton formed the Black Panther Party in Oakland, California. They took the name for their organization from the drawing of a black panther that Carmichael had adopted as the emblem for his earlier Lowndes County Freedom Organization, formed in Alabama in 1964. The Black Panthers at their height had chapters in several major cities and a membership that may have approached two thousand. They saw themselves as radicals who openly harassed the police, including engaging in several shootouts with the police. Brown left SNCC and joined the Black Panther Party, as did Carmichael. Ultimately, Carmichael became the group's "honorary prime minister." He adopted a second slogan, "Black Is Beautiful," and began wearing traditional African forms of dress and an Afro hairstyle to emphasize a feeling of black pride and a rejection of white society and white values.

The Black Panthers moved in a Marxist, revolutionary direction, drawing intellectual support from angry radicals. At the same time, Malcolm X gave voice to the Black Muslim movement, a movement that rejected whites as a "beast" against whom blacks were locked in warfare. Then the FBI, under orders from director J. Edgar Hoover, placed the Black Panthers under surveillance after determining that the group represented a threat to America's internal security. A feeling of confrontation was intensifying.

On April 4, 1968, Martin Luther King Jr. was assassinated in Memphis, Tennessee, shot on the balcony of his hotel while in town to lead a nonviolent labor union march of striking sanitation workers. In response to the outrage over King's assassination, another wave of race riots swept across America's inner cities. On June 5, 1968, only two months after King's assassination, Robert F. Kennedy was assassinated in Los Angeles. Kennedy had just left the celebration in the ballroom of the Ambassador Hotel after announcing his victory in the Democratic Party's California presidential primary. Kennedy had become a major voice in the antiwar movement, as the politics of opposing the Vietnam War had begun to merge with the politics of opposing racism.

Within the span of two months, the nation lost both Martin Luther King Jr. and Robert Kennedy, two of the most effective leaders who had pressed together for racial justice. With these two killings, the nation experienced again spasms of trauma that began in 1963 with the assassination of John F. Kennedy. The politics of the civil rights movement radicalized even more, joining forces with the antiwar movement and moving farther than ever toward the political Left.

In August 1968, the Democratic National Convention in Chicago was marred by violent confrontations in the streets between city police and demonstrators protesting the Vietnam War. Bobby Seale of the Black Panthers was one of the so-called Chicago Seven, charged with criminal conspiracy for disrupting the convention. Seale stood alongside white radicals Jerry Rubin and Abbie Hoffman in a raucous trial before Judge Julius Hoffman. The antiwar violence of the 1968 Democratic National

Convention in Chicago, followed by the Kent State killing of protesting students by the National Guard, caused the image of race riots and anti-war riots to merge in the national consciousness. When Richard M. Nixon won the 1968 presidential election, the nation appeared to split between those who supported the Vietnam War and a revolutionary an-tiwar movement that had co-opted whatever was left of the 1950s civil rights movement. Now with Robert Kennedy and Martin Luther King Jr. both gone, the radicals in the antiwar movement joined forces with the radicals in the civil rights movement as both became more revolutionary in word and deed.

That summer, on July 23, 1968, a gun battle broke out between po-lice and black militants in Glenville, Ohio, in Cleveland's racially trou-bled East Side, not far from where the Hough riots had occurred in 1966. A relatively innocuous incident with police attempting to remove an abandoned car with a tow truck led to a shootout between police and a group of armed black militants under the leadership of radical Ahmed Evans. The group had been under surveillance by Cleveland Po-lice, who were suspicious that the black militants were buying illegal automatic weapons. In the gun battle that resulted, three police officers were killed and twelve wounded; casualties among the black militants included three killed and one wounded. As the gun battle wound down around midnight, arson began. What followed was a typical 1960s ghetto race riot characterized by burning and looting.

What made the Glenville incident important was the gun battle be-tween the police and the black radicals. Prior to the Glenville incident, race riots had been dominated by black property damage, arson, and looting, all limited to the black ghetto. Now, black militants began with person-oriented violence, a gun battle with the police. Moreover, here there were more white casualties than black, something that had not happened in the previous race riots. America had never experienced an interracial civil war; the shootout in Glenville raised the possibility that interpersonal violence between blacks and whites could happen.[10]

Since the 1970s, racial violence has largely subsided in the United States. Yet the possibility lies just below the surface. In the aftermath of Hurricane Katrina in 2005, the looting that broke out among poor, mostly black residents who had not evacuated New Orleans prior to the storm was reminiscent of the looting of the typical 1960s-style race riot. The limited arson experience in New Orleans could easily have been more widespread had the city not been flooded. Because we have not experienced an outbreak of racial violence in recent years does not mean that the underlying problems of poverty and racial injustice have been solved. The racial violence of the 1960s intensified the argument that white racism was "at fault" for the inequality and lack of justice suffered by African Americans. The moral argument has great validity and force. Still, the path of blaming white America has not worked if the goals are to restore racial justice and equality. We have been emphasizing here that, if anything, many problems of racial inequality have actually intensified since the 1960s and grown more difficult to change.

In one sense, the radical revolutionary aspect of the civil rights movement of 1968–72 died when the race riots stopped. What really happened was more subtle. The radicals themselves aged, but the radical nature of their thinking transformed the tenor of the political Left in a permanent way. "White racism" became the only politically correct argument that could be advanced when discussing the cause of African American inequality; any other argument justified the political Left's labeling the argument's proponent a "racist" by definition.

Thinking from guilt and wanting to redress the problems of racial injustice, President Lyndon B. Johnson initiated a massive effort to evoke change. Still, we have argued that four decades of waging the War on Poverty are enough to declare that the experiment with government bureaucracy and massive federal spending has failed to eliminate poverty. Regardless of the validity of the moral argument that white racism is the cause of racial injustice and racial inequality experienced by African Americans, we have to realize that blaming whites is not enough to end racial inequality.

White prejudice may have so clouded our thinking as a nation that, prior to the 1960s, we could not even identify the problem. Still, today we have to admit that confronting white prejudice directly since the 1960s has not been an effective tactic in solving the problem. Calling out the problem of white racism in clear and unequivocal terms has not ended poverty or the related problems caused by racism. If white racism was the clear and accurate description of the cause for racial discrimination in America, correctly identifying and defining that cause did not mean we would be equally as effective in clearly and precisely defining a solution. The politics of guilt, rage, and violence have now had more than four decades of robust expression in America. Yet making white America feel guilty for the racial discrimination suffered by African Americans has not worked, not if we judge by objective or measurable results. What confidence do we have that another four decades of guilt and rage would produce any better results?

## BILL COSBY AND BLACK RESPONSIBILITY: THE PROBLEM OF "BLAMING THE VICTIM"

AT A 2004 meeting in Washington DC commemorating the fiftieth anniversary of *Brown v. Board of Education*, comedian and actor Bill Cosby made some remarks that were sharply critical of the African American poor. He challenged poor blacks by charging, "The lower economic people are not holding up their end in this deal. These people are not parenting. They are buying things for kids—$500 for sneakers for what? And won't spend $200 for 'Hooked on Phonics.'" He ridiculed the poor English of the black ghetto: "They're standing on the corner and they can't speak English. I can't even talk the way these people talk: 'Why you ain't,' 'Where you is.' . . . And I blamed the kids until I heard the mother talk. And then I heard the father talk. . . . Everybody knows it's important to speak English except these knuckleheads. . . . You can't be a doctor with that kind of crap coming out of your mouth!" He suggested that African American criminals were being incarcerated not because of racism but because of crimes: "These are not political criminals. These are people going around stealing Coca-Cola. People getting shot in the back of the head over a piece of pound cake and then we run out and we are outraged, [saying] 'The cops shouldn't have shot him.' What the hell was he doing with the pound cake in his hand?"

The controversy began as soon as the *Washington Post* published Cosby's comments.[11] The controversy gained momentum as the wisdom of Cosby's remarks was debated in the blogosphere.[12]

Cosby dared to challenge African American responsibility for the conditions suffered in the black ghetto underclass. This attack went against the grain of politically correct rhetoric that defines white racism as the cause and black inequality as the result. Cosby was attacked both for his flippant tone and because his argument appeared to "blame the victim" for the racial inequality and racial injustice suffered. Cosby was attacked as being a successful elitist, an African American who had achieved success and was now embarrassed by less-fortunate African Americans. His comments were seen as "a relentless attack on poor and working-class African Americans."[13] Writing in the *Village Voice,* Ta-Nehisi Coates charged that Cosby was long on his moral attacks and short on solutions:

> When the Coz came to Constitution Hall last week, he was one up on his audience. He had no solutions, and unlike his audience, he knew it. And so he fell back on what elitists do best—impose condescending lessons on ethics and etiquette. He fell back on *Fat Albert,* and a world where poverty can be beaten through sheer force of blithe axiom. Morality becomes the answer when you don't have another one. Maybe we are everything the racists say we are—dumb, fat, and cute, in a really ugly and childish sort of way. But if we could just pay attention in school, stop stealing, learn proper English, and correctly apply deodorant, we'd be all right. Well, maybe not all right, but at least we wouldn't make Cosby look so bad.[14]

Bill Cosby issued a press release to defend himself, claiming that he felt he could no longer remain quiet. He was concerned that the conservative media was beginning to speak negatively of African Americans on the question of personal responsibility and that he wanted to lead the charge by "ringing the bell to galvanize those who want change in the lower economic community."[15] As the press release elaborated:

> Mr. Cosby explains that his comments were intended to be a call to action, to "turn the mirror around on ourselves." "I think that it is time for concerned African Americans to march, galvanize and raise the awareness about this epidemic to transform our helplessness, frustration and righteous indignation into a sense of shared responsibility and action.

"I travel the country and see these patterns in every community—stories of 12 year old children killed in the cross fire between knuckleheads selling drugs, the 14 year olds with a sealed envelope as their first step into the criminal justice system, the young males who become fathers and not held responsible, the young women having children and moving back in with their mothers and grandmothers, and the young people who choose not to learn standard English.

"My question: Is Bill Cosby hoping that the dropout rate will reach 70% soon and teenage single parenthood will grow to 80% in the lower economic neighborhoods? Or is he clanging a bell and warning that this is an epidemic that has to be stopped? Are we so worried about what others think about us that we are unwilling to address this disease that is infecting our people more and more every day?"[16]

The criticism did not stop Cosby from voicing his charges. In October 2004, while visiting some public schools in Richmond, Virginia, with former Governor L. Douglas Wilder, who was then running for mayor, Cosby emphasized to the students the importance of their education: "Study. That's all. It's not tough. You're not picking cotton. You're not picking up the trash. You're not washing windows. You sit down. You read. You develop your brain." He commented on the problem of teenage pregnancy: "Everybody knows about sex. Not too many people know about algebra. Let's think about love. Let's think about where you can get it, but not sex. You're too young for sex." He spoke out against drugs and alcohol: "There are still old people who drink, do drugs—who will stop and take the time to tell you don't be like them. Have you heard them? Pay attention to them."[17]

Cosby was clearly trying to connect with a message that black poverty would only end when and if black people themselves took responsibility for changing their lives. This was a very different message from the politics of guilt, where the message had been that white racism had placed barriers to African American progress, and these were the causes of racial injustice and inequality. Since the 1960s, many barriers had been removed; still the problem of black poverty persisted. Cosby argued that his intent was not to "blame the victims" but to encourage the victims to use their own moral resolve and determination to work themselves toward justice and equality now that the barriers of racial discrimination were substantially reduced. The message was one of self-help.

Bill Cosby is not alone in voicing the message of responsibility. Over the past few years an increasing number of African American conservatives have been expressing this theme, countering the rhetoric of anger and blame. The Reverend Jesse Lee Peterson is an African American pastor who founded BOND—the Brotherhood Organization of a New Destiny—a national nonprofit organization dedicated to "rebuilding the family by rebuilding the man."[18] Peterson's focus is on family issues, approached through reinforcing the moral and economic role of African American males as the head of traditional families. He has argued that Democratic politicians have exploited the affinity African Americans have felt toward Democratic politicians since the New Deal. While Peterson's tone is more seriously and directly expressed than Bill Cosby's, his message is fundamentally in agreement:

> Our biggest barrier as black Americans is no longer the law, white Americans, or black leaders. It is ourselves. We must solve the problems in our own community. Seventy percent of black children born out of wedlock is unacceptable. Celebration of drugs and perverse sex in rap music must be rejected.[19]

In moving terms, Peterson described his own evolution from welfare dependence to a life based on themes of responsibility:

> In a way, my life was a preview of much to come for many black Americans. I was born into a broken family in the tiny town of Comer Hill, Alabama. I did not know my father, and my mother had left me with her mother when I was a toddler and moved to Gary, Indiana, with another man.[20]

Peterson explained how the trap of welfare dependency had captured him in a downward spiral:

In fact, I found it amazingly easy to get on welfare and simply live off the system. I signed up in Los Angeles and started receiving $300 a month. In addition, the system paid my rent and supplied me with food stamps, free medical coverage, and other benefits. I was making the white man pay me back for all the oppression I thought I'd been subjected to in the past. So I partied with that money, caroused with women, and lived a fairly degenerate life. I thought I had it made.

But while on welfare, things didn't get better. They got worse. The more money I got from welfare, the less desire I had to work. It became spiritually and morally suffocating.[21]

For Peterson, the key to breaking out of this debilitating welfare dependency demanded that he reject the rage he felt almost unconsciously for whites.

That themes of African American responsibility are being openly expressed and debated marks a shift in the debate on racial injustice in America. Up to now, liberal Democrats, who have defined the politically correct themes that may be expressed without criticism, have largely owned the terms of the debate. Anyone arguing themes of black responsibility, even if the critics are themselves African Americans, runs the risk of being labeled as racists, part of the problem, not the solution. Raising his voice in opposition to what he considers a black leadership that exploits African Americans has not been easy for Jesse Lee Peterson. He is regularly ridiculed and scorned by black leaders on the political Left. His thinking, according to the standards of liberal politics, is politically incorrect precisely because his themes call upon African Americans to use available opportunities to improve themselves. The politically correct theme would be to continue articulating the politics of rage against white racism, with the expectation that more government welfare programs are not only the solution but are required as a payback for the centuries of discrimination and racism suffered by African Americans.

Affixing the cause of poverty and racial injustice is a moral judgment, but the judgment that white racism is to blame for racial inequality has not been sufficient to solve the problems of racial discrimination that we have been trying for decades to address as a society. Behavioral social scientists argue that we must change what we do before we can change what we think. In other words, no matter how much we argue about who is at fault for causing racial injustice, nothing will change until we begin to change some of the realities themselves. From a behavioral perspective, we will not eliminate poverty in America, or in the black ghetto, until we begin to implement programs that register measurable improvements in the underlying conditions we are trying to change. Until a school program actually graduates more poor children, it doesn't matter how much we argue about placing blame for the failure. We must begin to see more job prospects from our urban poverty ghettos actually get jobs before we will change attitudes about employment, but pointing fingers will get us nowhere. We can rail on moral issues for decades more, but we will not begin to see attitudes toward family and marriage change among the poor until we find successful methodologies that result in poor families forming and staying together.

From a behavioral perspective, the argument about blame is largely irrelevant, a rationalization for failure at best, not a productive path for solution. The War on Poverty is to be rejected, from a behavioral perspective, simply because it did not achieve its stated goal, that is, the elimination of poverty, regardless of whether the effort was right or well intentioned.

## THE BLAME GAME AND THE QUESTION OF IQ: A POINTLESS AND DANGEROUS ARGUMENT

IN 1984 Charles Murray published *Losing Ground*,[22] an important indictment of the welfare system that we analyzed in chapter 2. And we agree with Murray that the welfare system produces a dependency that is unlikely to succeed in reducing poverty regardless of the welfare reforms that are implemented. Ten years later, in 1994, Murray worked with Harvard University psychology professor Richard J. Herrnstein to write *The Bell Curve*,[23] a book dedicated to exploring a link between low IQ and the social underclass. The key argument was that cognitive differences as measured by intelligence tests play a determinative role in causing black inequality in a variety of arenas, including education, employment, income, welfare, poverty, and even family formation. Almost immediately, Herrnstein and Murray were attacked by scholars who pointed out that intelligence tests are biased by their nature so that the results of intelligence tests tend to reflect rather than explain social and economic inequalities and disadvantages.[24]

We raise the issue here to advance our theme that the blame game is not a productive path to pursue if our real goal is to reduce or eliminate poverty. The eugenics theme that results from an argument that race is linked by intelligence to underclass characteristics takes us down a path of hatred and destruction that has produced the worst in human nature, including Hitler and the Holocaust. Moreover, we find that the argument ignores the progress that has been made. Under the administration of George W. Bush, we have had two African American secretaries of state, Colin Powell and Condoleezza Rice. Blacks in recent decades have also succeeded in the highest ranks of business, sports, and entertainment. Our argument here is that a dysfunctional environment produces dysfunctional results regardless of the race of the people involved. We want to attack the problem of black inequality and racial injustice not because we believe poverty is somehow intrinsic to the nature of African Americans. On the contrary, we believe that blacks have suffered injustice and inequality because of white racism—on this we agree with the liberal argument. Our point is that no argument on blame will advance us toward greater equality or justice for all in America. If we want to eliminate poverty, we have to find an approach that works, an approach that produces results, regardless of the "right and wrong" moral arguments that are being slung from both the political Left and the political Right.

## THE WELFARE STATE AND THE DEMOCRATIC PARTY:
## A NEW DEPENDENCY?

AFRICAN AMERICANS have gravitated toward the Democratic Party since the New Deal presidency of Franklin D. Roosevelt. When John F. Kennedy embraced the civil rights movement, African Americans overwhelmingly identified themselves as Democrats. Lyndon B. Johnson's

War on Poverty solidified the political identification for a new generation of African Americans. For more than five decades Republican politicians have not been able to depend upon more than a small percentage of black votes. Republican presidents from Richard M. Nixon through George W. Bush have expanded welfare programs and supported civil rights initiatives. Still, as conservative Republicans have articulated traditional themes of families, employment, and religion, a gap has grown with black voters whose views continue to be strongly influenced by the political Left.

In many states, black voters can and do swing close elections simply by demographics. Many states are predominately Republican, especially in their suburban and rural areas. Yet the metropolitan areas within these states increasingly have large population concentrations that are predominately African American. If a state's white population divides nearly evenly between Republican and Democratic votes, then the large numbers of African American votes concentrated in the urban areas can become the swing votes that determine the outcomes of elections. Strategists in both the Democratic and Republican parties are well aware of these voting demographics. Many Republican politicians abandon campaigning in urban areas, knowing that no matter what they do, they will pick up no more than 5 percent of the African American vote. When urban African American voters change to vote 8–10% Republican, then Democratic strategists know their chances are vastly diminished.

These dynamics have led to a new dependency—Democratic politicians can be counted on to support the expansion of government-funded welfare programs simply because many urban African Americans remain dependent upon those programs. Arguments that the programs have not worked, despite forty years of massive bureaucracy and federal spending, make no impact on Democratic Party politicians who know that objecting to welfare may undermine a critical voting constituency upon whom their electoral success hinges.

What we are arguing for here is a new approach. We believe conservative themes may yield measurable improvements in solving the problems of poverty and racial inequality. Our argument is that we must change our thinking away from depending upon government to solve the problems. Relying on government to solve social problems has only generated self-perpetuating bureaucracies whose survival instincts depend on continuing the social problems they were created to eliminate.

As we proceed with the discussion, we want to move beyond blame arguments. We agree that conservative arguments of responsibility are an important corrective to the debate. Still, these arguments by themselves will not solve a problem that is resistant to moral judgments. We must develop methodologies that result in fundamental changes— methodologies that produce measurable results in reducing poverty and eliminating racial inequality. When initiatives fail, the program should be abandoned. Our argument at this point in the book is that we need to get off the blame game and move beyond the politics of rage, guilt, and violence. Those approaches have not worked. We need to look beyond, to a new solution set, otherwise we are merely setting ourselves up for more decades of angry finger-pointing.

# 4

## The Attack on the Black Family

The shattering blows on the Negro family have made it fragile, deprived and often psychopathic.

—Martin Luther King Jr., 1967[1]

Forty years of the welfare state have resulted in a state of extreme social dysfunction that threatens to destroy the African American community by destroying the African American family. This chapter is perhaps the most difficult chapter we have written. At the outset, we want to state clearly that the social dysfunction we are describing results from the structure of the welfare system itself. Our social science training comes from a behavioral perspective. If people of any race were placed in the identical conditions of urban poverty, we would expect the same behavior to result. The problems we are going to describe in this chapter are inherent to the welfare system and the dysfunctional behavior that results from the liberal political thinking that has guided the welfare system, not from anything inherent in African Americans themselves.

We have already seen that more than 70 percent of African American babies are born to unmarried mothers, of whom about one-third are teenagers. Black families have been under unimaginable stress, and as many households are headed by women today as there are married couples in the black community. Since the U.S. Supreme Court issued

97

the *Roe v. Wade* decision in 1973,[2] we have seen an estimated 13 million African American abortions in a population of 37 million African Americans in the United States. In the Holocaust during World War II, Hitler's Germany exterminated 6 million Jews. The staggering number of African American abortions since *Roe v. Wade* would suggest that the "abortion upon demand" insistence of the political Left is permitting genocide to be waged against blacks in America.

The populations of our prisons are disproportionately black, and within the prison system, homosexual violence is rampant and unchecked. With the breakup of the African American family, we have seen a rise of sexual promiscuity in the African American community. AIDS has increasingly become a disease of that community. Nearly 40 percent of all reported AIDS cases since the epidemic began involve African Americans, even though African Americans make up only about 13 percent of the U.S. population.[3] The impact of AIDS inflicts further violence upon the African American community, threatening to compound the impact of abortions by advancing a subtle and unspoken policy of implicit genocide.

We have already argued that much of our failure to eliminate poverty has come not from a lack of caring or a deficiency in effort. But we believe that the principles of the political Left are doomed to failure. Our goal is to eliminate poverty, build families, and eradicate deadly sexually transmitted diseases, such as AIDS. As we continue to note, the political Left has argued since the writings of Karl Marx and Vladimir Lenin that the family is an arbitrary social unit whose primary function is to socialize children into acceptance of a class society where workers are exploited for the benefit of capitalists who lack any social consciousness. Human experience throughout recorded history argues differently. The human family has been the primary unit of all societies for thousands of years. Still, the Left posits that homosexual and lesbian families are equivalent to traditional families composed of one woman and one man. Our society has had relatively little experience with homosexual or lesbian alternative family structures, and as a result there is little empirical evidence to compare these alternative social units to traditional families. In the next few decades, social scientists will have the opportunity to see how alternative family structures fare on the important questions of how children are educated, what types of jobs they are able to secure, and what types of incomes they are able to earn.

What we have in hand, though, are the results of the welfare state created since President Johnson declared war on poverty in 1964—the largest experiment ever undertaken in human history—by which we can assess the social assumptions of the political Left. If we look at the black community, we can see that the welfare state has caused poor black families to disintegrate. The huge number of abortions in black communities since *Roe v. Wade* is shocking. The sexual agenda promoted by the political Left has allowed AIDS to reach epidemic proportions in African American communities. We do not believe that liberals have ever had a conscious agenda to cause black genocide in America. Instead, our concern is that liberal policies regarding abortion and sexual freedom have had unintended genocidal consequences for African Americans.

These are extreme statements, but we believe the severity of their expression is merited by the extreme social dysfunctions we are about to describe. Nor do we feel our concerns are limited to African American families. White families today are in many ways where black families were twenty or thirty years ago. Teenage pregnancies, the number of babies being born to single mothers, the frequency of abortions, and the threat of AIDS are all problems that threaten soon to be as severe in America's white families as they are today in America's black families. Unless we recognize these problems and design effective programs to reverse the trends, the destruction of poor black families will be followed by the destruction of white families. The adverse consequences resulting from the liberal attack on the family are enormous for all Americans concerned about advancing a morally sound and economically productive society.

## GENOCIDE BY ABORTION

MARGARET SANGER, the founder of the organization that today is Planned Parenthood, began her crusade for abortion on the theme of eugenics. Her journal, *The Birth Control Review,* is filled with articles advocating the elimination of the "unfit," including those with mental and physical disabilities, to produce a superior race of human geniuses. Her slogan, "Birth Control: To Create a Race of Thoroughbreds," appealed to the type of racist thinking that gave rise to Hitler's propaganda and the resultant "racial purification" violence of the concentration camps. Her writings are filled with a mix of the popular ideas of her day, drawn from early sexual psychology and Darwinism. She advocated that women separate sex from childbearing so as to preserve the "right" to have an abortion when childbearing does not suit their economic or psychological needs. Her views were extreme to the point where almost any reason expressed by a woman justifies abortion, even when the need is simply inconvenience. Sanger's writings strongly attack Christianity, often expressing a vehement anti-Catholicism. She wanted sexual freedom to replace religion. She intended the combination of birth control and abortion to produce more children from the "fit" and fewer children from the "unfit."

In 1939 Sanger launched what came to be known as "the Negro Project," a concerted attempt to build birth-control clinics in black areas across the country. The underlying goal was to limit the rising number of African Americans by reducing African American birthrates throughout the rural South as well as in the urban cities of the North. By placing birth-control centers in or near black communities, Sanger sought to convince African Americans that by having fewer babies more carefully "spaced" in a family, African Americans would enjoy an improved standard of health that would be measured in a reduction in maternal and infant deaths. Sanger's letters of the time outline a plan to convince black religious leaders to preach the virtues of birth control. The tone of her letters conveys a thinly disguised racism aimed at attacking the "reproductive practices of black Americans." In a 1939 letter to Dr. Clarence J. Gamble, prominent for creating the soap-manufacturing company of Proctor and Gamble, Sanger wrote, "We do not want word to go out that we want to exterminate the Negro population, and the minister is the man who can straighten out that idea if it ever occurs to any of their more rebellious members."[4] Obviously, this needed to be written precisely because Sanger's message did sound like an extermination attack. Gamble was then serving as southern director for Sanger's Birth Control Federation of America, a predecessor to Planned Parenthood.

The statistics on African American abortions are shocking. Even though African Americans are only about 13 percent of the U.S. population, one of every three abortions in the United States is performed on a black woman.[5] Three of every five African American women will abort a child. Some 1,452 African American babies are killed each day in abortions. Let's compare these statistics to the number of African Americans who have been killed by crimes of racial violence. Statistics show that between 1882 and 1968, 3,446 blacks were lynched in the United States. That number is bypassed by the number of African American abortions every three days. Let's project the favorable consequences had the aborted babies been allowed to live. Had the 13 million babies aborted since *Roe v. Wade* in 1973 been allowed to live, today's African American population of 37 million could reasonably be projected to exceed 50 million today. In other words, today's potential African American population has been reduced 25 percent by abortions. And the 13 million African American abortions are estimated to have enriched the U.S. abortion industry by some $4 billion since *Roe v. Wade*.

Supporters of abortion like to argue that the incidence of abortion may simply be a timing issue. In other words, if a woman aborts a child, she may later have a child, supposedly when her life circumstances are more suitable for her to be a mother. This argument attempts to say that abortions do not reduce long-term population growth trends; abortions merely change the timing of births. U.S. government data present contrary evidence. Fertility, defined as the number of births per 1,000 women, was identified at 84.9 for black women in 1980; by 2002, the fertility rate among black women had fallen to 65.8. Similar reductions did not occur among white women. For white women, the fertility rate in 1980 was 65.6 births per 1,000 women; by 2002, the fertility rate for white women was 64.8, little changed.[6] Granted, abortions are not the only reason black women may be having fewer babies. Yet the statistics would indicate that the birthrate trend is downward for African Americans. In 1980 the higher fertility among blacks should have indicated a growing African American population. The straight-line downward progression since 1980 suggests that the African American population, as a percentage of total U.S. population, is unlikely to increase from births. Abortions since *Roe v. Wade* have taken a far greater toll among African Americans than among whites. Of some 40 million abortions in the United States since 1973, some 30 percent are African American, even though African Americans are only about 13 percent of the population.

If abortions were being supported by conservative Republicans instead of by liberal Democrats, African Americans would be loudly arguing that the true goal of abortion was to eliminate the African American race from the United States through attrition. But that is not the case. Abortion has been one of the central causes advanced by the political Left since the 1960s.

To "market" abortion, the political Left has packaged the concept around "pro-choice," the supposed right of a woman to self-determine her own body, including the right to choose even a late-term abortion, regardless of whether the woman had taken any steps to prevent pregnancy. In 2005 David Kupelian argued in his important book, *The Marketing of Evil,* that the political Left has waged a war on marriage, determined to advance an agenda of sexual license that includes same-sex marriage and teaching homosexuality and lesbianism in our schools, an agenda whose forefront argument is the "right" to demand an abortion:

> What if reporters and editors cut through the high-flying rhetoric of civil rights and constitutional freedom and women's health and brought the issue down to little, perfectly formed human babies— three thousand of them every day, the same number of people as perished on 9/11—being painfully ripped apart, suctioned, chemically burned, sliced up, or decapitated?
>
> What if the press diligently reported on the proven and devastating physical and psychological effects abortion has on women or on the many studies that show abortion leads to an increased risk of breast cancer? What if the press actually broadcast pictures or videos of abortions?[7]

Kupelian answers his own questions. Presented with the cold reality of abortions, Americans would "see the truth once again, and the realization of the horror of abortion would, as it did for centuries before this generation, seep into and eventually pervade the public consciousness."[8] As a result, abortions would again become illegal, recognized as barbaric and criminal acts of murder, except in rare and carefully defined circumstances. Politically correct thinking as defined by the Left demands that we accept "abortion upon demand," allowing even unmarried teenagers to kill their unborn babies simply because the pregnancy is not the best decision for the moment.

Margaret Sanger would be among the first to argue that babies born into poverty constitute an economic and health burden that justifies killing the fetus. Nowhere will the pro-abortion movement accept responsibility for what is obvious, that these arguments result in more African American abortions. Since the political Left blames white America for black poverty, the political Left believes white America is responsible for perpetuating the economic and health conditions that "cause" abortion to be disproportionately a problem today in African American communities. Victimization is the main perspective through which the Left sees all racial problems. For the Left, the victims are always the minority and the culprits are always the white majority. The truth is that the political Left's almost religious adherence to a policy of abortion on demand has unleashed abortion doctors to kill unborn babies almost indiscriminately in the black community.

Contrary to what the political Left wants us to believe, unwanted pregnancies are not a "disease," nor is the appropriate "medical treatment" an abortion. Abortion is not justified by the argument that there are inadequate economic resources to care for all unwanted babies unless they are killed by abortion. Families wanting to adopt babies frequently are blocked from doing so, often by the cumbersome nature of adoption rules and regulations, but rarely because there are no babies available to adopt. The population of the United States is not "improved" when unborn black babies are killed. How many business leaders, academic luminaries, artistic geniuses, future mothers and fathers were lost to America when 13 million African American unborn babies have been killed since 1973? This loss is a loss not only to the African American community but also to America and the world as a whole.

## BILL BENNETT CALLED A "RACIST"

IN 2005 economist Steven Levitt coauthored a best-selling book entitled *Freakonomics,* in which he argued that lower crime rates in the United States were a direct result of the *Roe v. Wade* decision allowing abortions. This was an argument the political Left loved. If allowing an abortion to any woman who wanted one resulted in reducing crime, then obviously abortions had to be good. Here's how Levitt expressed the argument:

> Perhaps the most dramatic effect of legalized abortion, however, and one that would take years to reveal itself, was its impact on crime. In the early 1990s, just as the first cohort of children born after *Roe v. Wade* was hitting its late teen years—the rate of crime began to fall. What this cohort was missing, of course, were the children who stood the greatest chance of becoming criminals. And the crime rate continued to fall as an entire generation came of age minus the children whose mothers had not wanted to bring a child into the world. Legalized abortion led to less unwantedness; unwantedness leads to high crime; legalized abortion, therefore, led to less crime.[9]

As usual, the political Left went along with Levitt in turning a blind eye to an underlying link in the chain, a correlation a numbers-oriented economist who was thinking objectively should have been expected to explore. Crime rates are higher among African Americans than for whites, and abortion rates are higher among African Americans than for whites, so why did Levitt leave out a discussion of race? What we might consider concluding is that the political Left has been willing to see the African American community decimated by abortion as long as nobody talked about it.

On September 28, 2005, conservative talk-show host and former secretary of education Bill Bennett explored the politically incorrect topic on his Salem Radio Network's nationally broadcast show *Morning in America.* Here is the transcript of the discussion:

CALLER: I noticed the national media, you know, they talk a lot about the loss of revenue, or the inability of the government to fund Social Security, and I was curious, and I've read articles in recent months here, that the abortions that have happened since *Roe v. Wade,* the lost revenue from the people who have been aborted in the last 30-something years, could fund Social Security as we know it today. And the media just doesn't—never touches this at all.

BENNETT: Assuming they're all productive citizens?

CALLER: Assuming that they are. Even if only a portion of them were, it would be an enormous amount of revenue.

BENNETT: Maybe, maybe, but we don't know what the costs would be, too. I think as—abortions disproportionately occur among single women? No.

CALLER: I don't know the exact statistics, but quite a bit are, yeah.

BENNETT: All right, well, I just don't know. I would not argue for the pro-life position based on this, because you don't know. I mean, it cuts both—you know, one of the arguments in this book *Freakonomics* that they make is that the declining crime rate, you know, they deal with this hypothesis, that one of the reasons crime is down is that abortion is up. Well—

CALLER: Well, I don't think that statistic is accurate.

BENNETT: Well, I don't think it is either. I don't think it is either, because first of all, there is just too much that you don't know. But I do know that it's true that if you wanted to reduce crime, you could—if that were your sole purpose, you could abort every black baby in this country and your crime rate would go down. That would be an impossible, ridiculous, and morally reprehensible thing to do, but your crime rate would go down. So these far-out, these far-reaching extrapolations are, I think, tricky.[10]

The reaction from the political Left was immediate and vociferous. Bennett predictably was called a racist. House minority leader

Nancy Pelosi, a California Democrat, called Bennett's comments "alarming." Even White House press secretary Scott McClellan was forced to tell reporters that President Bush considered Bennett's comments "not appropriate."[11] In the firestorm of criticism that followed, Bennett appeared on Fox News's *Hannity and Colmes* television show, stating that he had only meant the argument to be advanced as a "morally impossible hypothesis," an argument he considered "ridiculous and impossible," an argument he advanced so it could be refuted, a technique Bennett said that he commonly used when he was teaching philosophy.[12]

In the chorus of disapproval that occurred over the next few days on talk radio and cable news television, Bennett was excoriated by liberal politicians and spokespersons who called him racist because he dared venture into the forbidden topic, the politically incorrect link liberals wanted to ignore in their determination to protect abortion from political attack by moral conservatives. If Bennett were right, and the reason abortions were resulting in a lower crime rate was in part attributable to the high incidence of abortions among African Americans, then the average American who is not a racist might see the issue clearly and still logically conclude that abortion was bad. Racial genocide is no solution to the problem of crime. Is this the argument that the political Left wants to advance but still keep hidden in its support of abortion?

Steven Levitt felt compelled to defend his book. He argued that he did not mean to imply that African Americans were somehow more intrinsically criminal by nature. Still, his troubled explanation took pains to step around the argument without offending liberals in their frenzied support of abortion:

> It is true that, on average, crime involvement in the U.S. is higher among blacks than whites. Importantly, however, once you control for income, the likelihood of growing up in a female-headed household, having a teenage mother, and how urban the environment is, the importance of race disappears for all crimes except homicide. (The homicide gap is partly explained by crack markets.) In other words, for most crimes a white person and a black

person who grow up next door to each other with similar incomes and the same family structure would be predicted to have the same crime involvement. Empirically, what matters is the fact that abortions are disproportionately used on unwanted pregnancies, and disproportionately by teenage women and single women.[13]

Bennett had not claimed that blacks as a race were criminals by nature, an inherent character trait determined by race. Yet this is the argument Levitt took pains to refute. Bennett simply made the link the Left wants defined as politically incorrect. African Americans do live disproportionately in low-income levels. Births to teenage women who end up raising their babies in female-headed households are characteristics experienced disproportionately by African Americans. Also, African American abortions are disproportionately high. Bennett had a point that Levitt was quick to sidestep, assuming perhaps that nobody would notice and challenge him on the ground shifting he was attempting to support his position.

If the situations were reversed, such that abortions among whites were disproportionately high while abortions among blacks were disproportionately low, then we probably would not see a reduction in crime rates despite an increase in abortions. Why? Because it is true that African Americans experience a disproportionately high crime rate and whites do not. These are empirical observations, matters of fact, not conclusions Bill Bennett was arguing are necessary because of race. Bennett would agree that if we put white people in the same inner-city poverty neighborhoods as blacks live in today, with the same incidence of teenage pregnancy and single mothers raising children, then whites would be expected to suffer the same social dysfunctions and crime rates blacks suffer from now.

Today a disproportionately large number of unmarried and teenage black girls get pregnant and do not want their babies, often because they have no idea how they can afford to raise the babies when they lack employment skills and have no husband to assist them. Crime rates go up because young black men raised in poor economic situations without fathers to impose discipline tend to join gangs, beginning a pattern of social interaction that ends up in crime, often violent crime. This is not a racial indictment of African Americans; it is an indictment of the dysfunctions that result from inner-city poverty.

Liberals do not want to discuss this problem because they do not want abortion criticized, and they do not want to admit any racial links between abortion and crime. They want us to believe that *unwanted babies* grow up disproportionately to become criminals. So, the liberal conclusion is that unwanted pregnancies are bad and abortion is good. The problem is that babies born to poor unwed teenager mothers tend disproportionately to become criminals, regardless of whether they are wanted or unwanted, regardless of whether they are black or white. Women who do not want babies should take steps not to become pregnant. The argument Levitt makes—that killing unwanted unborn babies reduces crime—is nothing more than a prescription for abortion at will. He is right in that teenage pregnancies result in more babies who turn to crime later in life; he was wrong to claim his argument had no relation to race.

Bennett was attacked as a racist because he mentioned the topic. His critics ignored that he brought up the argument in order to refute it. Since liberals could not refute his argument, viewed as an empirical argument or a simple matter of fact, they chose to label him, hoping to characterize him as a racist in order to discredit him and deflect attention from their cherished endorsement of abortion. Again, as we have noted, ad hominem attacks are always a sign that the person being attacked has scored a point his or her opponent probably cannot answer, a point so sensitive that the attacker cannot afford to have objective listeners consider the objection seriously.

The criticism of Bill Bennett was unfair precisely because he has a long record of being adamantly opposed to abortion in any form, as anyone knows who has listened to his radio show for any period of time or read his best-selling book, *The Book of Virtues*.[14] Bennett's point was that the oddball associations typically made by economist Steven Levitt are often problematic. Possibly Bennett would have been better advised to have made his point by advancing for refutation the extreme statement of Levitt's equally ridiculous and morally unacceptable correlation. Bennett could have charged that Levitt's contortions in suspect statistical correlations would lead us to conclude absurdly that we could reduce crime significantly if we simply aborted *all unborn babies*, regardless of race. No babies, no young hoodlums to turn into criminals—that would be the true reductio ad absurdum of Levitt's argument. Reducing crime rates should never be used as an argument to justify abortion. Moreover, there is a racial element to Levitt's argument, whether he wants to admit it or not.

Our argument here is different. We argue that *Roe v. Wade,* by allowing abortion on demand, has resulted in black genocide, whether the political Left wants to acknowledge this horrible empirical consequence of its twisted policy of murdering unborn babies or not.

Ironically, there is another twist the Democratic Party should consider in its enthusiasm to embrace abortion upon demand. Considering the 40 million abortions that have been performed in the United States since *Roe v. Wade,* the Democratic Party's enthusiasm for abortion may be costing them future voters. An estimated 12.3 million potentially eligible voters were missing from the voting-age population during the 2000 presidential elections because of abortions from 1973–82. Very possibly this number would have been more than enough to have tipped the balance in favor of Al Gore. In the 2004 presidential election, the number of voters missing because of abortions was estimated at 18.3 million; in 2008, the number of missing voters may exceed 24 million.[15] If we assume that children tend to absorb the political views of their parents (which is a reasonable assumption of political science) and that those with conservative views are less likely to seek abortions, Democrats, by supporting abortion, have unconsciously eliminated much of their future base of voters. As abortion rates continue to rise, liberal Democratic Party supporters of abortion are disproportionately killing off future Democratic Party voters. And many of the "missing voters" who were killed as unborn babies would be reaching childbearing age today, had they been permitted to live. So Democrats, by supporting abortion, are killing off their base of potential voters at rates approaching a geometric progression, not an arithmetic progression—all this at a time when conservative criticism of liberal principles continues to gain ground with the American public. From this analysis, we would conclude that the Democratic Party's rigid adherence to supporting abortion on demand has led, not only to genocide against black Americans, but also to suicide upon themselves.

### THE AIDS EPIDEMIC: ANOTHER FORM OF BLACK GENOCIDE?

THE CENTERS for Disease Control (CDC) leaves no doubt that HIV/AIDS has hit the African American community hard:

> The HIV/AIDS epidemic is a health crisis for African Americans. In 2002, HIV/AIDS was among the top 3 causes of death for African American men aged 25–54 years and among the top 4 causes of death for African American women aged 20–54 years. It was the number 1 cause of death for African American women aged 25–34 years.[16]

No matter how the statistics are analyzed, the results are always the same. HIV/AIDS impacts the African American community with disproportionate severity. In an important book entitled *The Secret Epidemic: The Story of AIDS and Black America,* journalist Jacob Levenson commented that when he began his investigations in 1999, HIV/AIDS had already "been designated as a largely black disease by the government, the public health community, and even the Congressional Black Caucus."[17]

Teenage sexual promiscuity has led to increasing rates of HIV/AIDS infection, a trend that again is accentuated in the African American community. This is how the Black AIDS Institute summarizes the CDC data:

> The U.S. Centers for Disease Control and Prevention (CDC) estimates that about 40,000 people become infected with HIV every year, with more than half of them occurring among people under the age of 25. No matter how you chop those numbers up, African American young people are heavily overrepresented. African Americans account for 66 percent of HIV infections among those 13 to 19 year olds. Among 20 to 24 year olds, it's only slightly better, with Blacks accounting for 53 percent infected. Through 2003, 62 percent of all reported AIDS cases in children under the age of 13 were found among African Americans.[18]

The Black AIDS Institute noted that the problem was most severe for African American male youths who had sex with other males, many of whom were bisexual, engaging as well in heterosexual sex with African American women. The institute noted that young black men were "the driving force behind a surge in new HIV infections among gay and bisexual men in recent years."[19] A shocking 46 percent of African American men of all ages who had sex with men in a study of five major U.S. cities tested positive for HIV.

The disproportionately high number of African American men imprisoned makes the HIV/AIDS problem in the black community more severe. According to statistics maintained by the U.S. Department of Justice, in 2004, black inmates represented 41 percent of all state and federal prison inmates with a sentence of one year or more.[20] The impact is particularly serious among African American youths. Of black males aged twenty-five to twenty-nine, an estimated 8.4 percent were in prison on December 31, 2004, compared to 2.5 percent of Hispanic males and about 1.2 percent of white males in the same age group. About one in three African American males can anticipate being in prison at some time during their lives. Again, these high rates of incarceration largely reflect the dysfunctions of ghetto poverty and rigid law-enforcement standards that result in especially strict pursuit of criminal infractions committed by ghetto residents. For this discussion, our concern is that blacks in prison are subjected to high rates of homosexual activity, often violent homosexual activity imposed upon incarcerated victims, with the resultant high risk of HIV/AIDS infection.

CDC data shows that more than 50 percent of HIV/AIDS infection in black men comes from male-to-male sexual contact. As we have noted, many black men engaging in homosexual contact also have heterosexual contacts. More than 80 percent of black women infected by HIV/AIDS are infected by heterosexual contact. Here's how the CDC summarizes the data:

> African American women are most likely to be infected with HIV as a result of sex with men. They may not be aware of their male partners' possible risks for HIV infection, such as unprotected sex with multiple partners, bisexuality, or injection drug use. According to a recent study of HIV infected and noninfected African American men who have sex with men (MSM), approximately

20% of the study participants reported having had a female sex partner during the preceding 12 months. In another study of HIV-infected persons, 34% of African American MSM reported having had sex with women, even though only 6% of African American women reported having sex with a bisexual man.[21]

Injection drug use was the second leading cause of HIV infection for African American women and the third leading cause for African American men (after male-to-male sexual contact and heterosexual contact). An obvious risk was shared needles. The CDC also noted that chronic substance users are "more likely to engage in high-risk behaviors, such as unprotected sex, when they are under the influence of drugs or alcohol."[22] Drug use also affects treatment success. Drug users are less likely than nonusers to take antiretroviral medicines as prescribed.

No matter how we slice the data, the conclusion remains the same. The impact of HIV/AIDS infection is especially high in the African American community. The Black AIDS Institute reports these statistics:

- African Americans account for two-thirds of all new AIDS cases among teens.
- African Americans account for two-thirds of all diagnosed female AIDS cases.
- One-third of all black gay and bisexual men under the age of thirty are HIV positive.
- African Americans now account for half of all new HIV infections, even though blacks make up only 13 percent of the population.[23]

Report after report documents an epidemic of HIV/AIDS infections in the black community.

What we see is a pattern of dysfunction, not the elimination of poverty the Great Society has been promising for more than four decades. The reality of life experienced in inner-city black communities is a picture composed of many troublesome and difficult pieces. What we find is a breakdown in the black family, an increase in teenage sex and pregnancies, more and more single-parent black families generally headed by unemployed or marginally employed females, a growing number of black youth gangs that terrorize inner-city ghetto residents, a high rate of unemployment among black men, and a disproportionately high rate of crime and imprisonment for African American men and women. The Black AIDS Institute published an emotionally charged paragraph that describes the plight:

> We know that young people who live in poverty, who have dropped out of school, and who are homeless are more likely to be forced to make decisions that will put them at risk for transmission of the virus. Every time a young woman who lives in poverty feels like she cannot demand that her male partner use a condom when they have sex, because she worries that he will leave her and stop providing the financial support on which she depends, then the potential for transmission of the virus increases. And every time young people who are homeless or in need of a fix decide to trade unprotected sex for food or drugs or shelter, they put themselves and others at risk of infection. Our fight against AIDS is not a singular one; it must include, and make central issues of, poverty, jobs, education, housing and other factors.[24]

Pleas like this sound all too familiar to anyone who has read the drumbeat of repetitive analyses of the problem that have come forward since 1964. Again we have to emphasize that, after spending some $10 trillion on welfare programs over the last four decades, we appear to be losing ground, not gaining ground.

The RAND Corporation conducted a telephone survey with a random sample of African Americans aged fourteen to forty-four years old.[25] The results indicated that a significant proportion of respondents believed in HIV/AIDS conspiracy theories. The wildest of the conspiracy theories charge that the HIV/AIDS virus was created by white society in order to kill "undesirables," including homosexuals, drug users, and African Americans. That conspiracy theories are seriously entertained does not prove they are true. Yet the prevalence of conspiracy theories is a further indication that HIV/AIDS is recognized as an epidemic with serious life-threatening implications within the black community.

The RAND Corporation study concluded that conspiracy beliefs form a barrier to HIV/AIDS prevention among African Americans. Those holding conspiracy beliefs also tend to be those with negative attitudes toward condoms. Inconsistent condom use among sexually active people is simply not safe. The study recommended that to counter the conspiracy beliefs, government and public-health entities "need to work toward obtaining the trust of black communities by addressing current discrimination within the health care system as well as by acknowledging the origin of conspiracy beliefs in the context of historical discrimination." Clearly, attacking discrimination is always important. Still, this conclusion echoes the "blame-guilt" thinking we have seen throughout the past four decades of the welfare-state discussion of race-related problems. The fundamental question is this: if the black family remains in shambles, how is the sexual behavior that leads to the spread of the HIV/AIDS going to change?

Our argument is that the deterioration of the African American family is one of the most important consequences of the welfare system itself, not a characteristic that results from race itself. At some point, America is going to have to examine the reality of the massive social dysfunction the welfare system has produced and recognize that no matter how well intentioned, the welfare state itself has not worked to change the poverty culture of chronically poor blacks, despite the many fixes its supporters have attempted to put into place.

## REVERSING THE ATTACK ON THE BLACK FAMILY

FROM A behavioral-science point of view, we need to ask what we need to do differently if we are to stop the attack on the black family. Sociologists have thoroughly tested the conditions that correlate with poverty with some clear results: "Limited education, living in a single-parent family and giving birth out of wedlock are among the most familiar correlates of poverty."[26] These conclusions apply regardless of what race is being considered.

Sociologists have noted that we can easily convert these empirically tested conclusions into a set of rules of behavior that need to be followed to avoid poverty.[27] In other words, if the goal is to get out of poverty or to avoid poverty in the first place, certain behaviors are simply a "bad idea" while other behaviors can be identified as a "good idea." Or, to put the point in a slightly different way, people who are not poor make decisions with their lives and take steps that people who are poor do not take. While making good decisions is not 100 percent certain to result in improved economic decisions, the probabilities of economic advancement dramatically increase when certain decisions are made. Conversely, the probabilities of economic advancement dramatically decrease when other decisions are made. This thinking is core to studies that examine, for example, successful business leaders or successful entrepreneurs to identify the decisions they make and how they think in order to understand the keys to their success.

Charles Murray, author of *Losing Ground,* which we have discussed previously, summarized this line of analysis as follows:

> If you follow a set of modest requirements, you are almost surely going to avoid poverty. . . . For women, one option is to get an education, acquire skills, and get a job. . . . Another option is to marry a man who will be a good and conscientious provider. . . . Whatever else she does: A poor woman who wishes to get out of poverty ought not to have a baby out of wedlock. This is not a moral statement but an empirical one. . . . The main policy question is: *"How can policies affecting poor people encourage them to do the very ordinary things that need to be done to avoid poverty?"*[28]

Sociologist and poverty expert William Julius Wilson argues that, since the 1940s, inner-city neighborhoods have undergone a profound transformation where middle-class black professionals and blue-collar workers have largely moved away, leaving behind "a much higher concentration of the most disadvantaged segments of the black urban population, the population to which I refer when I speak of the black urban underclass." As a result, the inner-city black ghettos have experienced "increasing rates of social dislocation," including crime, joblessness, out-of-wedlock births, female-headed families, and welfare dependency.[29] Wilson concludes that low-income residents of black inner-city ghettos experience a "concentration effect" in that the social concentration of the most disadvantaged segments of the black urban population create an environment in which families and economic opportunity disintegrate:

> Thus, in a neighborhood with a paucity of regularly employed families and with the overwhelming majority of families having spells of long-term joblessness, people experience a social isolation that excludes them from the job network system that permeates other neighborhoods and that is so important in learning about or being recommended for jobs that become available in various parts of the city. And as the prospects for employment diminish, other alternatives such as welfare and the underground economy are not only increasingly relied on, they come to be seen as a way of life. Moreover, unlike the situation in earlier years, girls who become pregnant out of wedlock invariably give birth out of wedlock because of a shrinking pool of marriageable, that is, employed, black males.[30]

Again, children born in these disadvantaged situations rarely emerge successfully. Wilson continues:

> Thus, in such neighborhoods the chances are overwhelming that children will seldom interact on a sustained basis with people who are employed or with families that have a steady breadwinner. The net effect is that joblessness, as a way of life, takes on a different social meaning; the relationship between schooling and postschool employment takes on a different meaning. The development of cognitive, linguistic, and other educational and job-related skills necessary for the world of work in the mainstream economy is thereby affected. In such neighborhoods, therefore, teachers become frustrated and do not teach and children do not learn. A vicious cycle is perpetuated through the family, through the community, and through the schools.[31]

The vicious cycle of teenage pregnancies and single-parent families is compounded by abortion rates that approach genocide by offering a ready escape from family formation and parenting. Children raised in an inner-city environment face further difficulties of an inadequate education and minimal preparation to enter the employment pool. These disadvantages are compounded by the lack of a solid family structure from which they can derive moral education and positive values that might offer some hope of escape from the downward spiral of poverty and unemployment into which they were unfortunately born. Reversing this trend will demand making conscious decisions to move away from abortion on demand, avoid teenage pregnancy, and heal broken families.

What we have established in the last forty years is that a government bureaucracy spending trillions of dollars is not a solution. The social and economic dysfunction we have described in these pages is the result of that failed government bureaucracy. At some point, we as a society have no choice but to admit that the welfare state has failed. The principles of the political Left have not only failed to solve the problem of poverty in American, liberalism has actually made the problem worse. We, as political conservatives, know that we are bound to be castigated by the political Left precisely because we are attacking head-on a key pillar of its politics. The welfare state has not only produced dependency of the poor in America upon a government bureaucracy, the welfare state has also launched a direct attack upon the African American family. We will never make real progress until we resolve that the end of the welfare state is at hand, not simply symbolically, as President Clinton articulated (the end of the welfare state "as we know it"), but once and for all, so that no welfare state remains at all, not even an altered welfare state that is radically different from the one we have today.

We firmly believe that the problem of poverty in America will not be resolved until the African American family is restored. Forty years and $10 trillion spent without measurable results is enough justification to dismantle the massive government bureaucracy the welfare state has created. Our goal is to end the welfare state altogether and to replace it with the family. The family for all of recorded history has been society's bedrock for creating the conditions necessary for political freedom and economic advancement. Replacing the independence of the family with dependency upon government to solve the problem of poverty has been a bad idea, probably the fundamental reason the modern liberal welfare state has failed. As we will discuss in the next chapter, the courts in the

United States have struck down the legal barriers of racial discrimination to the point where discrimination in America is a crime. Today the time has come for putting in place the de facto conditions of economic opportunity for all Americans, regardless of race, color, or previous conditions of inequality and disadvantage. Now is the time for the political Left to stand down and admit, as President Reagan encouraged us to concede, that President Johnson's War on Poverty, no matter how noble in intent, has nonetheless been lost in practice.

# 5

## Victory in the Courts

### What Really Was Achieved?

In the eyes of government, we are one race here. It is American.
—Justice Antonin Scalia, 1995[1]

In 1954 CHIEF JUSTICE Earl Warren, writing for the majority of the Court in the landmark case *Brown v. Board of Education*,[2] articulated a principal of racial equality that lit up a new day in American racial relationships. The chief justice's words left no doubt. American schools had to be racially integrated, and they had to be integrated immediately: "We therefore conclude that in the field of public education the doctrine of 'separate but equal' has no place. Separate educational facilities are inherently unequal."

These two sentences should have been sufficient by themselves to cause a dramatic and fundamental reordering of America's then racially segregated school system. Moreover, by relying upon the "equal protection of the laws" principle of the Fourteenth Amendment to outlaw any state action that caused schools to be racially segregated, the Court gave a clear signal that the justices would not accept state-sanctioned discrimination of any kind—not in schools, not in employment, not in housing, not in voting, not anywhere. What the majority of the Supreme Court was telling the nation with this decision in 1954 was that the day of officially sanctioned racial discrimination was over.

119

If Supreme Court opinions could cause an immediate transformation of society, then *Brown v. Board of Education* should have done just that. Someone looking in from the outside, someone who did not know how America truly works, might reasonably have concluded that, with all due speed, the problem of racially segregated schools would pass from the landscape as a historical mistake from a bygone era. That same outsider might also have reasonably concluded that soon America would face equal rights in the workplace, in residential neighborhoods, in polling precincts, and throughout society. Unfortunately, racial equality and social justice required more than the waving of a magic wand by the chief justice.

In truth, nothing much changed after *Brown v. Board of Education*, at least not right away. We did get a wave of Great Society laws passed by Congress. We did get a series of Supreme Court decisions extending the principles of *Brown v. Board of Education* to other areas, including employment, housing, and voting. Still, fifty years after *Brown v. Board of Education*, we have only begun to realize how resistant the problems of racial discrimination have been to change. Many of the legislatively and judicially crafted solutions contained unanticipated problems of their own. Adverse reactions and resistance to change have made progress difficult, if not impossible, in a great many arenas where racial discrimination was attacked.

Looking over the past fifty years, we should try to identify where our attempts at social engineering went wrong. The fundamental question is again one of behavior. How can we make people live and act in ways that are truly "color-blind," especially when we know that laws and rules will not by themselves perform the required transformation? What then are the necessary and sufficient conditions to produce change such that we end racial discrimination in America and usher in the sought-after era of racially equal opportunity and racially equal results, not just racially equal rights as defined by the laws and the courts?

## SCHOOL DESEGREGATION

FOLLOWING *Brown v. Board of Education*, court-ordered busing to integrate schools became the order of the day, especially in major cities across the nation. Intellectually, the idea of busing children seemed an obvious solution. If the problem was that schools were divided into two camps, nearly all-black and all-white, the solution to create a racial mix by busing students according to a master plan seemed like the answer. The problem was that busing necessitated moving children from neighborhoods where they lived to distant neighborhoods that were strange to them and away from their parents and homes. Moreover, the neighborhoods to which the children were bused were inevitably neighborhoods where the residential pattern remained segregated. So black children were bused to white neighborhoods, and white children were bused to black neighborhoods. As a result, state and local governments found their school districts transformed into one of the largest social experiments ever attempted in America, in most cases without a thoroughly vetted plan and without proper training for the likely consequences they were soon to experience.

The anger of parents intensified when they realized that their children were going to be bused even if the parents objected. In other words, to enforce racial integration in the public schools, the courts ordered state and local governments to override family decisions, asserting the authority of government to tell children where they were going to go to school and with no regard for the wishes of the parents. Never before in our history had government so overruled the family. Millions of parents believed busing deprived them of a most fundamental freedom to be the primary decision makers responsible for their children's welfare and upbringing. The affront to the authority of the family that busing entailed meant that, for millions of Americans, busing overrode their basic rights in order to achieve a socially engineered goal many may have agreed with abstractly, but not when the implementation of the goal involved their lives directly or the lives of their children.

The hostility against busing was perhaps best expressed in 1974 when U.S. District Court Judge W. Arthur Garrity Jr. ordered massive busing to force integration in the Boston Public Schools. Judge Garrity implemented the Massachusetts State Board of Education's master plan designed to achieve racial balance in the public schools by ordering a crosstown busing plan that moved children from white neighborhoods to black neighborhoods and vice versa. A crisis developed the instant parents in Boston's Irish and Italian Catholic neighborhoods, including Charlestown and the North End, realized their children were going to be bused in exchange for African American children being bused from Roxbury. An alternative plan prepared by Boston school superintendent Frederick Gillis would have involved an "open enrollment plan" that would have allowed families to choose which school their children would attend. Judge Garrity did not consider this alternative; instead, he gave Boston eleven weeks to begin the busing master plan that he admitted he had not read prior to ordering its implementation.[3]

The ensuing protest was led by angry mothers who believed that liberal courts had taken their freedom away, supplanting their authority over their own children with a judge's edict that forced education officials to bus their children away. Matthew Richer, writing in the Hoover Institution's *Policy Review,* provided a graphic description of the outcry:

> One day in fall 1975, about 400 Charlestown mothers marched up Bunker Hill Street, clutching rosary beads and reciting the "Hail Mary." They knelt in prayer for several minutes on the pavement between Charlestown High and the Bunker Hill Monument. And then they stood up and walked toward the police line, still in prayer, handbags held high to shield their faces. Soon a scuffle broke out between the mothers and the police. Some women were tossed to the ground.
>
> Although the women's movement was on the rise, the feminist establishment had no interest in the working-class woman's struggle against forced busing. They were indifferent to the wailing mothers who were throwing themselves down in front of delivery trucks owned by the *Boston Globe* (the pro-busing newspaper) or fleeing from the dogs that police used to enforce curfews. The same people who celebrated when the Supreme Court recognized a woman's "right to choose" to have an abortion were unmoved when a federal court revoked a mother's right to choose where her children could go to school. When anti-busing mothers attended a rally for the Equal Rights Amendment downtown, one mother addressed the gathering to ask whether the ERA would guarantee a woman's authority over her children's schooling. They were all asked to leave.[4]

The Boston busing experiment was a disaster. Police were forced to escort and unload buses at Boston high schools every morning and afternoon, while law-enforcement snipers were positioned on roofs to prevent assaults. Metal detectors were installed in schools, and police patrolled school corridors. Parents adopted the civil disobedience tactics of the civil rights movement, blocking buses with sit-ins, staging protest marches, picketing, and finally even rioting. The images of angry protesters in South Boston hurling rocks and bottles at school buses bringing black children into their neighborhood schools remains haunting even today.[5]

The results of the Boston busing experiment presaged the experience that would be repeated around the country. Judge Arthur Garrity became the de facto school superintendent of the Boston schools. White families moved to the suburbs in droves, exacerbating a phenomenon that became known as "white flight." Public-school enrollment dropped by nearly half, as thousands of white families placed their children in private schools. Seventy-eight Boston schools closed entirely, including Roxbury High, and the proportion of white students in public schools dropped from 65 percent of total enrollment to just 28 percent.[6] Still, the experiment was widely copied around the country as judge after judge was forced into the position of acting school superintendent, a role few judges had any training or experience to justify. Busing became a leftist venture into social engineering, with the result that parents were denied a right to choose where their children went to school.

In 1991 the Supreme Court changed direction. In the case *Board of Education of Oklahoma City v. Dowell,* the Court, in a majority decision written by Chief Justice William H. Rehnquist, permitted a return to neighborhood schools, even if that decision was certain to reinforce patterns of racial segregation rather than integration.[7] This decision allowed communities to back away from a continuing program of busing to integrate the schools. As a result, school districts across America began to re-segregate. With the *Dowell* decision, the Supreme Court admitted defeat. Even if the principle of *Brown v. Board of Education* was right, that segregated schools were inherently inferior, the Court acknowledged that judicially mandated social engineering by means of busing children did not work.

In reality, the courts had no choice but to admit defeat. The courts could not stem the tide of fundamental demographic changes sweeping the country. Today there is no major city in America with a remaining non-Hispanic white majority. Whites have fled the cities in large part to escape forced school integration. After fifty years of trying to implement *Brown v. Board of Education,* the nation's public school system remains predominately segregated, especially in our cities. Schools that the law forced to desegregate are today resegregating after *Dowell.* Writing in *Harper's Magazine,* author Jonathan Kozol makes the case clearly:

> In Chicago, by the academic year 2002–2003, 87 percent of public-school enrollment was black or Hispanic; less than 10 percent of children in the schools were white. In Washington, D.C., 94 percent of children were black or Hispanic; less than 5 percent were white. In St. Louis, 82 percent of the student population were black or Hispanic; in Philadelphia and Cleveland, 79 percent; in Los Angeles, 84 percent; in Detroit, 96 percent; in Baltimore, 89 percent. In New York City, nearly three quarters of the students were black or Hispanic.
>
> Even these statistics, as stark as they are, cannot begin to convey how deeply isolated children in the poorest and most segregated sections of these cities have become. In the typically colossal high schools of the Bronx, for instance, more than 90 percent of students (in most cases, more than 95 percent) are black or Hispanic. At John F. Kennedy High School in 2003, 93 percent of the enrollment of more than 4,000 students were black and Hispanic; only 3.5 percent of the students at the school were white. At Harry S. Truman High School, black and Hispanic students represented 96 percent of the enrollment of 2,700 students; 2 percent were white. At Adlai Stevenson High School, which enrolls 3,400 students, blacks and Hispanics made up 97 percent of the student population; a mere eight-tenths of one percent were white.[8]

America remains residentially segregated. As a consequence, our schools remain segregated.

That schools are slipping back into segregated patterns in the decade since the *Dowell* decision is one of the main conclusions of the exhaustive studies of the school integration battle as reported by Professor Gary Orfield of Harvard's Graduate School of Education and the civil rights project he directs at the university. Today, white students constitute only 60 percent of all students in public schools, in large part because of the dramatic increase in Hispanic immigration, especially in the Southwest and the cities. Fully 25 percent of all U.S. public-school students are in states with a majority of nonwhite students. The vast majority of our intensely segregated schools remain in central cities, a consequence of the concentrations of African American ghetto poverty to which our core urban areas have been abandoned. Ironically, the "white flight" that was exacerbated by court-ordered busing to integrate the schools has reinforced the failure of the welfare system by concentrating the problem of urban poverty. Intensely segregated African American schools are associated with concentrations of urban poverty, which in turn produces the type of inadequate schooling opportunities that were the core concern at the heart of the *Brown v. Board of Education* decision fifty years ago. As Orfield notes:

> Concentrated poverty turns out to be powerfully related to both school opportunities and achievement levels. Children in these schools tend to be less healthy, to have weaker preschool experiences, to attend classes taught by less experienced or unqualified teachers, to have friends and classmates with lower levels of achievement, to be in schools with fewer demanding pre-collegiate courses and more remedial courses, and to have higher teacher turnover. Many of these schools are also deteriorated and lack key resources. The strong correlation between race and poverty show that a great many black and Latino students attend these schools of concentrated poverty.[9]

Orfield and his colleagues on the Harvard civil rights project implore America to have the political resolve to resume the campaign to desegregate our nation's schools, believing resolutely that separate schools will remain inherently unequal and to the disadvantage of minority students.

Some African American commentators have questioned whether the forced integration efforts imposed by the courts were the right solution. Thomas Sowell, a Rose and Milton Friedman Senior Fellow, observed:

> *Brown v. Board of Education* did not prescribe compulsory busing for racial balance. But the logic of its argument led inexorably to that conclusion, whether that was the original intent or not.
>
> More broadly, both the explicit language and the implicit assumptions of the Supreme Court in *Brown* depicted the answer to the problems of blacks in general as being essentially the changing of white people. This was yet another line of reasoning that led straight into a blind alley.
>
> Today, there are all-black schools that succeed, all-black schools that fail, and racially mixed schools that do either. Neither race nor racial segregation can explain such things. But both can serve as distractions from the task of creating higher standards and harder work.
>
> The judicial mythology of racial mixing has led to an absurd situation where a white student can get into a selective public high school in San Francisco with lower qualifications than a Chinese American student. This farcical consequence of judicial mythology about a need for racial mixing does nothing to improve education for blacks or anyone else.[10]

It made intuitive sense to the jurists that the courts, with the best intentions, should engage in a great social experiment by implementing a forced-busing solution. Unfortunately, the jurists lacked behavioral evidence that people would respond as the judges believed they should. Anyone acquainted with the judges in the forced-busing error would not doubt their sincere conviction that forced busing would work. Few judges anticipated the degree to which their "just" solution "justly imposed" would backfire, creating angry protests from both the majority and the minority communities, as well as leading to such unanticipated results as "white flight," a phenomenon that compounded the problem by creating schools even more racially segregated in the cities.

Few racial issues in America have received as much attention as the judicial campaign waged over the last fifty years to desegregate our public schools. A Web site exists (www.s4.brown.edu) that links comprehensive information about desegregation court cases in individual school districts and provides current data on trends in the racial composition and segregation of the schools in those districts nationwide.[11] You can enter the state and select the school district in which you live, and the Web site will give you access to comprehensive data on any relevant court cases and the racial-ethnic makeup of the schools in that district. The volume of available data is overwhelming. Results can be calculated to estimate the economic and class disparities between schools in any district as well as various indexes to calculate the isolation or mixture of students in the district by ethnic and racial characteristics. School desegregation is one of the most comprehensively studied and documented issues in social science. Yet, in the final analysis, the conclusion remains the same. As long as residential patterns remain segregated, schools will be segregated. Where school districts have the choice to abandon busing, schools tend to drop busing and resegregate according to residential patterns. Court-ordered busing over the last fifty years has largely failed to achieve the purpose of integrating America's schools as *Brown v. Board of Education* ordered in 1954.

## AFFIRMATIVE ACTION

In 1965 President Johnson issued an executive order requiring federal contractors and subcontractors to take specific steps to increase the employment opportunities of preferred ethnic groups, racial minorities, and women. The idea was that specific "affirmative action" was necessary, in the form of preferential treatment, simply to establish "equal treatment" for those who had endured decades of discrimination. The Johnson administration was anxious to achieve equality for those who had suffered what was considered systematic discrimination, often called "structural" discrimination, because the pattern of discrimination had become so customary that unequal treatment had virtually been built into the fabric of key social structures, including employment, education, housing, and voting. Government intervention was seen as necessary to force preferential treatment so a balance could be restored. From the beginning, affirmative action was considered a temporary strategy, so that, after a generation or two, governmental intervention to

127

force preferential treatment would no longer be needed for minorities to receive equal treatment and equal results.

Again, the theory of affirmative action was well intentioned. The problem came when implementation resulted in opportunities being awarded preferentially to minorities because they were minorities. Majority Americans, generally white Americans, were denied opportunities because they were majority Americans. Lawsuits were inevitable when minorities, who were less qualified on objective standards, were given opportunities in what amounted to a "zero-sum game." In other words, somebody won and, as a consequence, somebody else lost. In game theory, the rub of affirmative action was that—especially in employment, education, and housing competitions—few opportunities were set up so that win-win solutions were possible. A minority candidate, for instance, might get a job in preference to a white candidate who had more job training or experience. In these cases, the preferential treatment for the minority being favored ended up being unfair to the better-qualified majority who was denied the opportunity. When the Johnson administration implemented affirmative action, the social benefit to be derived from eliminating minority injustice was seen as outweighing the social harm that would be done to better-qualified majorities who now had to step aside so that minorities could advance.

Over the last forty years, the courts have struggled with how to set the rules for affirmative action. One of the most hotly contended arenas involved applications to graduate educational programs, including law school and medical school. In the 1950s and early 1960s the proportion of minorities in law schools and medical schools was virtually negligible. The situation began to change after professional graduate programs began implementing affirmative-action selection systems designed to give preference to minority admissions. Expectedly, qualified majority students who lost admission to minority students began filing lawsuits, charging that they were victims of "reverse discrimination," in that minorities with inferior entrance qualifications were admitted when they were not.

A case in this area involved Allan Bakke, an applicant who was twice denied admission to the medical school at the University of California at Davis (UCD) despite having higher undergraduate grades and medical school admission test scores than those minority candidates who were admitted. After being rejected the second time, Bakke filed suit in the Superior Court of California seeking an injunction to compel his entry into UCD's medical school. He charged that his rights had been violated under the equal protection clause of the Fourteenth Amendment and Title 6 of the 1964 Civil Rights Act.[12] The case ultimately resulted in a complex Supreme Court decision, *University of California Regents v. Bakke*,[13] in which the justices filed six different opinions, filling more than 120 pages with judicial reasoning on the case. Associate Justice Lewis F. Powell Jr. cast the deciding vote and announced the Court's decision. The Court's holding, as articulated by Powell, was that while race could be a factor in admissions decisions, quotas were unacceptable. The Court ordered that Bakke would have to be given a place in the class. In discussing quota systems based on race, Justice Powell wrote: "Racial and ethnic distinctions of any sort are inherently suspect and thus call for the most exacting judicial examination."

The *Bakke* decision marked a give-and-take process in which Justice Powell affirmed the principle of affirmative action while commenting that racial and ethnic quotas were unacceptable guides. Increasingly, the Court began to apply a standard of "strict scrutiny" to affirmative-action preference schemes, weighting the matter with a presumption that only narrowly limited plans would be constitutionally acceptable. In the 1989 case *Richmond v. J. A. Croson Co.*,[14] the Court rejected a plan by the city of Richmond, Virginia, that required prime contractors on city construction projects to subcontract at least 30 percent of the work to one or more minority businesses. In a separate opinion to this case, Justice Antonin Scalia agreed with the majority and articulated an important principle that addressed the core of the difficulty: a preference scheme based on racial classifications was no different than the discrimination that had caused the problem in the first place:

> The difficulty of overcoming effects of past discrimination is as nothing compared with the difficulty of eradicating from our society the source of those effects, which is the tendency—fatal to a Nation such as ours—to classify and judge men and women on the basis of their country of origin or the color of their skin. A solution to the first problem that aggravates the second is no solution at all.

In Justice Scalia's view, race could be used as a decision principle only in extreme and limited conditions, namely, where there is no color-blind alternative. The example he gave was "a prison race riot, requiring temporary segregation of the inmates."

In the four decades since President Johnson established affirmative action by executive order, the courts have worked to limit racial preferences as a means of redressing problems of inequality caused by racial discrimination. In 2003 the Supreme Court handed down two companion affirmative-action decisions on the same day. *Grutter v. Bollinger*,[15] a case in which the Court decided that a University of Michigan law school admissions scheme designed to create "diversity" did not violate the equal protection clause of the Fourteenth Amendment largely because the decision process was loosely defined and did not involve the application of any quota or mathematical formula to ensure admission of a minimum percentage of minorities defined by particular racial groupings. In the other case, *Gratz v. Bollinger*,[16] the Court struck down the University of Michigan's undergraduate admissions program because the program assigned points to every "underrepresented minority" as part of the plan to establish "diversity" in the undergraduate school.

Justice Scalia voted against both affirmative action plans.[17] In *Grutter*, Scalia stated his desire for "a clear constitutional holding that racial preferences in state educational institutions are impermissible." The conservative reaction to affirmative action crystallized around this principle—using racial categories to reverse problems caused by using racial categories was internally inconsistent and bound to be unfair to one racial group or another. Put even more simply, affirmative action schemes by definition entailed handing out unequal benefits to favor minorities at the expense of majorities. Justice Scalia saw this as a trap. Instead of emerging from problems of racial discrimination, we were simply creating new problems of racial disadvantage. Interestingly, Justice Scalia embraced a principle articulated by Justice John Marshall Harlan in his 1896 dissent to *Plessy v. Ferguson*,[18] the case in which the Court's majority decision established that racial segregation could be considered equal, the case finally overturned in 1954 by *Brown v. Board of Education*. Quoting Harlan's famous dissent, Scalia underscored, "Our constitution is color-blind, and neither knows nor tolerates classes among citizens." This was the principle, so Scalia argued, that had been embodied in the Fourteenth Amendment's extension of equal protection of the laws to all Americans, regardless of race. Any deviation from this principle, including affirmative action, was intrinsically self-defeating.

In November 2004 Professor Richard Sander of the UCLA Law School published a paper in the *Stanford Law Review* analyzing empirical data regarding the experience of African American students admitted to law school through affirmative-action efforts.[19] Sander's findings were highly controversial. He concluded that black law students admitted to law school preferentially through affirmative-action admissions programs did poorly in law school, compared with white students. In top-tier law schools, 52 percent of all black first-year students ended up in the bottom decile of first-year grades, compared to 6 percent of all whites. Only 8 percent of black first-year students ended up in the top half of their classes.[20] But Sander stressed, "The collective poor performance of black students at elite schools does not seem due to their being 'black.'"[21] Instead, the poor performance was seen to be a function of the heavy racial preferences allowing black candidates with weaker credentials to enter elite schools where they might not have been admitted except for affirmative action.

Because black students received poorer grades, dropout rates were higher for African American law-school students admitted through racial preferences. In other words, "Black attrition rates are substantially higher than white rates, simply because racial preferences advance students into schools where they will get low grades."[22] Failure to pass bar exams tends to increase for law-school students who get poorer grades. Because African American students who were preferentially admitted tend to get poorer grades, they also were found to have lower rates of passing the bar exam after graduation from law school. Some 45 percent of all African American law students who began law school in 1991 graduated and passed state bar exams on their first try, compared to nearly 80 percent of the white students.

Ironically, Sander concluded that more African Americans might have become lawyers had there been no affirmative-action programs. He wrote:

> For most blacks benefiting from affirmative action by law schools,
> the issue is not whether they will get into a law school but, rather,
> how good of a law school. Going to a better school, we have seen,
> carries with it a higher risk of getting poor grades; going to a much
> better school creates a very high risk of ending up close to the bot-
> tom of the class. Prospective law students tend to assume automat-
> ically that going to the most prestigious school possible is always
> the smart thing to do, but we can now see that there is, in fact, a
> trade-off between "more eliteness" and "higher performance."[23]

If the goal was to pass the bar and secure good employment opportunities in law, Sander recommended that applicants with lesser qualifications are better served by entering less-than-top-tier schools, where
the competition is less and their chance of success is higher.

> The next legal challenge to affirmative action practices by law
> schools could very plausibly be led by black plaintiffs who were
> admitted, spent years and thousands of dollars on their educa-
> tions, and then never passed the bar and never became lawyers—
> all because of the misleading double standards used by law schools
> to admit them, and the schools' failure to disclose to them the
> uniquely long odds against their becoming lawyers.[24]

Venturing into this quagmire, Sander knew he would criticized and
inevitably his most strident critics would call him a racist simply because
he dared examine the possibility that the objective results of minority-
student preferential law-school admissions might be disappointing.

Responsible critics have argued that minority affirmative-action
admissions to law schools have also produced several success stories.
A study of minority and white graduates from the University of Michigan Law School showed that in 1965 only one African American was
counted among the 1,000 students then studying law at the university. Over the next three decades, between 1970 and 1998, some 800
African American, 350 Latino, 200 Asian American, and nearly 100
Native American students have graduated from the law school. The
study reported two major findings. The first conclusion was that the

minority students who graduated ended up having successful legal careers.[25]

> We have two principal and related findings to report. The first is
> that our African American, Latino, and Native American alumni,
> though, on average, admitted to the Law School with lower numer-
> ical entry credentials than those of whites, have fully entered the
> mainstream of the American legal profession. As a group, they earn
> large incomes, perform pro bono work in generous amounts, and
> feel satisfied with their careers. The initial and current job choices
> of minorities and whites differ somewhat, but across time the
> achievements of the minority graduates are quite similar and very
> few differences between them are statistically significant.[26]

The second conclusion followed logically from the first: lower-entry
qualifications might predict law-school grades, but for those who
graduated, these lower-entry qualifications did not predict ultimate success in legal careers.

> Our second finding is related to the first. It is that although Law
> School Admission Test (LSAT) scores and undergraduate grade
> point averages (UGPA), two factors that figure prominently in ad-
> missions decisions, do correlate strongly with law school grades,
> they seem to have no relationship to achievement after law school,
> within the range of students admitted to our law school, whether
> achievement is measured by earned income, career satisfaction, or
> service contributions. For both our minority and white alumni,
> those numbers that counted so much at the admissions stage tell
> little if anything about their later careers.[27]

There is no doubt that affirmative-action programs have resulted in
an important increase in the number of minority graduates from universities and professional schools in America. Moreover, attacks on
affirmative-action programs have led to a weakening of preference systems away from specified targets or quotas, with the result that high
points of minority admissions may have been reached in the late 1990s.[28]

If affirmative-action programs were eliminated entirely, minority admissions would undoubtedly decline even further, perhaps precipitously.[29]

The disadvantage that begins for African American students in segregated inner-city schools remains a disadvantage of concentrated ghetto poverty itself. Affirmative-action programs were designed to reverse this disadvantage by extending preference to minorities seeking entrance to college and professional schools. Yet affirmative action always entailed the problematic result that qualified majorities would be disadvantaged when less-qualified minorities were preferred. So judges never embraced affirmative action with the enthusiasm with which the courts embraced school desegregation.

These are fundamental conclusions we cannot avoid. Our elementary schools and high schools remain largely segregated. Our colleges and professional schools remain in a position where preferences still have to be extended to minority applicants or minority admissions will decline. This would not be the case if minority applicants had advanced to the point where their qualifications were equal or superior to those of majority applicants. Affirmative-action programs were originally conceptualized to be necessary only for a while, until society itself had eliminated the fundamental inequities that resulted in discrimination against minorities. That we still need to retain affirmative-action programs reveals how little fundamental progress we have made as a nation in eliminating the root problems of racial inequality itself.

An easy answer is readily obtained if we revert to the themes of blame and guilt. An argument that white racism remains the culprit can be expected from the political Left. A more difficult argument would be the one we are pressing here. The major solution designed to relieve poverty in America, the welfare state, has failed. As long as the welfare state remains in place, we should expect to perpetuate fundamental inequalities suffered by minorities. Nor are laws and court decisions enough. Few would have believed that conclusion in 1954 when *Brown v. Board of Education* was decided or in 1964 when President Johnson inaugurated the War on Poverty. If the welfare state and favorable judicial decisions were all that was truly necessary, problems of racial inequality and injustice would have passed from the scene over the last four or five decades. But conventional solutions and politically correct thinking have not solved the problems of poverty and racial discrimination. We must look deeper if true solutions are ever to be found.

## FAIR HOUSING RIGHTS

DENYING SOMEONE the right to buy a home because of race, religion, or age is clearly illegal. Yet since our communities remain largely segregated, especially in our larger urban areas, America has not pursued "fair housing rights" to the point where anything near racial equality has been achieve in home-buying patterns. The issue of purchasing or renting a home is much more complex. More affluent, predominately white suburbs tend to be where higher-priced homes can be found. Given the disparity in income most minorities continue to suffer, economic qualifications for homeownership or for renting impose a type of financial barrier that mitigates against residential integration. Then, too, patterns of discrimination are more subtle. Realtors, motivated by their own economic gain, tend to predetermine which homes to show to which customers, so that minorities typically are not shown higher-value suburban properties unless the Realtor has already determined that the minority buyer will qualify for a mortgage to buy the property or has met income-verification requirements to rent.

In 2000 the U.S. Housing and Urban Development Department conducted a national study of discrimination in the nation's metropolitan housing markets.[30] The results were based on forty-six hundred research matched "pairs" in twenty-three metropolitan areas nationwide during the summer and fall of 2000. Random samples of advertised housing units were drawn from newspapers, and the testers made inquiries about the advertised units. White and minority partners were paired, matched for income, assets, and debt levels to make them equally qualified to buy or rent the advertised units. The test partners were also assigned comparable family circumstances, job characteristics, education levels, and housing preferences. The researchers visited sales or rental agents and systematically recorded the assistance they received about the advertised unit or similar units they were offered. Research pairs did not compare their experiences with one another; they simply recorded the details of the treatment they experienced and the offers they were made, presenting themselves as experienced home seekers.

The study concluded that "discrimination still persists in both rental and sales markets of large metropolitan areas nationwide." The incidence of discrimination was found to have declined moderately for African Americans renters since 1989, but Hispanic renters faced essentially the same incidence of discrimination they did in the earlier 1989 study.

> African Americans still face discrimination when they search for rental housing in metropolitan markets nationwide. Whites were consistently favored over blacks in 21.6 percent of tests. In particular, whites were more likely to receive information about available housing units, and had more opportunities to inspect available units.[31]

For homebuyers, the study found discrimination patterns still persisted, but this varied from one metropolitan area to another.

Researchers focused on the practice of "steering," a subtle process whereby minorities and ethnics are guided to minority and ethnic neighborhoods. The study distinguished *information steering,* where minority prospects were given restricted information on available opportunities to buy homes or rent in higher-value or majority neighborhoods, versus *segregation steering,* where the opportunities shown to minorities were largely in minority neighborhoods, versus *class steering,* where minority and ethnic prospects were not shown higher-value opportunities. The conclusion was that discrimination via steering was occurring to reinforce segregated residential patterns:

> Editorializing is by far the most prevalent mechanism of black/white steering, and it occurred consistently across all three types of steering and at all geographical levels. In at least 12 to 15 percent of tests, agents systematically provided gratuitous geographic commentary that gave more information to white home seekers and encouraged them to choose areas with more whites and fewer poor households. In addition, black/white segregation steering and class steering were most prevalent when the advertised home and/or agent's office were

located in neighborhoods with a high percent white population, and were least likely to occur when advertised homes or agents' offices were located in less well-off areas.[32]

Clearly, refusing to show someone a housing opportunity because of race or ethnic identification constituted a violation of law. The more subtle practice of "steering" operates to produce the same result, but with practices that stay below the radar of the type of outright racial discrimination that could be actionable with litigation.

Another discriminatory practice that has reinforced segregated residential patterns is "redlining," or the drawing of a red line around a minority or ethnic area, such that lenders are reluctant to provide mortgages and insurers are hesitant to provide homeowner's or renter's insurance. When mortgage lenders avoid certain areas or provide only more expensive mortgage loans in those areas, home buyers are disadvantaged. Without homeowner's insurance, a minority or ethnic buyer might not be able to get a mortgage loan to buy the property. Both practices are illegal. Under the Home Mortgage Disclosure Act, for instance, mortgage lenders are generally required to disclose a wide range of information about their mortgage lending, including how many loans are made by census tract in the geographic area the lender is covering.[33] Again, blatant violations are rare; more subtle patterns of discrimination that make more difficult the process of obtaining mortgage loans or homeowner's insurance in minority or ethnic areas remain more difficult to detect and prove.

Equally difficult to remove by passing laws or by obtaining favorable court decisions is a public-planning process that has come to be termed "exclusionary zoning." Here zoning ordinances are passed that exclude low-income or multifamily housing from more affluent suburbs.[34] The end result is that low-income housing, including "project housing" complexes such as were commonly built in the 1960s, are relegated to inner-city neighborhoods, with the result that poverty and minority-ethnic segregation effects are compounded, thus reinforcing an "inner city" downward spiral effect. As a result of the Supreme Court's 1976 decision *Hills v. Gautreaux*,[35] concentrating public housing in segregated African American neighborhoods became a suspect practice. Since 1976, public programs to provide "Gautreaux assisted-housing" have provided voucher programs to allow a certain number of poor families to obtain rental properties in nonpoverty neighborhoods.[36] These programs have tended to wind down, however, when desegregated housing opportunities have been provided to some typically specified number of poor families that have been relocated out of public housing in disadvantaged neighborhoods.

Another approach has been called "opportunity-based housing," defined as a "Gautreaux-type program of 100,000 federal housing vouchers a year to relocate poor black families from high-poverty, opportunity-poor ghettos to low-poverty, opportunity-rich communities."[37] Proponents have also urged the passing of inclusionary zoning laws (IZ laws) that require developers to build somewhere between 10 to 15 percent of the new homes they are constructing for modest- to low-income families. In the attempt to engage market forces, some IZ laws provide "automatic density bonuses" that allow builders to put up more homes than the underlying zoning laws would otherwise permit in an effort to encourage builders to "squeeze" their IZ homes into developments without having to give up the number of homes they would build for higher-income families purchasing their homes through conventional financing.

A problem hounding the public-housing dilemma since the 1960s has been that those living in projects tend to remain in poverty, including the disadvantages of education and job skills that limit advancement out of poverty. Moving a poor family into a more affluent area may well produce positive results. For the family moved, however, adjustment in a relocated area can prove difficult both for the family moved and for those already residing in the new area. As we have pointed out repeatedly, racial segregation remains a reality in America despite legislation and court decisions to the contrary.

## VOTING RIGHTS

ANY DISCUSSION of voting-rights violations inevitably brings to mind the Florida vote in the 2000 presidential election. The central charge from Democrats was that systematic efforts to disenfranchise the African American vote in Florida had cost the election for Al Gore. A six-month investigation by the U.S. Commission on Civil Rights, headed by a fiercely partisan Democrat, Mary Frances Berry, concluded in June 2001 that statistical evidence and anecdotal evidence pointed to "widespread disenfranchisement" and "denial of voter rights" among Florida's African American voters.[38] While the report acknowledged that "it is impossible to determine the extent of the disenfranchisement," the commission recommended that the U.S. Department of Justice and the Florida attorney general should investigate a wide range of alleged civil-rights violations involving African American voters who were supposedly turned away from the polls, had their ballots disqualified disproportionately, or who otherwise were prevented a fair opportunity to vote. Unstated in the report, but clear in the underlying politics, was the assumption by the Democratic Party that African Americans who would have voted for Al Gore were turned away by the systematic efforts of Florida's Republican governor, Jeb Bush, the brother of the Republican Party candidate, George Bush, who won the election. Had the blacks been permitted to vote, or had all their votes been counted, Gore would have won—such was the argument of countless Democratic Party apologists.

On June 7, 2002, U.S. Assistant Attorney General Ralph F. Boyd Jr. of the Justice Department's Civil Rights Division wrote a letter to Senator Patrick Leahy (D-VT) of the Judiciary Committee in response to the senator's inquiry into what action, if any, had been taken to investigate the allegations of misconduct made by the Florida commission.[39] Boyd's letter made clear that Justice Department investigations found most of the allegations of intentional official misconduct were unsubstantiated. For instance, regarding allegations that police roadblocks in the Tallahassee area were intended to intimidate African American voters, Boyd wrote:

> The Voting Section received a complaint on Election Day that the Florida State Police had set up a traffic checkpoint near a polling place in or near a predominately black neighborhood outside Tallahassee, Florida. Our investigation, which included contact with the Florida Attorney General's Office on Election Day, showed that the police had not received the usual supervisory approval for the checkpoint, but that such checkpoints were not unusual in the area. The Voting Section also learned that (a) the checkpoint existed for about 3 hours; (b) the checkpoint was in fact several

miles from the nearest polling place; (c) a higher number of white motorists were stopped than African-American motorists; and (d) interviews with minority drivers indicated that the motorists themselves considered the checkpoint routine, that the police had been cordial, and that minority drivers proceeded to vote without incident. Based on this information we concluded there was no evidence of a violation of the Voting Rights Act and decided not to pursue the matter further.[40]

With regard to virtually all the allegations—that a majority of the ballot spoilage had involved minority voters, that older voting machines were more often placed in predominately minority precincts, that police had blocked access to minority polling places or had otherwise intimidated black voters—the Justice Department found no evidence of any systematic pattern of official action aimed at disenfranchising black voters. Peter Kirsanow, a Republican member of the U.S. Commission on Civil Rights, argued that the issue had become a political issue such that Democrats sought to gain electoral advantage by perpetuating the "urban legend," the unsubstantiated myth that black voters in Florida were systematically harassed, intimidated, and prevented from voting in the 2000 presidential election. Kirsanow concluded:

The myth holds that Governor Bush, in league with Secretary of State Katherine Harris, either by design or incompetence, failed to fulfill their electoral responsibilities, resulting in the discriminatory disenfranchisement of thousands of black voters. This was purportedly a key to the overarching Republican plot to steal the election from Al Gore.

Again, reality intrudes. The uncontroverted evidence shows that by statute the responsibility for the conduct of elections is in the hands of *county supervisors,* not the governor or secretary of state. County supervisors are independent officers answerable to county commissioners, not the governor or secretary of state. And in 24 of the 25 counties that had the highest ballot-spoilage rates, the county supervisor was a Democrat. (In the remaining county the supervisor was not a Republican, but an independent.)[41]

Kirsanow speculated that Democratic Party pundits were seeking to gain political advantage by perpetuating this urban legend, despite facts to the contrary, because they were calculating to increase black voter turnout in the 2004 presidential election under the assumption that black voters would vote disproportionately for John Kerry.

In the 2004 presidential election, the focus shifted from Florida to Ohio, where a narrow statewide majority of some 117,000 votes proved decisive in George Bush's reelection. This time, Democrats charged that Ken Blackwell—the coauthor of this book and then the African American Republican who was Ohio's secretary of state and in charge of supervising elections in Ohio—took steps to disenfranchise African American voters in his state. John Kerry reportedly had thousands of lawyers ready to swoop down on any state where he felt minority disenfranchisement or other voting irregularities had cost him victory. The Reverend Jesse Jackson intervened in Ohio, helping to raise enough money to call for a recount. John Conyers—an African American congressman from Michigan with a history of supporting leftist causes stretching back to his joining John Kerry by supporting Vietnam Veterans Against the War rallies in the 1970s—issued a report prepared by the Democratic staff of the House Judiciary Committee, of which he is the ranking Democratic member. As with the Florida report issued by Mary Frances Berry's committee, Conyers issued partisan findings, this time charging Blackwell and numerous other Ohio election officials with irregularities that had resulted in disenfranchising black voters in the 2004 presidential election.[42]

Again, the results in Ohio in 2004 were the same as had been the case in Florida in 2000. But this time the Democratic candidate, John Kerry, decided not to launch a legal challenge, especially not after his legal team advised him there was no evidence in Ohio of sufficient irregularities of the magnitude needed to reverse the election result. Again, no charges of any violations of the law were filed by either Ohio's state authorities or the U.S. Department of Justice. A major reason Democrats were upset with Ohio was that George W. Bush received approximately 17 percent of the black vote in 2004, which was a large increase over the 8 percent of the black vote that Bush had won in 2000. Democrats were also upset that Blackwell had fought to keep the Ohio Marriage Amendment on the ballot, an initiative that made Bush voters 26 percent more likely to vote, to reaffirm traditional marriage, versus Kerry voters, who were only 17 percent more likely to vote because the Marriage Amendment was on the ballot.[43]

John Fund, a columnist for the *Wall Street Journal*'s Internet-based OpinionJournal.com, examined election fraud and concluded that there is a responsibility side to the disenfranchisement debate:

> Discrimination can take many forms: turning away voters already in line when polls close, intimidating or misinforming voters when they arrive at the polls, using badly flawed or poorly designed ballots, failing to provide bilingual materials and failing to fix problem voting machines. We must guard against all these practices. But we must also recognize that voters have a responsibility to acquaint themselves with the election process and they cannot expect that their vote will be counted no matter what mistakes they make in casting it. Better voter education in schools, literacy programs and public service announcements before an election reminding people what they must do to cast a valid vote can all help reduce the number of spoiled ballots and ensure that as many valid votes as possible are cast.[44]

Liberals tend to repeat black disenfranchisement urban legends until they are accepted as truth, knowing that even unsubstantiated claims can still drive voters to act in a partisan manner. Kirsanow further cautions us to correct these disenfranchisement claims because "these toxic claims join a host of other pernicious urban legends that filter through the black electorate each election cycle, such as the perennial claim that the Voting Rights Act is about to expire."[45]

The spreading of urban legends to inflate claims of racial discrimination was perhaps never more evident than in New Orleans after Hurricane Katrina in the summer of 2005. Rumors ran rampant—body counts reporting that thousands had been killed, horrible accounts of rapes and assaults in the overcrowded Superdome and the convention center, wild rumors of infants being chopped up or stuffed in refrigerators, even claims that sharks from Lake Pontchartrain were devouring corpses in the business district. Mayor C. Ray Nagin told Oprah Winfrey's national television audience of people "in that frickin' Superdome for five days watching dead bodies, watching hooligans killing people, raping people."[46] The initial impression broadcast worldwide by an overwrought mainstream media created a false image of violence and lawlessness that fostered a politically motivated conclusion that a white-majority-oriented Bush administration did not care about the suffering of the poverty-stricken racial minorities of New Orleans. Even when these and countless other rumors were proven to be wild exaggerations, if not simply outright fabrications, too much damage had been done to correct the story. Because the media amplified these stories unfiltered, broadcasting myths, rumors, and lies, without making any attempt to substantiate the information, nothing could be done to clarify what had actually happened. Belated corrections of the stories by the media did little to correct the political damage that had been done.[47]

Ironically, we have moved from a 1950s environment, where images of Bull Connor and attack dogs gave truth to the racial injustice suffered by America's minorities, to a twenty-first-century reality, where lies are advanced to perpetuate charges that America remains racially unjust. The truth is that, since the 1950s, our laws and courts have made racial discrimination a crime. Still, while we may have achieved de jure racial equality, we still have abundant de facto racial inequality. As we have argued, the logic of blame and guilt will not in the future solve the problem any more than we will solve the problem by continuing to spend trillions of dollars in the most massive government welfare state bureaucracy ever created in human history. Simply put, it is time for a new approach.

## THE END OF RACISM

IN WRITING *The End of Racism,* a challenging 1995 book, Dinesh D'Souza argued that the civil rights movement beginning in the 1950s had succeeded in eliminating the legal barriers that supported racial discrimination only to find that racial inequality persisted. In response, the liberal refrain from the civil rights era transformed from embracing color-blind laws to endorsing policies that discriminate in favor of minorities, giving birth to a wide variety of affirmative-action programs and racial-preference schemes, again without achieving any fundamental result in de facto racial equality. D'Souza poses the question, Is racism the main problem blacks are facing today? He answers:

> No. The main contemporary obstacle facing African Americans is neither white racism, as many liberals claim, nor black genetic deficiency, as Charles Murray and others imply. Rather it involves destructive and pathological cultural patterns of behavior: excessive reliance on government, conspiratorial paranoia about racism, a resistance to academic achievement as "acting white," a celebration of the criminal and outlaw as authentically black, and the normalization of illegitimacy and dependency. These group patterns arose as a response to past oppression, but they are now dysfunctional and must be modified.[48]

D'Souza called for a fundamental change within the African American community, and he reached for a solution that transcends the typical boundaries of a language defined by "blame" or "rage."

Today, as opposed to 1954, white Americans almost universally have some kind of personal experience with African Americans. We see African Americans prominent in sports, television, movies, even politics. Every industry in America can point to many African Americans who have achieved prominence. African Americans have headed New York Stock Exchange–listed companies and earned millions of dollars for that achievement. African Americans have graduated with advanced degrees from virtually every university in the nation, in virtually every field or discipline. While we still have segregated communities, most schools even in the most exclusive, predominately white upper-class neighborhoods have some African Americans as residents. And their children attend the nearby public schools, and their families are admitted on an equal basis to the community's hospitals when they need medical care. White patients themselves are frequently treated by African American doctors and physicians. Lawyers and judges are African Americans, even on our highest federal and state courts. African Americans are elected to public office at the highest levels. Both of our major political parties have prominent African American candidate and officials. In all these senses, America today is not the racially segregated America of 1954.

For D'Souza, achieving de facto equality in results depends upon African Americans advancing to meet competitive standards across the board. He argued that America's real problem is both "a race problem and partly a black problem."

> The solution to the race problem is a public policy that is strictly in-different to race. The black problem can be solved only through a program of cultural reconstruction in which society plays a support-ing role but which is carried out primarily by African Americans themselves. Both projects need to be pursued simultaneously; nei-ther can work by itself. If society is race neutral but blacks remain uncompetitive, then equality of rights for individuals will lead to dramatic inequality of results for groups, liberal embarrassment will set in, and we are back on the path to racial preferences. On the other hand, if blacks are going to reform their community, they have a right to expect that they will be treated equally under the law. Al-though America has a long way to go, many mistakes have been made, and current antagonisms are high, still there are hopeful signs that the nation can move toward a society in which race ceases to matter, a destination that we can term "the end of racism."[49]

The solution then lies internally. Or as D'Souza observed, "Black success and social acceptance are now both tied to rebuilding the African American community." Achieving equal results, in other words, begins with being equal in all measured respects. As we have seen here, changing laws is not enough, nor will court decisions con-demning racial discrimination be enough to result in racial equality. Yet progress in de jure equality has been made. We have made racial dis-crimination a crime such that no American can knowingly deny an-other an important social, economic, or political advantage because of race, religion, age, or sex. Americans today are accepting of racial dif-ferences to an extent that would have been virtually unimaginable in 1954. Now we have to deal head-on with the legacy of a poverty under-class that still remains a problem of race. Our call here is to look be-yond the welfare state and admit finally that the government-waged war on poverty has failed.

We turn again to Jesse Lee Peterson's *From Rage to Responsibility:*

> As much as some people hate to admit it, and as angry as it makes
> many black people, *the undeniable fact is that the greatest enemies to
> black progress today are within the black community itself, not in
> American society at large.* As black people, we must recognize that
> our real battle is with ourselves, not with society. It is not racism
> but the civil rights establishment, with its victim-centered mental-
> ity and irrational fury at white America that mentally cripples
> blacks, teaching them to find the means of success outside of
> themselves in government programs, and urging them to find the
> origin of their greatest problems in white society.[50]

African Americans have "journeyed through the pothole-ridden
road of liberal promises and social reforms, and found that it ends in a
frustrating dead end."[51] We have crossed the threshold into a world
"armed with the moral and legal victories of the civil rights movement,
as well as a national conscience attuned to racial fairness."[52] These are
cornerstone accomplishments without which de facto equality could
never be hoped for, let alone attained. Government action may have
been indispensable in the battle to eliminate the de jure barriers that
had institutionalized racial discrimination. That we can no longer rely
upon government action alone to achieve de facto racial equality is our
fundamental theme here. The solution that will be needed will not be
easy to implement; we doubt we can fully imagine today all the ele-
ments that will be necessary for success. We know the journey begins
with restoring the family and rebuilding the African American communities that reside at the core of our urban metropolitan areas. We believe
the journey will only end when private enterprise has been fully engaged. As long as the driving energy of private enterprise remains on
the sideline, genuine racial equality will never be achieved in America.
Until we crack the code of achieving racial equality in America, we will
never fundamentally solve the problem of poverty residing as an un-
movable cancer in our midst.

# PART 2

# The Solution

# 6

## The Blackwell Initiative

We must begin to bring the talents, skills, and resources of the private enterprise system into the struggle to end poverty and deprivation in urban and rural America.

—Robert F. Kennedy

FEW AMERICANS ARE MORE identified with the War on Poverty in the 1960s than Robert F. Kennedy. As attorney general in his brother's administration, and later as a senator from New York, Kennedy was a tireless champion of the poor. He fought alongside Martin Luther King Jr. to end racial discrimination in America. Today we must remember one of Kennedy's most important insights: we will never defeat poverty in America or establish racial equality until we find a way to engage the full creative genius of capitalism. "Government must join in a partnership with industry," Kennedy instructed us, "permitting private enterprise to help solve the problems of housing and unemployment in our deprived areas."

We have seen the dead end produced by reliance on government bureaucracy to solve these social problems. After decades of massive federal spending, we continue to live in a society where poverty has not been diminished and patterns of racial segregation and disadvantage persist.

Reliance upon government has produced a culture that undervalues self-reliance, and that culture has detracted from the ability of our poor and minorities to advance. Rather than build communities, we have allowed inner cities to deteriorate further. Rather than educate children so they could develop the needed skills to advance as productive employees, managers, and executives, we have destroyed families. Social success is tied to one's self-worth, which in America is tied to a job. Teenage pregnancies and abortions are the legacy of a welfare system that cannot solve the daily worsening problems of unemployment and crime that distinguish our poor and segregated inner-city neighborhoods.

The only way this downward spiral will be reversed is if we can find a way to engage fully private business and the profit motive to attack these persistent social and economic problems we cannot otherwise shake. Perhaps the problems will prove too recalcitrant and entrenched even for private enterprise to solve, yet that case has not yet been demonstrated. Instead, we are going to make a case here for a partnership between government and private enterprise, with the understanding that government's role is to set up the framework in which private enterprise can flourish of its own initiative. Government cannot direct this effort successfully any more than government could run a welfare state that produced measurable reductions in poverty. Government can enable business, but if government crosses the line and tries to direct or control private enterprise activities, those enterprises themselves will inevitably fail. This then is the difficult balance we must find. What is the proper role for government, if that role is not to run a publicly financed, massive welfare bureaucracy?

## THE BLACKWELL INITIATIVE

How can government best enable business to become engaged in rebuilding America? We must start at the state level, not the federal level. Since the Great Depression, Americans have turned increasingly to Washington for the solutions to problems that are fundamentally local in nature. Here we argue that the problem of poverty is best understood as a problem of neighborhoods and cities. When Washington tries to mandate national solutions, the inevitable result is bureaucracy—more rules and paperwork mandated as requirements for funding. Yet truly solving the core problems of poverty has to involve the smallest units of society, particularly families. The welfare state has failed to put in place programs that motivate families to educate children in a way that reverses the downward spiral of poverty. The failure is not the failure of poor families; the failure is the failure of the welfare system itself. The solution we propose involves the state government's enabling banks and businesses to get involved, to revitalize impoverished communities with the end result being the creation of jobs, thus creating more homeowners and educating children with the fundamental skills they will need to be gainfully employed as adults.

The goal is to find new state funds that can be applied to stimulate jobs and homeownership in Ohio. We call the plan "the Blackwell Initiative." After consultation with nationally renowned investment bankers, we propose to raise several billions of new state dollars in a "Rebuild Ohio Now" program that we will outline in this chapter. The Blackwell Initiative described in the next paragraphs will be a key strategic component of Ken Blackwell's 2006 gubernatorial campaign.

The Blackwell Initiative involves unleashing the power of the global private-equity capital markets on what has until recently been a state and local government capital market dominated almost exclusively by state and local governments entering into debt to pay for purposes such as roads, sewers, and most important, jobs and economic development. As we will discuss in this chapter, we propose that the state of Ohio take a national leadership role in authorizing the private sector to invest the proceeds of leasing Ohio's toll road—the Ohio Turnpike—and thereby provide for an immediate cash infusion of potentially billions of dollars into a trust fund or funds that will be dedicated to jobs and economic development for Ohioans.

We expect the investments from these trusts will particularly emphasize investment in those urban and rural areas of Ohio that have become underinvested as a result of the failures of the welfare state. Currently, governments throughout the United States have either pursued or are actively reviewing proposals similar to the one we will discuss in this chapter. What we hope this book will do is to stir a national debate about what to do with these funds once received. Our plan is to

invest these newly found state dollars in jobs and economic development. We believe we can show that conservatives are ready to commit
significant resources to twenty-first-century strategies to better families
and communities decimated by the forty years of investment in the
failed bureaucracies of the welfare state. The foundation of the Blackwell Initiative is our respective commitment to involving private enterprise in a constructive manner to create new jobs, generate more
income for Ohioans, and expand the number of Ohioans who are successful homeowners.

Our goal in leasing the Ohio Turnpike is to establish, under Ohio
law, trust funds that will work with the private-capital markets, including banks, venture capital firms, real estate investment trusts (REITS)
comprised of property owners, and businesses whose job it will be to
put the funds to work in Ohio's communities. The benefit of the Blackwell Initiative is that it can be pursued without raising taxes in Ohio. In
fact, our objective is to lower taxes. We believe the increased economic
activity we will generate with the *Rebuild Ohio Now* program will increase tax revenues, thus permitting us to examine tax cuts. Likewise
the Blackwell Initiative will be put in place without increasing the size
or cost of the state bureaucracy.

## LEASING THE OHIO TURNPIKE: FINANCING
## THE REBUILD OHIO NOW PROGRAM

ON APRIL 30, 1992, President George H. W. Bush signed Executive Order
No. 12803 on infrastructure privatization, clearing federal barriers for
cities and states to lease public works infrastructure to private investors.
Several advantages can result: the state government offering an infrastructure project will generate a substantial one-time payment when the
facility is leased; continuing revenue can be realized in taxes or other
usage fees that may still be charged; the leased facility enters the market
economy, and updating and maintenance charges are removed from the
state budget. A primary candidate for leasing in Ohio is the 241-mile
Ohio Turnpike, which might bring a one-time initial payment of $4–6
billion on a ninety-nine-year lease. Toll road privatization is like selling
someone the right to operate a business that you still own. The lease-

holder gets the right to operate the Ohio Turnpike, keeps the toll revenue, and is responsible for maintenance and upkeep on the turnpike. Ohio's state government could reduce the bureaucracy and tax burden necessary to operate the turnpike while receiving continuing tax revenue from the turnpike leaseholder.[1] Even with the lease in place, the state of Ohio continues to own the turnpike.

Critics argue that leasing the turnpike is like selling the capitol dome. State assets are being sold to handle current budgetary needs, foregoing the continuing revenue the infrastructure asset could generate. Yet a lease is not an outright sale; the state still owns the infrastructure asset. What is being sold is the right to operate the turnpike, not the turnpike itself. The goal is consistent with the Blackwell Initiative's overall intent: to move the state government away from providing services that can better be delivered by private enterprise. By generating a higher level of business activity, Ohio's tax revenues will increase without increasing taxes. We continue to doubt that a government bureaucracy is the efficient way to run any enterprise, especially not one that could be turned over to private business for operation.

Other candidates for privatization in Ohio include airports, water departments, even school systems. Those infrastructure facilities owned by municipalities could be leased by the municipalities. All contracts written to privatize infrastructure governmental assets must be bid openly and competitively to assure the best financial deal is received in the lease and to eliminate opportunities for fraud or bribery.

There is no intrinsic reason to believe that a state government bureaucracy can operate the Ohio Turnpike better than a private business can. If a private road company operating the turnpike charges exorbitant tolls, usage will decline and market forces will drive pricing adjustments. The most fundamental change required is one of mentality: we have to change from thinking of government as a taxing-and-spending entity to conceptualizing government in investment banking terms. Government has a unique ability to structure public projects so that investment bankers can find private financing, with the ultimate result being to create new businesses or to encourage the expansion of existing businesses. Government conceptualized from an investment-banking framework plays primarily a structuring function, not the primary role of operating the enterprises created. So Ohio's state government would work with investment bankers (selected through open bids and competition) who would structure and arrange the turnpike lease, deriving a maximum one-time payment for the state plus finding an operator with a track record likely to generate maximum subsequent tax revenue to the state. Using this methodology, we are able to find new monies that the state government can apply to economic development, again without raising taxes.

The movement to consider leasing toll roads began in January 2005, when the Chicago Skyway let a ninety-nine-year lease concession to a private-operator consortium for $1.8 billion. Then, on January 23, 2006, the state of Indiana opened bids to enter into a seventy-five-year lease concession with a private operator to operate the Indiana Toll Road (which connects to the Ohio Turnpike). In both cases, the maximum toll schedule for both roads was set in the award of the agreement. The private operator under the terms of the lease is responsible for all upkeep and maintenance of the road at agreed-upon standards. The operator must also pay for the policing of the road. The Chicago Skyway agreement is more than a thousand pages long, with stringent terms and conditions. In both the Chicago and Indiana cases, the lease-bidding process was completely open, conducted to achieve the highest possible price.

On January 24, 2006, Ohio secretary of state Ken Blackwell announced a dramatic new plan to boost the state's economy by leasing the Ohio Turnpike to private investors and creating the JOB (Jobs for Ohio Businesses) Fund with the proceeds. Given the cash flow of the Ohio Turnpike (which produces approximately $100 million annually of earnings before interest, taxes, depreciation, and amortization [EBITDA]), the expected price of the lease should be in the $4–6 billion range. All the monies will be received by the state of Ohio on an upfront basis. Approximately $675 million of the proceeds from the lease concession are planned to be used to reduce the outstanding debt of the turnpike; the remaining money will be used for economic development and other critical job-creating infrastructure improvements.

In announcing the leasing plan, coauthor Ken Blackwell issued a statement:

Recently published reports indicate Ohio has dropped to 47th nationally in job creation. As our economy continues to falter, we can no longer rely on business as usual. We must innovate. We must take risks. Ohio must use every resource available to create jobs. This proposal will allow an unprecedented push for economic development without depleting funds needed for other state services. By soliciting bids and segregating the proceeds, we can provide for market-driven activity free from political influence. Nothing is more important to the future of our state than the creation of jobs. We must do everything we can to restore economic opportunity and hope to the families and communities of Ohio.

Leasing the turnpike will require legislative action to authorize the transaction after the completion of the open-bidding process. The plan is to keep all service plaza agreements in place until expiration; advertising rights will be retained by the state. The Ohio Highway Patrol will remain responsible for policing the road, with all the costs of policing being paid by the private operator. Operating standards—maintenance, repairs, engineering standards, capital improvements, safety, handling of traffic and emergencies, environmental issues, and landscaping—will be set out in a detailed schedule in agreement with the operator. Maintenance will be regulated and inspected annually by a consulting engineer. If operating standards are not met, the operator's lease is subject to termination and the road will be reclaimed by the state of Ohio.

Funds from the turnpike lease can also be allocated to a revolving development loan fund that can be administered by participating banks in the *Rebuild Ohio Now* program. Expecting that the loans made in the *Rebuild Ohio Now* program will be repaid by the borrowers, the development fund will be "revolving," meaning that interest and principal payments on *Rebuild Ohio Now* loans will be returned to the Ohio economy by participating banks making new loans. This allows us to utilize the one-time upfront lease proceeds to stimulate new jobs and homeownership in Ohio on a continuing basis. Funds from the turnpike lease are also planned to create a venture capital fund to stimulate job creation. Turnpike lease proceeds are also planned to be allocated toward energy development, including funding alternative energies and clean coal resources, as well as conservation and efficiency improvements. Additionally, turnpike lease funds will go toward a higher education scholarship for Ohio's engineering, technology, and science students.

We say that the turnpike lease may be the best alternative for financing the *Rebuild Ohio Now* program because the lease promises to provide a large sum, somewhere between $4–6 billion, new money that is totally outside Ohio's general revenue tax basis, funds that can be available relatively quickly. The lease then would function to leverage a state asset, the turnpike, into much-needed funds for jobs. Realizing that people are Ohio's greatest resource, the investment we plan to make in the *Rebuild Ohio Now* program has the greatest return imaginable. We are making an investment in Ohio's future by providing today an expanded opportunity for gainful employment, homeownership, and educational advancement in Ohio. Jobs and the advancement of Ohio's citizens, in the final analysis, are the ultimate goal of *Rebuild Ohio Now*.

## WHAT WILL WE ACCOMPLISH WITH THE *REBUILD OHIO NOW* PROGRAM?

THE *Rebuild Ohio Now* program, what we have also termed the Blackwell Initiative, is designed to attract profitable businesses into troubled areas and to foster successful homeownership there. We recognize that many of the areas we will first target are inner-city neighborhoods that are currently characterized by African American poverty. The strategy is to get profitable business activity started in these areas and to expand the base of independently viable homeownership. In Ohio, Cleveland's Hough community was hurt badly by the race riots of the 1960s. Many properties were abandoned and many lots were left vacant. Property values dropped and business closed. In recent years, economic recovery in Hough has been stimulated by the growth of the Cleveland Clinic, which has expanded into a world-class health services complex. Redevelopment efforts in Hough have also benefited from the close proximity to Case Western Reserve University's top-ranked medical school.

The Cleveland Clinic has stimulated the economic redevelopment of Hough in the same way that commercial developers seek "anchor tenants" to develop a new mall complex. When building a strip mall, an anchor tenant is typically sought as part of a strategy designed to attract additional tenants. The principle is that business activity is needed to attract additional business activities.

Over the past fifty years, downtown Cleveland has been largely in decline. Economic revival occurred in the 1980s when the new investment in the city's sports teams attracted fans downtown to new facilities, such as Jacobs Field, which was constructed at Ninth Street and Carnegie Avenue. Next, Municipal Stadium, an aging complex badly in need of repair, was demolished, and a new stadium was built for the Cleveland Browns. Then the basketball Cleveland Cavaliers moved back to downtown, and Gund Arena (now known as the Q Arena) was constructed in an expanded Jacobs Field complex. New downtown skyscrapers were constructed, such as the Key Bank Tower and the BP America (Sohio) Building. Still, large sections of Euclid Avenue remain abandoned, with vacant lots standing on what in the 1950s and 1960s had been the major commercial street in downtown Cleveland. The further development of downtown Cleveland will demand attracting new businesses, including attracting businesses now in outlying suburbs to relocate their headquarters operations downtown.

Business owners will have many considerations about any move downtown. Is there sufficient parking? What are the relative costs per square foot for office space versus the outlying suburbs? What is the anticipated commute time for employees? Cleveland's Rapid Transit Association (RTA) still connects much of the 1960s suburbs to the downtown hub at the Terminal Tower. The limited-access highway system also connects the major interstate highways into Cleveland's downtown, with a strong beltway system that connects east and west at various wheel-rim distances around Cleveland. Proposals to redevelop downtown Cleveland have been discussed for years. Cleveland even today is a major center for the paint industry; plans for a thirty-story downtown Sherwin-Williams skyscraper at West Third and Superior have been on the drawing board for years. Additional office space yet remains available in the Renaissance and North Point buildings, as well as new buildings that were built in the 1980s in the space behind Terminal Tower. Cleveland's downtown has development possibilities. What is required is the availability of development dollars, such as we plan to provide with the

*Rebuild Ohio Now* program, together with old-fashioned city planning and marketing skills.

The governor, the mayor, and banks, together with various business-planning groups, need to work together to identify target businesses that might move operations into the downtown and other greater Cleveland metropolitan target areas. Armed with *Rebuild Ohio Now* loans and investments, companies willing to establish a business in a target area should be able to get competitive pricing. With some experience, the participating financial institutions will be able to determine the pricing on a financing package that provides sufficient pricing incentives to attract businesses while still allowing the investments to be profitable. Making the program work will not be as simple as putting an advertisement in the *Plain Dealer* and waiting for prospective businesses to form a line and apply for loans. Much thought, considerable marketing, and creative hard work will be needed to identify businesses willing to examine the opportunity. Negotiations will have to take place regarding location decisions, financing packages, and other support service concessions that need to be made. To make the program work, the governor will need to establish working partnerships with local officials, appropriate bankers, and business leaders.

By its very nature, we intend the *Rebuild Ohio Now* program to be significantly different from previous redevelopment efforts. Our goal is not to finance minorities to create businesses in poverty-stricken neighborhoods. Nor is the idea that minorities who lack any financial resources or who are unable to provide the income verification needed for conventional home financing will receive subsidized homeowner's assistance. A wide variety of public welfare, public housing, and community-development programs exist to fulfill those needs. The *Rebuild Ohio Now* program proposes keeping all existing welfare, public housing, and community-development programs in place, operating just as they currently do. The *Rebuild Ohio Now* goal is to find anchor businesses that will relocate in the target areas, regardless of whether they are majority or minority owned, regardless of whether they plan on employing the area's minority workers or not. Our goal is to start the development process in the target areas on a strictly private-enterprise basis. The corporations that decide to participate in the *Rebuild Ohio Now* program will *not* have to meet special requirements, such as a commitment to hire minorities who live in the communities where they locate or to employ a quota of local welfare residents who will receive retraining at the company. Such requirements would put added costs on companies that will need economic incentives, not economic burdens, to make the decision to participate.

Billions of dollars have already been spent in a vast array of community development efforts.[2] We are arguing here that target neighborhoods remain poor today because they lack profitable businesses that create a hub of economic activity around which the neighborhood can build. Torn-down schools and abandoned lots will not attract profitable companies to troubled neighborhoods. A combination of supportive government efforts, demanding the time and personal involvement of mayors and city council members, will be needed. Participating financial institutions with creative financing alternatives will need to work to attract prospective businesses. Business owners must be made to see that competitive gain can result from below-market financing and other support concessions that local and state government officials can and are willing to make in order to get businesses to set up operation in the target areas.

The idea is to create an environment where public welfare and community development programs can work in conjunction with *Rebuild Ohio Now* business activity. Public welfare organizations will be encouraged to approach *Rebuild Ohio Now* companies to see if they can assist the corporations willing to establish businesses in the target areas. Corporations may not be enthusiastic about a job-retraining program if that program is imposed as a quota or a requirement. But if a welfare program has a need to retrain people who can only stay on welfare for a limited time, the welfare program itself can provide incentives to local businesses that are willing to provide job training on favorable terms. Majority employees of a *Rebuild Ohio Now* company may decide to relocate their homes into a target area so they can live closer to their place of employment. The resulting urban homesteading should raise property values for many current minority property owners in the target area, whether or not those residents are employed by the participating businesses. The principle we are pursuing is that economic activity is going to generate increased economic activity.

Problem neighborhoods are today in a downward spiral of business flight and increasingly depressed property values. This downward spiral deepens poverty blight and reduces the opportunity for support businesses, such as restaurants, supermarkets, and retail shopping stores. Moving profitable businesses into economically troubled target areas is a move designed to reverse the downward spiral by setting in motion a business multiplier effect on the upward side.

Not every troubled area in a city as complex as metropolitan Cleveland will jump at the opportunity of participating in *Rebuild Ohio Now* program. Yet if even one mayor does, the model can be established so that increased economic build-out can proceed from there to other target areas that want to follow the example and decide to participate later.

Participating businesses can be new companies or established companies, companies currently doing business in Ohio, or companies operating elsewhere that are attracted by the opportunity. Even international companies can apply. Ironically, economic development in troubled areas may be easier to accomplish than in already well-developed areas. Installing sophisticated infrastructure, including computer and telecommunications infrastructure, may be easier in areas where there are vacant lots to be occupied. Rather than replacing an outmoded infrastructure in an area that is already economically profitable, a business relocating in a current poverty area may be able to put in place the most modern systems more cheaply, as part of the initial design, without having to replace anything. The *Rebuild Ohio Now* program is designed not just for Cleveland but also for cities throughout Ohio, large and small. Opportunities will exist statewide from Youngstown to Toledo, from Columbus to Cincinnati, throughout the Akron-Canton area, and beyond. Rural areas seeking development can and will participate as well in these investments. We look forward to working with the Ohio legislature to determine the rural focus of participation.

The business opportunities attracted to target areas will not all be high tech. Ohio has many industrial zones that can be revitalized. The Great Lakes are accessible to oceangoing shipping via the St. Lawrence Seaway. Even today, oil refinery operations continue in Cleveland, south of the downtown area along Interstate 77, for example. Yet some 60 percent of America's refineries are situated in the Gulf of Mexico. Regional diversification of oil refineries is needed, if only to reduce the impact hurricanes can have on gasoline and heating-oil supplies. Moreover, America has not built a new refinery in thirty years.

Light manufacturing is another opportunity sector. Steel plants in Cleveland's Flats were once a major economic boost to the city. Those industrial areas remain, many of which would be adapted to light manufacturing at competitive economic advantage, simply by redeveloping Cleveland's industrial areas, such as the Flats. For *Rebuild Ohio Now* to be successful, we will need creative thought that involves city managers, commerce organizations, and banks. Marketing will be essential to get the word out that opportunities exist in Ohio and that Ohio government and banks are open to make deals.

Again, we emphasize that money alone will not solve the problem of developing economically troubled target areas. The *Rebuild Ohio Now* program provides a reason for bankers, government officials, corporate officers, and entrepreneurs to talk with one another. Knowing that financing will be made available through the *Rebuild Ohio Now* program will provide an incentive for all parties to see how they can economically benefit themselves and others by participating.

## UNDERSTANDING THE *REBUILD OHIO NOW* PARTICIPATING BANK PROGRAM

BILLIONS OF dollars have been spent by banks throughout America on community development efforts[3] and in Community Reinvestment Act funds.[4] The *Rebuild Ohio Now* program is not just more of these same dollars. Banks that embark on traditional community development and community reinvestment projects typically create special departments or groups within banks to undertake the effort. Bank senior management often does not expect community development or community reinvestment initiatives to contribute strongly to bank profitability, if at all. Bank officers who succeed in managing community development and community reinvestment programs can become highly valued employees. Future presidents of major commercial banks, however, even today, still tend to come from commercial lending. Why? Commercial lending is typically where commercial banks make the most profits. Banking stars tend to be those managers who generate the most profits. Looked at objectively, managers of community development and community reinvestment units in banks are good candidates to receive recognition and to be the honored guests at community public relations dinners. Senior commercial bankers who manage the banks' largest commercial accounts, by comparison, receive fewer plaques and larger annual bonuses.

The *Rebuild Ohio Now* loans and investments are designed to fit into the major commercial banking and residential mortgage banking operations of participating financial institutions. The senior officers running these programs will have the opportunity to advance their careers and benefit themselves and their families economically, especially when they succeed in attracting and growing profitable businesses in target areas. When senior bank management understands that the program is designed for banks to develop major new commercial banking clients, then even the banks' boards of directors can be expected to become interested. Banks operate as bureaucratic structures, especially today, when government-reporting requirements mandate additional documentation and reports to be filed. Bank managers take direction from the top. New programs may be implemented without the involvement of bank senior management, but the enthusiasm and dedication of senior bank management, including bank presidents, needs to be visible supporting a plan for that plan to have a chance of succeeding in a big way.

We intend that the *Rebuild Ohio Now* program will justify the attention even of a commercial bank's most senior management because the program will be designed to offer strong profit opportunities in areas previously neglected by bank management. Under *Rebuild Ohio Now,* community development is not intended to be charity work in disguise. Community development and community reinvestment bank officers who decide to team up with *Rebuild Ohio Now* commercial and residential lenders can build strong teams within banks, with the result that all the bankers involved have the chance to advance their careers. If we are to follow Robert F. Kennedy's advice, we must engage the private enterprise system at all levels, including within the banks that participate. Everything of significance that happens positively in a bank tends to result from senior management commitment, and that commitment depends upon profits.

Participating financial institutions will be cautious at first, suspecting that the *Rebuild Ohio Now* program is destined to become just another report-ridden bureaucratic nightmare. This is why the *Rebuild Ohio Now* program has been designed to be administered through a small government staff. To be successful, each participating financial institution must have flexibility on exactly how *Rebuild Ohio Now* loans and investments are constructed. This flexibility should include the ability to tailor each loan or investment with different mixes of bank funds, equity funds, *Rebuild Ohio Now* funds, and community reinvestment dollars as part of the equation. For the program to work, competitive *Rebuild Ohio Now* packages must be presented with sufficient economic incentives to attract prospect companies. Depending upon the prospect company involved, the incentive that may finalize a decision may be the availability of land at a reasonable price within a target area, the offer of a town to develop the local public infrastructure of roads, or police and fire services to benefit the business. The incentive that wins the deal might be a willingness of local welfare agencies to provide retraining at agency expense, with the goal that minority residents in the community will be developed as an important part of the company's workforce. Because each incentive package has to be custom designed, the structure of how *Rebuild Ohio Now* loans are put together will itself have to remain adaptable.

The state government's major responsibility will be to disperse funds to the trust. The board of trustees of the trust will be comprised of leaders in the field of business creation, business growth, and economic development. These trustees will be responsible for identifying the private banks and financial institutions that will participate in the *Rebuild Ohio Now* program. The responsibility of the board of trustees will be to make sure the trust receives the benefit of the state's investment in terms of new jobs, return on principal and interest, capital appreciation, and so forth, according the expectations of the state set forth in the trust agreement and Ohio law. The goal will be to transform the initial substantial payment from leasing the Ohio Turnpike into a permanent fund that continues to create jobs and enhance the attractiveness of Ohio as a business location and a good place to raise and educate a family.

No large bureaucracy at the state level will be created to impose demanding rules, regulations, or formulas on the financial institutions and banks participating in the *Rebuild Ohio Now* program. Extensive government regulation would only serve to quash the flexibility these participating banks and financial institutions need to negotiate creative business solutions within the targeted economic areas. Abuses, if they occur, will be investigated by the state, as the maker of the trust fund, just like any other abuse would be investigated. The state government's role will be to hold its experts, the trustees of the *Rebuild Ohio Now* trust, accountable for the state's expected performance from the trust in terms of job creation and business growth. The state should have few oversight expectations on the trustees of the trust other than seeking the highest possible return on its investment, consistent with the state's purposes when it forms the trust pursuant to Ohio law. As long as *Rebuild Ohio Now* loans and investments are performing according to the trustees' and state's expectations, the state government should be largely satisfied that the program is working, even if each participating bank or financial institution chooses to use its expertise to use the *Rebuild Ohio Now* program differently.

Complex government bureaucracies are a primary reason state welfare programs failed over the last four decades. The *Rebuild Ohio Now* program must avoid developing a large state government bureaucracy, or the program will inevitably fail.

## EXPECTED ECONOMIC BENEFITS TO TARGET COMMUNITIES

CRITICS WILL charge that the point of the *Rebuild Ohio Now* program is to bring majority-controlled businesses favoring white Americans into poor African American inner-city areas because land values are cheaper and business opportunities are being created on preferential terms. The argument will be that these companies will not employ poor blacks, nor will African Americans own the companies. Moreover, young affluent whites will be encouraged to buy the best residential opportunities, again taking advantage of favorable bank financing, permitting majority whites to redevelop the best homes. As a result, so the argument will go, poor blacks currently occupying residential units in target areas will simply be dislodged from their homes and forced to go elsewhere.

In responding, we must note several important points. The *Rebuild Ohio Now* program will encourage businesses owned by African Americans to apply. The *Rebuild Ohio Now* program will also expect African American residents of the target community to apply as homeowners to take advantage of the new financing available. The goal is *not* to displace poor blacks but to raise the economic level of the economically depressed neighborhoods for the benefit of everyone, including the African Americans currently residing in the target areas.

Expanded business opportunities should benefit everyone. Anchor businesses should stimulate the opening of additional support businesses, including restaurants and shopping centers. New job openings should encourage local residents to apply. Even if current homeowners sell, the new economic activity brought into the area by the *Rebuild Ohio Now* program should result in higher prices from which all current residents should benefit. Moreover, the *Rebuild Ohio Now* program is not intended to terminate or replace any existing welfare or community development program now operating in the target areas. If anything, our goal is to establish partnerships between the businesses attracted to the target areas and the welfare or community-development programs operating there now. As a result, we intend for new job training and other skill-development opportunities to surface for target-area residents. Current residents of economically troubled target areas should advance economically in conjunction with the new businesses taking hold in the area.

The *Rebuild Ohio Now* program is designed to be an "add to," not a "take away from," approach to advancing economically troubled areas. The *Rebuild Ohio Now* program design is a win-win structure. By bringing new financing into troubled areas and by establishing new businesses in those areas, more money should be available in local communities, with a resulting economic benefit to minority residents currently residing there. Since welfare and community-development expenditures will continue, the target community is not suffering any loss of current funding, nor are residents currently benefiting from various social programs intended to be removed from those programs. The vision is that poor neighborhoods will only advance when profitable private enterprise takes root in those neighborhoods. This is the entire goal of the *Rebuild Ohio Now* program, with the expectation that the increase in profitable private enterprise will lift the economic horizon for everyone, the new businesses and their employees, as well as the current residents of these communities.

## WHY THE *REBUILD OHIO NOW* PROGRAM SHOULD PERMIT TAX CUTS IN OHIO

ULTIMATELY, INCREASED business activity in Ohio should, by its own momentum, increase state tax revenues. At the same time, expanded employment opportunities should reduce welfare and other social assistance programs in Ohio. As we have mentioned, the ultimate goal is to provide the basis so that taxes in Ohio can be cut without cutting public expenditures. Even in welfare and social assistance programs, the *Rebuild Ohio Now* initiative has no intent of cutting programs or services. We expect these programs will need to spend less, but only because we expect that the increased business activity resulting from *Rebuild Ohio Now* loans will enable more people to get off welfare. Our goal is to reduce the expense of welfare and social service payments that are needed without reducing the program definitions of social welfare benefits provided or the people who remain eligible. Fewer people on welfare means reduced state revenue expenditures in welfare programs. Reduced social welfare expenditures enable tax cuts, which should, in turn, stimulate more business activity in Ohio and larger tax revenues. The stimulus effect of tax cuts has been demonstrated over and over again since the Kennedy administration. The stimulus effect of tax cuts that are permitted by decreasing welfare expenditures should be positively dynamic for Ohio.

A government-driven welfare bureaucracy creates a downward economic spiral that further depresses problem neighborhoods. We have amply documented this in our earlier discussion of the War on Poverty. We repeat for emphasis that the goal of the Blackwell Initiative is to set in motion an upward economic spiral that should raise the economic level of every participating neighborhood with an anticipated economic benefit to the current residents of those neighborhoods. *If the state government is able to realize any savings in welfare or community development outlays, tax cuts might be considered, a move that would further stim-*

*ulate the economy of Ohio. Our ultimate goal is to increase public spending through the* Rebuild Ohio Now *program while at the same time cutting state taxes.*

## PRIVATIZATION OF LOCAL GOVERNMENT PUBLIC SERVICES

HISTORICALLY, MOST towns in America have been responsible for performing a number of public-service functions, including garbage collection, police and fire departments, maintaining streets, libraries, and public education. Lately, we have seen many communities turn to privatization, especially with garbage-collection services. If the *Rebuild Ohio Now* program is as successful as we believe it will be, we will also be open to assisting local governments in Ohio that may wish to consider how privatization might be beneficial to their communities. We believe that there may be a special opportunity in the area of education. As we have seen earlier, a continuing problem in economically troubled target areas is that public schools continue to be segregated. These "separate" schools continue to be "unequal," providing a lower standard of education and obtaining, as a consequence, less-than-adequate results. Forced busing has failed to integrate inner-city schools. Nor have decades of public-program innovations solved the problem.

If a target community so chooses, we would be willing to hold out the opportunity to experiment with proposals from private companies to operate its schools. Several advantages should result from these experiments. Communities deciding to pay private operators to run public schools might save on overall expenditures to the extent that competing companies can be attracted to submit competitive bids to obtain the opportunity. Moreover, to retain the opportunity, private operators will be expected to demonstrate results according to educational standards set by the appropriate municipal government body overseeing the public schools. We believe that the private enterprise system should be encouraged at all levels to get involved in the rebuilding of our economically troubled areas. Economically troubled areas now face the problem of how to maintain public services when their tax revenues are declining. *Rebuild Ohio Now* intends to reverse the downward spiral of the local tax base by attracting profitable businesses and tax-paying homeowners into neighborhoods. If, additionally, we can remove public-service burdens, such as paying for public schools, we might attract private companies to run the schools utilizing a version of the leasing model we have proposed for the Ohio Turnpike. Private companies that contract to perform public services will also pay state and local taxes.

The last services a community would want to privatize are fire and police services. This reflects a basic intuition that the core value of government is public safety. Other services—including garbage collection, road maintenance, water departments, even schools—might be privatized. Again, we see a partnership between local government and financial institutions as being critical to defining whether and how any local government might consider privatizing its public-service activities.

This effort is at the core of what the *Rebuild Ohio Now* program at the state level is all about. We want to improve the quality of life within economically troubled target activities by attracting private enterprise into these communities. Why not start with the provision of public services? A town nearing bankruptcy cannot provide adequate public schools, let alone other needed public services. A target area will need public infrastructure advancement to attract the businesses we want to come into the target areas. A good start would be for target communities to identify public services that might be privatized so the community can put out its own contracts for competitive bids. A bid might even be put out to install high-tech computer and telecommunications infrastructure into corporate parks established in poverty areas planned for *Rebuild Ohio Now* business redevelopment. A private company seeing a combination of financing tools and other incentive options offered by a target community should see an expanding opportunity for its own investment in that target community.

The only way privatization should occur within a target community is with the target community's knowledge and consent. Any public services privatization, including the *Rebuild Ohio Now* program, must be subject to full public disclosure. No-bid contracts have created in Ohio an opportunity for corruption and scandal. Even at the level of special counsel, who are appointed to collect money owed the state of Ohio, candidates running for office in Ohio have been tempted to demand pay-to-profit campaign contributions, where the understanding is that no-bid government contracts will be awarded according to how generously prospective applicants contribute to election campaigns. In return for campaign contributions, lawyers and other pay-to-profit beneficiaries expected to personally benefit from no-bid contracts whose costs were inflated to provide compensation for everyone involved in the deal. Under the *Rebuild Ohio Now* program and any local government privatization efforts, all contracts given out to run schools, collect garbage, or provide water or other services to target communities must be open-bid contracts to assure the Ohio public that contracts have been awarded on the best prices available, with all selections made on competitive business principles and nothing else. When public-service opportunities are opened for bid, transparent "sunlight" provisions will apply to make sure only legitimate companies are selected to run operations in a businesslike, cost-effective manner that will benefit the citizens of the target communities.

The *Rebuild Ohio Now* program is about private enterprise operating at the highest moral level of professional business ethics.

### REBUILD OHIO NOW: A BEHAVIORAL APPROACH

WE HAVE noted earlier that, from a behavioral perspective, if a person does not want to be poor, then a person has to do what is necessary not to be poor. This is at least a necessary condition for escaping poverty; sufficient conditions include having economic opportunities available as well. The *Rebuild Ohio Now* program seeks to bring important business opportunities forward into Ohio's communities statewide.

To fulfill the necessary conditions of economic success, those living in target communities will still need to apply themselves to doing what economically self-sufficient people do. A person who is going to get and hold a good job needs education, appropriate skills, work habits conducive to everyday workplace productivity, dependable attendance, and a positive attitude. People who lack these qualities are not doing what is typically required to be productive employees. The lesson is basic, yet it merits statement. The formula needed to get a person out of poverty has been available for centuries. In America, we have made job discrimination a crime. Properly prepared minorities presenting themselves for work will be successful in an America where their right to work has been secured by law and court rulings.

So, too, if an impoverished community is to advance economically, private enterprise must take root within the community. This is why the focus of *Rebuild Ohio Now* is to attract profitable businesses into target areas.

Regardless of whether the business is owned or operated by minorities, regardless of whether the business employs minorities from the target area, benefits will rebound to resident minorities just because the business is there. Communities emerging from poverty must do the same things that economically successful communities do. What we are seeking to accomplish with the Blackwell Initiative is to take active steps to produce the incentives businesses need to make the decision to enter inner-city poverty neighborhoods. The *Rebuild Ohio Now* program will need some experience to determine what the right incentive packages should look like. Yet the principle is basic economics. Seats on airlines are filled with pricing structures designed to fly full planes. Similarly, the *Rebuild Ohio Now* program will fine-tune the incentives approach until the right formulas are found. Companies will make economically sound decisions when presented with the opportunities to do so. We expect that local residents of target communities will also see the opportunity and begin taking the necessary steps in their own lives to become productively involved in the companies attracted to their communities by the program.

We do not expect the *Rebuild Ohio Now* plan will be easy to implement, nor do we expect success to be immediate. We do believe that poor neighborhoods will be less poor when businesses begin operating there. This should be almost as obvious as observing that people, majority and minority alike, will earn substantial salaries when they begin doing the things people earning substantial salaries do today. We have spent decades believing that giving welfare checks to poor people will get them out of poverty. Instead, we have made continued participation in welfare programs effectively the "job" of poor people. People learn the welfare system's rules and are rewarded with welfare checks when they follow the rules. The *Rebuild Ohio Now* program aims to remove the ceiling the "welfare system job" pays to people who make the welfare system their livelihood. But let's not forget, by implementing *Rebuild Ohio Now*, we are not eliminating any welfare program or social service. The Blackwell Initiative aims to produce sufficient economic activity in target areas so that fewer welfare payments will be needed as a consequence over time. We are aiming to attract a target area's residents back to productive activity as a consequence of drawing private enterprise into the community. Our goal is not to displace minorities from inner cities but to employ minorities productively within inner-city neighborhoods where they also have the chance to become homeowners and to build families.

In four decades of the War on Poverty, private industry has tended to stay in the grandstands as observers. The Blackwell Initiative aims to get private industry onto the playing field as an active participant in the goal of reducing poverty and racial inequality in America. This is a necessary condition to eliminating poverty. But the condition will not be sufficient until poor people themselves decide to engage as the fully productive players, becoming the winners we know they can be in America's continuing economic development.

# 7

## Strengthening Families and Building Wealth

The children of our slums are being savagely cheated by society, which thinks it is too sophisticated to care about whether children have fathers and mothers have husbands.

—Daniel Patrick Moynihan, 1965[1]

PHOTOGRAPHS FROM THE EARLY twentieth century exist of busy downtown streets for most cities in America. Today the photographs are historical curiosities, documenting a bygone era. Yet, looking closely and suspending the one hundred years that have passed since the instant each photograph was taken, we are gazing on a single moment in time. Each person in that photograph was at that exact snap of the shutter moving with determination toward some destination, now long forgotten. Each person had a family, maybe a business or an occupation, which at that moment was foremost in his or her mind. Long gone too are their worries, their ailments, their hopes and fears. What we can be certain of in looking at virtually every one of these photographs is that everyone in these images is now dead. There was nothing any one of these people could have done, no matter how creative they were, how imaginative, gifted, or wealthy, that would have extended his or her life to the present. The same will be said of us one hundred years from now. Yet these people set up the conditions for economic advancement. Are we today doing the same? When we are gone, how will our children be living?

Another perspective that jumps out from these old photographs is how different were the styles of living then. The men in downtown areas

173

of major cities a century ago tended to wear suits, and women wore long dresses, generally with sleeves and high collars, even in summer. Almost everyone wore a hat. Transportation still depended on horses. Some trolley cars can typically be seen. Few of these people had experienced electricity, there was no television or radio, the vast majority were living within fifty miles of where they had been born, unless they were immigrants who had traveled great distances to settle and typically stay right here. Few of these people took vacations to Europe, though many came from Europe. In the streets are few African Americans, generally no Hispanics, and hardly ever a Native American. There may be telephone poles and wires prominent in some of these old downtowns, but few people then considered that a telephone would be a basic requirement of every home, let alone that cell phones would be carried everywhere, capable of connecting from anywhere to anywhere, allowing one to speak with nearly anyone.

Today, even for America's poor, color television is common and the world news carries our minds around the globe so that we can see into these distant worlds in real time. People may subsist on welfare, but few in our major cities ever starve to death because they cannot find food. Far too many lack health insurance or fear the loss of their health insurance, but few will die of diseases that never received medical attention. Almost everyone has attended school, even if they did not graduate. While yet too many among us are illiterate, being unable to read at all is rare. Our standard of life includes the ability to follow major sporting events all year round, even in the poorest homes, as long as there is a television. What we today judge as poverty would a hundred years ago have been considered a lavish lifestyle. Few Americans have ever experienced true poverty or starvation such as can be found today in third-world countries within our own hemisphere. We have advanced as a society in technological sophistication and knowledge. We must now work not only to reduce poverty but to eliminate poverty so that no minorities are excluded, not by race, age, ethnicity, sex, or any other classification that can be used to divide and categorize.

Still, we will not achieve true deliverance from poverty unless we can strengthen families. Strong families were an advantage most of those people in the photographs a hundred years ago had. Strong two-parent families even today remain fundamental to the moral and economic base upon which the future of America depends. These are not issues for white Americans or African Americans alone; the need to preserve strong family structures in which we can raise well-educated children is an issue for all Americans, regardless of race or ethnic heritage. What the Americans in the photographs of a hundred years ago knew, even more so than we do today, is that economic advancement depended upon families. Even if these people a hundred years ago suffered economically, they were determined that their children would advance in the American dream. This, more than anything else, was the foundational strength our ancestors used to advance society to the point we have reached today. To achieve the next levels of advancement, we need to recapture the family strength we have allowed to diminish, especially as we have abandoned our personal responsibility in the false hope that government bureaucracies could solve problems as historically difficult to eliminate as poverty. When the poor today resolve that their children will not be equally poor, we will begin to make real progress in eliminating poverty in America once and for all.

## THE POLITICS OF POVERTY IN AMERICA

ROBERT RECTOR, a senior research fellow in domestic policy studies at the Heritage Foundation, has done groundbreaking research on the politics of poverty in America. His perspective is that the word *poverty* and the designation *poor* carry a connotation that a person is living in dire straits. As Rector analyzes the poor in America, he makes the argument that America's poor are relatively well off, both by American standards and by global standards. Rector does not make this argument to minimize the hardship poverty can bring; his goal is to get the issue of poverty in America in proper perspective.

Let's begin with a key income statistic. Rector points out that the Census Bureau reported that 35.9 million persons "lived in poverty" in 2003.[2] The bureau also reported that in 2003 the top one-fifth of households had 49.8 percent of the total income, and the bottom one-fifth had only 3.4 percent. Read this way, the disparity is startling. The conclusion we are expected to draw is that the poor are desperately disadvantaged. The top 20 percent looked like they had $14.60 in income for every $1.00 held by the bottom 20 percent. Rector points out that these statistics ignore nearly all of the $750 billion in Social Security welfare and other safety-net payments received by low-income and elderly people in the United States. Also, the top 20 percent, measured statistically as a "quintile" segregated by income amounts, has 70 percent more people than are included in the bottom quintile. So, taking these important adjustments into account, "The apparent gap between the top and bottom quintile shrinks dramatically—the ratio of the income of the top quintile to that of the bottom quintile falls from $14.60 to $1.00 down to $4.21 to $1.00."[3] We end up with another example of "how to lie with statistics"[4] in that the initial impression of large numbers of people living in huge income disparity shifts into realizing that the real impact of income disparity in America is mitigated by public payments and the relatively large proportion of Americans who are ranked at the top.

Poverty also suggests that people are living without reasonable food, shelter, or clothing. We think of "abject poverty" as a deplorable condition where people may scramble even to find medical care should they be hit with a life-threatening disease or a medical emergency. Yet, looked at objectively, many of the poor in America today live in material conditions that would have been seen as comfortable one or two generations ago. Some of the advantages enjoyed commonly by those classed today as poor were not available to anyone only a few years ago, outside the pages of science fiction. Consider, the following list assembled by Rector as evidence for this conclusion:

- Forty-six percent of all poor households own their own homes. The average home owned by "poor" persons as classified by the Census Bureau is a three-bedroom house with one and one-half bathrooms, a garage, and a porch or a patio.
- Seventy-six percent of the poor have air-conditioning. Only thirty years ago only about one-third of all Americans enjoyed air-conditioning. Thirty years ago, many offices were still constructed with windows that opened, because the office buildings were then still being built without central air-conditioning.

- Only 6 percent of poor households live in overcrowded conditions. More than two-thirds of the poor live in homes with more than two rooms per person. The average "poor" American has more living space than the average middle-class resident of many European cities, including Athens, London, Paris, and Rome, even though these Europeans are not classified as "poor" or underclass in their own societies.
- Nearly two-thirds of America's poor households own a car; some 30 percent own two or more cars. Virtually every poor household has a color television (more than half own two or more color televisions), though color television was yet a novelty even for wealthy Americans in 1965 when Lyndon B. Johnson was president. John F. Kennedy's assassination was America's first nearly continuous twenty-four-hour news coverage, viewed over four days from November 22–25, 1963, by millions of Americans watching on black-and-white televisions.
- Seventy-eight percent of America's poor households own a VCR or DVD player; 62 percent have cable or satellite television reception. Seventy-three percent of America's poor own microwave ovens; more than half have a stereo system; and one-third have an automatic dishwasher.

In 1954, when *Brown v. Board of Education* was decided by the Supreme Court, few in America could have conceived that some fifty years later America's poor would be this well off. Yet Rector takes pains not to minimize the suffering of the truly poor:

> There is actually a wide range in living conditions among the poor. For example, over a quarter of poor households have cell phones and telephone answering machines, but at the other extreme, approximately one-tenth have no phone at all. While the majority of poor households do not experience material problems, roughly a third do experience at least one problem such as overcrowding, temporary hunger, or difficulty obtaining medical care. However, even in households in which such problems do occur, the hardship is generally not severe by historic or international standards.[5]

Granted, the suffering of the most extremely poor among us is unacceptable. Yet when we compare the standard of living of America's poor with the poor in Africa, Asia, or India, we see a world of difference.

Over the last fifty years we in America have made discrimination by race, religion, age, and sex a crime. Yet this historically great advancement in rights has not been enough to eradicate poverty. Robert Rector is right: poor children should be a great concern to all Americans, and advancement from poverty depends upon our children's ability to advance themselves in a world where higher education and technologically advanced skills are increasingly required.

Most children are poor because they are born into poverty. A person raised in a culture of poverty faces many barriers to advancing out of that condition. Without a solid education and training in some employable skill, a person may find it hard to land a good job or derive a substantial living. Again, as Rector stresses, the absence of a father is a major variable associated with a child's being poor:

> There are two main reasons that American children are poor: Their parents don't work much, and fathers are absent from the home. In good economic times or bad, the typical poor family with children is supported by only 800 hours of work each year: That amounts to 16 hours of work per week. If work in each family were raised to 2,000 hours per year—the equivalent of one adult working 40 hours per week throughout the year—nearly 75 percent of poor children would be lifted out of official poverty.[6]

Rector concludes his analysis by noting that each year an additional 1.3 million children are born out of wedlock. He notes, "If poor mothers married the fathers of their children, almost three-quarters would immediately be lifted out of poverty."[7]

Following the precepts of liberal thinking, we have created a large, expensive federal bureaucracy that has not solved the problem of poverty in four decades of trying to do so. Instead, it has allowed the truly poor to exist in a culture of unacceptable subsistence. Moreover, we have also created a moral culture of "abortion on demand" that has encouraged sexual license. We are experiencing a high rate of teenage pregnancy that is directly counter to the values and behaviors needed to build strong traditional families. While the political Left wants us to embrace family structure innovations, including same-sex marriage, no society has any lengthy experience of the consequences. After thousands of years of experience, even traditional marriages are difficult to maintain. A lasting marriage takes discipline and dedication, yet no other social structure has proven nearly as reliable for raising children so they can get the education they need to lead successful and productive lives. As basic as this point is, today we need to articulate once again the value of the family.

Never before in history has the family been under attack as directly and as viciously as it is today. From the openly avowed godlessness intrinsic to communism to the modern-day secularism of the abortion-on-demand advocates, we have pursued sex at the expense of the family. Communism tried to break up families and establish communes, but even communism failed where unchecked modern liberalism has succeeded. These lessons are so fundamental to human experience over thousands of years of recorded history that they should be self-evident, except for the unrelenting attack on the family launched by the radical political Left since the beginning of the last century. The wealth we have built as a nation will not be carried forward to our children if we do not take care to make sure we remain together as parents to raise our children in strong family structures.

Still, today, even the moderate political Left wants to portray the plight of the poor in America as nearly beyond hope, that is, unless the government intervenes and provides welfare. Poverty in America has become a battle of political elites, perhaps more than anything else. Of course, the victims of this battle of political elites are not the elites themselves, but the poor. If we were all concerned about truly eradicating or minimizing poverty, then programs that failed to work would be abandoned. Yet over the last four decades of the War on Poverty, the Democratic Party in America has made the poor a core constituency. Countless Democratic Party electoral candidates depend upon winning overwhelming majorities of voters in minority communities. In many states the large concentration of minorities in urban centers is enough to swing close elections Democratic simply because of the disproportionate impact of urban voters. In a state like Ohio, the minorities in Cuyahoga County alone can determine a close statewide election.

Minorities in poverty need to ask if remaining true to the Democratic Party is still the best policy. Yes, Democratic Party candidates for office depend upon the votes of minorities when they are running for office. But what actual results do the Democratic Party candidates produce for minorities once they have been elected? Maintaining welfare benefits at or above current levels is a formula for producing continued welfare dependency, not a formula for emerging from poverty and advancing into the first ranks of American life—the place where minorities truly belong. The modern welfare state was founded on a premise that the private enterprise system was part of the problem because corporations shut out minorities from equal opportunity. The state was called upon to fix the problem. While we agree that state action through the legislatures and the courts was needed to create a framework of equality for America's minorities, we believe the concrete results we are all seeking will only be achieved when the private enterprise system is fully engaged, not shut out.

As many as 90 percent of blacks regularly vote for Democratic candidates; many blacks overwhelmingly reject a Republican Party that they perceive as being racist.[8] Political Consultant Eloise Anderson argues that Republicans today must embrace the principles of the Declaration of Independence, as did Abraham Lincoln in his Gettysburg Address:

> The change I call for will not be an easy one for conservatives or for blacks. There is no easy ideological triumph for Republicans suggested here. Republicans, in order to fulfill the promise of their origins and have any hope of persuading blacks to join their party, must return to a proper understanding of the purposes of government as outlined in the Declaration of Independence. In addition, Republicans have to understand and admit the ways in which their party—in abandoning that original understanding—has failed blacks. Republicans are right to eschew guilty self-flagellation, but they would do well to embrace a more careful and sensitive rhetoric that re-examines their case for limited government and the recogni-

tion of individual excellence as called for in the Declaration. Blacks need to be reassured that Republicans view them as equals before the law. Above all, blacks need to be reassured that, as fellow citizens, they are held in equal esteem with all Americans. This last, of course, cannot be done with words alone. How we translate words into deeds requires first a look at past misdeeds. What I seek here is not mere co-existence between Republicans and blacks that generates enough black support to outdo the other side. What I hope to inspire is the basis for a kind of civic friendship and the ties of trust a political party should offer to all of its members.

In this spirit, the Blackwell Initiative is put forth here with the firm conviction that African Americans will advance to the first ranks of our society, our economy, and our politics once we break the dependency mentality that the welfare society has perpetuated. Strong black families have and will emerge from ownership opportunities in homes and in the workplace. We must share more than opportunities equally; we must strive to share successes equally.

Here Anderson provides another essential analysis of why the welfare society has failed. Deep in the logic of the welfare state is a presumption against minorities: liberals discount the ability of minorities to succeed unless the state tips the scale in their direction.

Republicans would also be smart to emphasize their strong belief in black intellectual capacity. It is no secret among blacks that liberal faith in affirmative action often comes from a deep-seated belief in black inferiority. In the eyes of many liberals, blacks need affirmative action to make it in society because their inferiority (whether natural or the result of oppression) means equal opportunity will never be enough. By the same token, there are some conservatives (not the vast majority, but enough to leave a bad impression) who believe blacks to be intellectually inferior and use that argument to justify their lack of attention to questions of civil rights. Both views are odious. Republicans need to disassociate themselves from them in forceful ways. George W. Bush started on this path when he campaigned in 2000 speaking of the "soft bigotry of low expectations."

That was a good turn of phrase but not much has been done to expand upon it.

The belief in minority achievement is at the heart of the Blackwell
Initiative. To the extent American private enterprise incorporates minority talent, private enterprise will be enriched for the experience. We
say this not to support a mindless or politically correct adherence to a
fuzzy notion of "multiculturalism," but because we believe the talent
pool and life experiences of minorities in America provide a rich resource that can drive private enterprise to new heights. In human en-
deavors, talent is always the scarcest resource. The underutilized talent
pool of America's minorities is a resource private enterprise must include if we are to reach new heights in the decades ahead.

## THE FAILURE OF PUBLIC HOUSING

PUBLIC HOUSING is another well-intentioned idea that does not work. In
2003, Howard Husock, the director of public policy case studies at Harvard University's Kennedy School of Government, wrote an important
book entitled *America's Trillion-Dollar Housing Mistake,* analyzing the
failure of public-housing projects. Husock charged, "Our low-income
housing policy is a mistake—over the decades, a trillion-dollar mistake—that, like so many other misguided antipoverty programs, has
harmed those it set out to help and has caused serious, and continuing,
collateral damage in our cities."[9]

By concentrating the urban poor in high-rise public-housing projects, the problem of African American inner-city ghetto poverty wors-
ened. Physically separated from jobs and schools, public-housing
projects became isolated communities composed mostly of single-
parent households in poorly maintained and dilapidated buildings that
were dominated by youth violence, gangs, and drugs. Moreover, by
dedicating large sections of urban land to public-housing projects, potentially valuable land was taken off the market while the projects
themselves tended to depress the value of the surrounding real estate.
As a result, poor communities became even poorer when public housing was constructed.

Husock studied the many different forms public housing took over more than six decades. He concluded that all variations had failed, ranging from high-rise apartment buildings dedicated to the poor to having nonprofit community groups running smaller, mixed-income apartment buildings for the poor. Providing the poor with better housing than they can afford only postponed the problem. Apartments built to higher standards ended up having fancier kitchens, more bathrooms, and larger living areas, all of which required additional maintenance that, not surprisingly, soon exceeded the ability of the residents to provide. Nor were vouchers successful. Vouchers that poor people could take to a landlord of their choice allowed the desperately poor to move among the working poor. Those working their way out of poverty felt, in turn, oppressed when a voucher allowed, for instance, a single mother who, for whatever reasons, failed to supervise her children to become their neighbor. This dysfunctional family could easily become a negative influence on the positive values they were trying to teach their children.

Still, liberal reformers refused to conclude that the concept of public housing did not work. Analyzing Clinton administration efforts to find some creative idea that might finally succeed in making public housing successful, Husock wrote:

> The response of reformers to drug- and gunfire-riddled projects has been not to reexamine the premise but to tinker with the model. Having long dwelt on design, they now devote equal attention to the social "environment." Thus Secretary [of Housing and Urban Development Henry] Cisneros dreamed of new, low-rise, mixed-income subsidized housing that would correct the mistake of concentrating the poor in apartment towers now said to have encouraged crime. So, too, the nonprofit, "community-based" management of renovated apartment buildings is touted as a nurturing environment in which the poorest are inspired by gainfully employed "role-model" neighbors to improve their habits and their lot.[10]

Yet mixing in the "bad apples" with the "good apples" ended up predictably being a formula destined to ruin the barrel for all the apples. Or, as Husock explains, mixing in the lawless—including juvenile delinquents, gang members, and drug dealers—with the lawful is based on the myth that the lawless are victims. The end result is that the lawful become victimized by seeing their neighborhood become unsafe and disorganized as the nonworking poor are placed among them.

Finally, Husock concluded about public housing what we have concluded about government welfare programs overall: "Maybe the whole idea is wrong." In other words, maybe our housing programs have not failed "because of some minor management problem but because they are flawed at the core."[11]

Husock's solution also fits comfortably at the heart of the Blackwell Initiative. He argued that the flaw was trying to solve the problem of housing the poor with a government program when the solution all along was to get private enterprise involved. Low-cost, unsubsidized housing can profitably be built for the poor, with the builder still making a profit. The market will provide adequate housing within the means of the poor, provided governments get out of the way and allow private enterprise to do the job. Husock argued back to a previous era in America where his principle had been proven to work.

> From the end of the Civil War until the New Deal and the National Housing Act of 1937, which gave public housing its first push, the private market generated a cornucopia of housing forms to accommodate those of modest means as they gradually improved their condition. In those years Chicago saw the construction of 211,000 low-cost two-family homes—or 21 percent of its residences. In Brooklyn 120,000 two-family structures with ground-floor stores sprang up. In Boston some 40 percent of the population of 770,000 lived in the 65,376 units of the city's three-decker frame houses, vilified by housing reformers.[12]

The idea is to allow the private market to build at a profit brand-new housing that is within the reach of those with minimal incomes or those living on public assistance.[13] We would encourage builders willing to explore such profit opportunities to apply for *Rebuild Ohio Now* loans.

Again, our goal with housing is to retain the profit motive. Lenders will plan to make profitable loans to home builders who plan to earn a profit by constructing low-income housing units in target neighbor-hoods. Potential homeowners applying for *Rebuild Ohio Now* mortgages will have to receive credit approval based on their ability to repay the mortgages and maintain the properties. The goal is to stimulate private-property homeownership on an economically sound basis so that all par-ties can gain economically and neighborhoods can be fashioned in target areas where properties have an opportunity to appreciate in value. This is a strong departure from the welfare model where public-housing proj-ects "radiate dysfunction and social problems outward, damaging local businesses and neighborhood values."[14] The goal of the Blackwell Initia-tive is "to bring inner-city neighborhoods into the mainstream economy" by financing private builders to solve the public-housing crisis.[15] Over time, we would like to see public housing phased out, just as we would like to see governmental welfare programs phased out.

## A POSITIVE PERSPECTIVE ON THE "WORKING POOR"

IN RECENT years a series of books has been written profiling the "working poor." As was noted earlier, by "working poor" the authors of these books typically have in mind unskilled workers who receive modest pay or even minimum wage for full-time work. Most of these authors have a liberal agenda in mind, generally arguing that the minimum wage needs to be raised so marginal workers can afford more than marginal lifestyles. The literature is filled with case studies documenting how hard it is to work a job for minimal pay that does not allow for adequate med-ical benefits, child care, or other necessities that make working more than just a paycheck. A single mother with an infant will have problems accepting a job that does not allow her to pay for child care during work-ing hours, especially if there is no family member or friend available to assist. Studies document how "on the edge" these marginal workers live, such that even a minor illness that causes time off from work can put one at risk for paying rent or putting food on the table. Typically, the working poor are seen as victims of a capitalist system that exploits their labor for the lowest pay and fewest benefits a company can get away with providing.

Our goal here is not to argue whether minimum wage should be set higher by law or whether a higher minimum wage ends up employing fewer workers. Our objective is to look at the working poor from a positive perspective. A key to getting private homes built and financed for the poor is the insight that owning a home is a step in the right direction. So, too, we want to argue that economic advancement must be taken in steps. We are unlikely to find a solution that simply lifts the poor from poverty to comfortable middle-class status in a single jump. The government welfare program of the last forty years has demonstrated that simply giving people money does not advance them from poverty; to the contrary, too many welfare recipients come to view that staying on welfare is a viable option for their lives and implicitly for the lives of their children. The result is that welfare families set an artificial income ceiling for themselves that is no greater than the welfare payments they qualify to receive. Our argument is that emerging from welfare requires beginning with some work, even at minimum wage, that puts a person on the path toward economic advancement. Once people are employed in the market economy, their experience on the job should result in further development of their skills such that possibilities of employment advancement open up.

We realize that economic downturns tend to hit hardest the minimally employed. We also realize that those employed at the lower ends of the economy tend to face the most disruption even from the normal business cycles of hiring and firing. Yet once people have organized their lives to be gainfully employed, a major step has been taken. We have stressed that those who succeed in getting out of poverty must engage in a set of behaviors that increase their chances of earning a gainful living. This includes even the fundamental attitudinal adjustments needed to get to work on time, properly prepared for work, with the ability to stay at work as many hours as may be required. Moreover, people must be prepared to repeat these work-oriented behaviors every day with sufficient discipline to earn and hold a job, even if the job offers only minimal pay. As basic as the idea is, those who advance from poverty must go through this discipline. Feeling victimized or believing that discrimination is a barrier are not arguments that will solve the problem. Again, we are focused on identifying behaviors that succeed. The Blackwell Initiative is premised on our conviction that the poor can be productive employees and successful homeowners even if today they are unemployed residents of public housing who are living on welfare.

As welfare moves toward being redefined as truly "temporary assistance" for needy families, we must resolve to appreciate step-wise improvements the poor need to make in their employment situation. Working a minimum-wage job for many of today's poor will either be seen as the classic half-empty or half-full glass. Those who successfully emerge from poverty will need to adapt a bootstraps perspective toward every employment opportunity, even one at a minimum wage, as being an opportunity to advance upward.

Remember, we are not advocating that any welfare programs currently in place be eliminated. We have advanced the Blackwell Initiative because we feel that private enterprise must become actively involved if we are going to eliminate or even substantially reduce poverty in America. Those who fall back from minimum-wage opportunities will still have the welfare assistance options that are in place today. Our thinking, however, is to advance to end the welfare state through productive enterprise, not through government assistance. This thinking, we believe, is in sharp contrast to the perspective that forty years ago believed a government bureaucracy could ever win a war against poverty. Our argument is that the war against poverty will only be won if and when we engage today's poor in the private economy, hopefully placing them on a path where families can be formed so children can be productively educated.

It is instructive to see how true socialists and communists portray the situation of the working poor. The *Socialist Worker* likes to paint a portrait that a huge segment of America is forced to earn below-poverty limits, despite working full time. Consider the following:

> According to a recent report by the Russell Sage and Rockefeller Foundations, some 34 million workers—more than a quarter of the U.S. workforce—earn less than $8.70 an hour. At full time, that works out to an annual income below the government's poverty line for a family of four.
>
> In other words, fully one-quarter of the U.S. workforce doesn't get paid enough, even for full-time work, to keep their families out

of poverty without help—other household members working, a second job or third job and so on.[16]

First, we have to question what is wrong with other household members working? For generations, pooling multiple incomes within a family has been a step in the right direction to emerge from poverty. Nor is there necessarily a problem with a person's working multiple jobs, especially in a functioning family environment where parents and relatives are available to help, possibly even to share living quarters. Moreover, there are abundant social welfare programs, many of which people can still receive even if they are employed. The underlying argument the socialists want to support here is that America is a capitalist society whose design is to benefit the wealthy by exploiting the labor of the lower classes. Socialists also face a political dilemma in that, if the poor really did advance from poverty, the socialists would lose their constituency. Again, our point is that the political Left has become dependent upon the poor. As the poor in America economically advance, socialists lose their audience.

This socialist author's point is that in "Bush's America" the poor are poor even if they work.

Even if the jobs picture begins to turn around, that won't necessarily have much of an impact on the lives of the working poor. According to the Department of Labor, of the 277,000 workers that were added to private payrolls in March, two-thirds were in the low-wage industries—retail trade, restaurants, janitorial services, home health nursing. In other words, many of the new jobs that are being created during this recovery aren't worth getting out of bed for.

Meanwhile, Congress is dragging its feet on new proposals to raise the minimum wage. The minimum wage was raised twice in the 1990s, but once inflation is taken into account, its value is now at the same level as it was before the hike. Since 1968, the real value of the minimum wage has dropped by 40 percent. If it had only kept pace with inflation, the minimum wage today would be $8.46 an hour today, not $5.15.[17]

Somehow, after reading this argument, we wonder if socialists would have us make every job in America guarantee $50,000 or more on an annual basis, with the government making up the difference between that amount and what a profitable business can afford to pay for the work being done. Working Americans are paying a substantial tax burden to provide social welfare benefits today. Income redistribution payments from higher-wage earners to those earning lower wages or no wages transfer tax payments that socialists and others on the political Left rarely take into account when arguing their poverty message. No country in the history of the world has been as generous to the poor as America, especially not since the 1960s. Yet what do we have to show for the effort? Despite the trillions spent on social welfare, the problem, especially of urban minority poverty, is only intensifying in America.

Moreover, the "working poor" argument from a leftist perspective is fundamentally flawed. Improving the economic ability to subsist at a minimum-wage level should not be our goal. We should aim higher. The goal is to get more of the poor to begin working and from there to advance to higher plateaus. Minimum-wage employment should be the end goal only for those in our society incapable of advancing beyond minimal skills or for those truly suffering serious disabilities. Even seniors who aspire to work should aim at employment higher than minimum wage if their skills permit them to qualify for more advanced work. The goal of the Blackwell Initiative is to bring profitable businesses into target poverty areas in order to establish a productive base of employment opportunity within these communities. We then encourage the social services, including welfare agencies, to adapt their available programs, including job-training programs, to support these businesses in their growth.

Our conclusion is that education is indispensable for economic advancement. If parents face skill-development limitations they cannot overcome, their responsibility remains to get their children as much disciplined education as possible. Advancing out of poverty through more government assistance only intensifies dependency thinking. Reversing the downward spiral of poverty can only be accomplished by education, skill development, and advancing within employment opportunities. Consider the following, written by Brian Jones, the president of the

Center for New Black Leadership, a member of the National Advisory Board of Project 21:

> Educational achievement is an essential component of upward mobility in America. The statistics are telling: while in the aggregate blacks tend to earn less than whites, controlling for educational achievement reveals that the disparity is closing rapidly, and that indeed, in some cases it has closed together. For example, the Census Bureau reports that in 1993, black men with college degrees working in managerial jobs earned 86 percent of what similarly situated white men earned. Black women with college degrees in managerial jobs actually earned on average 10 percent more than their white counterparts.[18]

Writing about what he calls "the working poor scam," Thomas Sowell, a Rose and Milton Friedman Senior Fellow, notes that "most people who are working are not poor and most people who are poor are not working."[19] A worker without skills and without education will have to struggle with low-paying jobs, but a worker with no job is headed nowhere, certainly not beyond continued welfare dependency. Moving in the right direction depends upon a determination to become employed and, from there, to improve skills so advancements in employment become a real possibility.

Liberal advocates of more welfare programs highlight only the negatives in government statistics. The *Statistical Abstract of the United States for 2004–2005* lists household income in table 665.[20] Yes, the table does show that in 2002 a larger proportion of white households had incomes of $100,000 or over (15 percent) than black households (6.4 percent), a statistic that can be used to continue the argument that racial inequality still persists in America. Yet the table also shows that in 1990 only 3.8 percent of black households made more than $100,000, reflecting a more than 65 percent improvement in twelve years. Why do we not tout this advancement? Why don't we encourage private enterprise to advance this impressive statistic? Even more important, we need to ask what these higher-income African Americans are doing that leads to their success? We rarely hear about the success stories, only the problems and crises.

Much more needs to be written to tell the stories of accomplishment, explaining in personal terms the life stories of our nation's increasing number of African American business leaders, African American lawyers and physicians, African American artists, musicians, and actors, as well as African American government officials. When our last two secretaries of state are African American—Colin Powell and Condoleezza Rice—the bar is raised for all African American children aspiring to achieve. Moreover, these appointments were made under Republican President George W. Bush, a president who is much maligned by liberal Democratic Party critics for not doing enough to improve the situation of blacks in America. If we focus on developing the African American success stories, we give hope and direction for African American youth who resolve to get ahead. For forty years we have heard the problem discussed and rediscussed. Focusing on failures has led to discouragement and a lessening of expectations, particularly with respect to the chronically poor. Now is the time to focus on the solution.

## STRENGTHENING BLACK FAMILIES

FORTIFYING BLACK families begins with a determination by African Americans that their families are important to them. There is no magic formula that will end teenage pregnancies. We need family structures and moral education that teaches young people in advance about the destructive consequences of teenage pregnancy. Editorial writer Joseph Brown makes the point that black leaders must speak up against self-destructive behavior:

> For example, everyone knows that low-income babies born out of wedlock stand a better than average chance of always living in poverty, and that these mothers virtually condemn themselves and their children to a lifetime of hardship. You don't need [Daniel Patrick] Moynihan's report to know this, just common sense. Yet, the so-called leaders lack the nerve and sense of morality to tackle the issue. Why? Because such talk is unpopular and would take away from the notion that all of this is the fault of the white man.

"We can't let white folks off the hook," they say. But we black Americans are the ones left hanging.[21]

After making life choices with negative economic consequences, each of us has to accept responsibility for the failures that result. Government welfare programs have been left to pay the economic costs of teenage pregnancies that result when government policies and court decisions create an abortion-on-demand culture in a sexually open society. We are going to have to realize as a society that these bold liberal social experiments with sex and reproduction have detrimental economic consequences. Along with our determination to engage private enterprise into the solution of poverty comes our determination to prepare the poor to participate in private enterprise, a conservative agenda we believe merits serious consideration not only for its intrinsic moral value but also for the positive economic consequences we anticipate.

African American conservatives are also speaking out on the family, encouraging fundamental principles of family building to be appreciated within the African American community so they can be internalized individually. Consider these words of Diann Ellen Cameron, a professional social worker in New York City who manages a foster care and preadoption division at a private child welfare agency:

> Not one family within the black community is a private entity; each family unit contributes to our community's well-being for better or for worse. Therefore, every aspect within the black community is needed to protect and preserve the black family as an institution. Churches, civic groups, community merchants, and residents themselves bear a responsibility for maintaining healthy families within the community. Furthermore, members of the black community must ensure that each family unit has the proper elements—parental stability, parent-child cohesiveness, and an environment filled with the proper balance of nurturance and discipline, to increase a family's social opportunity.[22]

She goes on to detail the personal involvement required to rebuild families in an environment where the family has been under attack.

192

Visible, consistent involvement in each other's family affairs reinforces our community and prevents any further family dissolution
within black America. No longer can the members of our community sit idly by and allow our fate and failure to be determined or
prejudged by others. We must be diligent in becoming foster parents, adoptive parents, and benefactors to adolescent youth living
in group homes or other residential communities. There are several
ways we can strengthen our children and create more stable families for our future. Also, we must not ignore the black extended-
family network (grandparents, aunts/uncles, godparents, and
friends), since it is the primary preserver of family history and resources within our community.[23]

These words paint a sharply different position from that conveyed
by high-rise public-housing apartment complexes where unsupervised
youth are left to join gangs and terrorize the women living alone and
the elderly in the community. The legacy of government welfare is a
culture of death both for dreams and for children, a culture of desola-
tion where even the prospect of opportunity ultimately dies. The future
of government welfare is likely to be more of the same in ever-
worsening inner-city ghettos abandoned to all but the minority poor.
Reversing this legacy is the goal of the Blackwell Initiative. We want to
end the dependency society created by forty years of government bureaucracy. Our objective is to stimulate independence by developing
employment opportunities, strengthening families, and educating children in a private-enterprise environment where individuals can advance
to the benefit of themselves and their loved ones.

In their important study of "high-impact" African American
churches, George Barna and Henry Jackson Jr. found that a large majority of blacks (85 percent) believe that their religious faith is very important in their lives. High-impact churches are those where the religious
leaders at the head of the congregation embrace theological principles to
shape Christian education for children and to guide parishioners in living moral lives. Generations ago, these principles would have been
commonplace to most Americans. Today, in our "postmodern" age, we
have reached a point of secular cynicism where belief in God and serious

devotion to religion applied in life are viewed as old-fashioned if not downright silly. Yet Barna and Jackson argue that effective African American churches can play a major role in transforming poverty communities into productive communities.

> Postmodern America is ripe for dramatic spiritual transformation but no serious change will occur unless courageous leaders redefine reality, developing the means to change and give people irresistible reasons for participating in the reengineering of their lives. The experience of effective black churches indicates that churches need not throw up their hands in despair and cave in to the prevailing culture. Instead, we must simply reach out to people in a slightly different manner and guide them along a different path of development.[24]

Barna and Jackson's message is an evangelical Christian message. They lend their voices to the increasing number of conservatives calling for strengthening the African American family as the path forward for helping not only African Americans, but all Americans.

> Is there hope for the black family? Absolutely! At the core of that hope are strategically-minded black churches that marshal their resources to impact black children under 12 years of age. Just as the black church has always adapted itself to meet the unique needs of its people, the church must now continue to equip the fragmented black family to minister to itself. Many of the problems that confront black families today—illegitimate births, cohabitation, divorce, child neglect and abuse, the absence of role models—can be overcome by ministry efforts that target the youngest of children with the strongest of medicines: carefully planned, well-conceived, consistently executed and continually monitored spiritual development provided by parents in partnership with their church.[25]

Again, the problems we see today in the minority communities are destined to become problems in the majority communities unless we return to these fundamental principles. If teenage pregnancies and single-parent households become the norm in America, we will have lost the family, the fundamental social unit upon which our nation has been built, both morally and economically.

The conservative reaction is gaining strength in black America in large part due to the bankrupt policies of the political Left. Conservative African Americans are speaking out today in larger numbers than ever before, finding a like-minded agreement with majority conservatives. America has moved beyond racism. The apartheid-like system of legally enforced racial segregation of the 1930s and the 1940s is gone. Today white Americans and African Americans have direct personal experience with one another and a base of agreement that opportunities must be open to all. Conservative African Americans are fighting back with concrete proposals to make Republican president Abraham Lincoln's dream that "all men are created equal" a reality in terms of education and incomes, not just in terms of opportunity.

The liberal formulas of government welfare dependence that have become conventional political wisdom since the Great Depression are being questioned today unlike ever before. Since Franklin D. Roosevelt was elected to his fourth term as president, we have been locked into an increasing dependence upon government to solve our social and economic problems. We must here and now reject the "declaration of dependency" that is inherent to government welfare programs. No government bureaucracy will ever create a truly "great society." Rejecting four decades of a failed government welfare bureaucracy will take honesty and courage, but we fully believe private enterprise can be engaged to pursue the goal of eliminating poverty. The next $10 trillion we spend should involve capital raised through the Blackwell Initiative, in programs where government provides a funding mechanism, which does not increase taxes, while private enterprise does the heavy lifting of providing jobs and incomes.

Fundamentally, we are all human beings who respond and grow best in families. From jobs and incomes, homes and families will follow. We all prosper best in productive jobs. We are all most fulfilled when we can spend our time developing our skills and advancing our wealth. Fifty years ago government involvement was needed to establish the de jure basis of equality. Today, private enterprise will be needed to solve the de facto inequality America still strives to achieve. One hundred years from now, our descendants need to look back and say that we, too, put in place the conditions necessary and sufficient for America's society and economy to advance. Continuing welfare dependency will not accomplish that goal.

# 8

---

# Revitalizing the
# Urban Landscape

East Cleveland is a city of single mothers and missing fathers.

—James F. Sweeney, *Cleveland Plain Dealer*,
February 20, 2005[1]

HOW CAN THE BLACKWELL INITIATIVE succeed in revitalizing our inner-city neighborhoods? As we have noted, inner-city poverty neighborhoods, all too often, have become segregated, African American ghettos. The trend since the end of World War II has been for businesses and more-affluent residents to move to the suburbs and beyond, establishing sprawling metropolitan areas that are connected by inner-belt limited-access highways. That this trend will continue in an era where gasoline has already spiked at three dollars a gallon remains to be seen. Core portions of downtown areas across America have been abandoned by corporate headquarters and turned over to poverty-plagued minorities. Yet this model does not have to continue, nor is the deterioration of our inner cities an inevitable or irreversible phenomenon. We have already witnessed how new sports facilities can bring renewed interest to downtown areas in a range of cities, including Baltimore, Chicago, Philadelphia, and even Cleveland and Detroit. We believe revitalizing the urban landscape is within our reach if only we can apply imagination and sound business principles to the project.

Our goal is to bring business activity back to our nation's downtowns and to create excellent neighborhoods in which to live and raise

197

families. Much of the rail rapid-transit structure is already in place to accomplish the goal in cities such as Boston, Chicago, Cleveland, and Washington DC, to name a prominent few. When commuter times to and from the outlying business areas require forty-five minutes one way, inner-city opportunities need to be reexamined. In many inner cities, universities and hospitals remain as centers around which development can be stimulated. Now we must find a way to attract inner-city businesses to be established and to grow.

Again, we think back to a time before the War on Poverty. At the end of World War II, many inner cities were centers of small manufacturing operations. Today, sixty years later, small manufacturing has again become a profitable and attractive area for business growth on a state and municipal level. Urban-renewal projects cleared many inner-city areas as they concentrated poverty into projects. Housing projects proved to be social and economic disasters, encouraging poverty rather than eliminating it. Many of these projects have now been taken down. Vacant and condemned properties, plus cleared land, offer many sites where businesses can be reestablished as the cornerstones around which urban neighborhoods can grow.

Here we must ask ourselves, How did we encourage our inner cities to become African American ghettos? In understanding that process, we may discover the very principles necessary to reverse the trend. Inner-city ghettos are a direct result of the dysfunctions caused by the welfare state and the government bureaucracy engendered by the welfare state. We believe there is nothing intrinsic about our inner cities that condemns them to second-class economic participation. Nor is there anything intrinsic to African Americans living in poverty today that condemns them to live in poverty tomorrow. African Americans living in poverty are an effect of the dysfunction caused by the welfare state. We strongly believe that any people—regardless of race, ethnicity, or age—that end up living dependently on the welfare state will end up in the grip of poverty's downward spiral. Government welfare programs have failed. Now is the time to get our inner cities and the inner-city minorities back to work, gainfully employed, living productive lives, and raising children in strong families positioned for the future.

## THE MAKING OF AN URBAN GHETTO:
## EAST CLEVELAND, A CASE STUDY

EAST CLEVELAND is a classic case of concentrated African American poverty in an inner-city neighborhood. Now, approximately 94 percent African American, East Cleveland was in a formally declared state of fiscal emergency from September 1988 until just recently, in 2006, a period lasting some eighteen years. The dynamics of change that began after the end of World War II in East Cleveland are being replicated in major metropolitan areas around the country. A study of what happened to East Cleveland is a study of inner-city neighborhoods in many of America's northern cities, from Boston to Chicago to Detroit, and reaching as well to Philadelphia, St. Louis, and even Washington DC. What does East Cleveland teach us about poverty in America?

In the 1920s East Cleveland developed as one of Cleveland's first suburbs, an area adjoining the city with easy access to the downtown area along Euclid Avenue, the major commercial artery for both downtown Cleveland and East Cleveland alike. The early homes built in East Cleveland were commonly two-family frame houses on relatively modest lots, priced in the 1920s to sell in the range of $8,000 to $20,000. Most residents who bought homes in East Cleveland during the 1920s were first-generation immigrants, largely European, including Irish, Italian, Polish, and German. Many spoke only basic English, but they brought with them their education, their skills, and their determination to raise their children as full-fledged Americans who would speak English as their first language. Until the Great Depression, East Cleveland was a thriving middle-class community that was nearly 100 percent populated by majority whites. Only the Depression-era social programs enacted by the Roosevelt administration permitted many East Clevelanders to save their homes when work opportunities became scarce in the 1930s. In the 1940s, after World War II, returning soldiers, many of them second-generation immigrants who had grown up in Cleveland's ethnic neighborhoods, settled in East Cleveland, ready to raise families of their own.

In the 1920s East Cleveland was enough of an elite suburb to attract the likes of oil magnate John D. Rockefeller, who built an estate home in sumptuous Forest Hill Park along Euclid Avenue. Rockefeller's home had a commanding view at the top of a large hill that gently sloped down toward the estate's Euclid Avenue entrance. To make Rockefeller's commute easier, a railroad station was built just off Euclid Avenue, near his residence. By the 1950s only the Rockefeller horse stables were left in Forest Hill, and the estate had become East Cleveland's largest public park. In the 1960s the Rapid Transit Association (RTA) extended light rail service from the downtown hub at the Terminal Tower to Windemere, the station that was then the RTA's easternmost rail terminal. From Windemere, buses formed a feeder system that spread throughout East Cleveland. Driving north on Shaw, motorists easily connected with the limited-access highway then known as the Shoreway, a main artery that provided an easy commute by car from East Cleveland to downtown Cleveland.

Through the mid-1960s, East Cleveland could be described as a middle-class ethnic community of immigrants with a growing African American population, a suburb where mortgages and rents were modest and $10,000–$15,000 a year was a good income. The homes were close together, but each home tended to have a two-car garage, and the streets were clean and lined with trees. Children growing up along Shaw and Hayden played sandlot baseball at Chambers Field each summer and swam in the public pool. The town was not as wealthy as neighboring Cleveland Heights and Shaker Heights, but public services were more than adequate, the neighborhoods were safe, and unemployment and crime were not major problems. East Cleveland from the 1940s through the late 1950s had few African American families. The early 1960s, however, brought an influx of African American families that grew larger by the mid-1960s.

By the mid-1960s, East Cleveland began changing from solidly middle class to lower middle class, still solidly white. Still, many of the city's more affluent white residents were beginning a "white flight" immigration into Cleveland's rapidly developing outlying suburbs, such as Rocky River on the west side and Euclid or Willoughby on the east side. As the 1960s ended, the racial pattern of Cleveland became firmly set, such that the east side was considered African American and the west side was predominately white.

The early African American families that entered East Cleveland in the 1960s tended to earn more money than their white counterparts. The civil rights movement of the 1960s had opened more doors to African American employees who were working for companies such as Ohio Bell, the Ford and GM plants, Republic Steel, University Hospitals, and the Cleveland Clinic. The election of Carl Stokes as mayor of Cleveland brought record numbers of African Americans into decent-paying city, county, and state jobs, as African Americans began to harness their political clout in a voting bloc. As the 1960s progressed, African Americans in increasing numbers were entering professions such as architecture, education, and law. East Cleveland became home to many middle- and upper-income African Americans who saw it as a thriving community in which to raise their families. White-collar African American professionals bought the homes that were once part of Millionaire's Row in East Cleveland, purchases that included many beautiful homes in the Forest Hill section of East Cleveland.

The downward slide in the economic profile of East Cleveland's residents accelerated after the Hough riots in the summer of 1966. African Americans were displaced from Hough because of the riots' fire damage and the continuing danger of racial violence, and they began moving from Cleveland into Glenville and East Cleveland. By the end of the 1960s, Cleveland's downtown was in economic decline, but East Cleveland was still an economically stable community. Even as the 1960s ended, East Cleveland's main economic contributors were still intact; businesses that ranged from Hough Bakery's plant at Euclid and Lakeview Road, several major car dealerships, and General Electric were all still major East Cleveland–based employers. Graduation rates at East Cleveland's high schools were still in the 90 percent and higher range.

Nevertheless, decline set in, and in the 1970s East Cleveland began losing the well-paying blue-collar jobs that kept most of the city's families, both African American and white, economically viable. By the early 1980s, GE began shipping jobs out of the city, Hough Bakery closed, the auto dealerships closed, even Bob's Big Boy restaurant chain closed its East Cleveland national headquarters. Then, as the city elected African American officials, many were convicted of crimes. African American voters in East Cleveland began to realize the need to scrutinize the capabilities of the individuals being elected to public office, learning the hard way the skills and honesty required to run what amounted to a multimillion-dollar municipal entity.

East Cleveland changed from a commission–city manager form of government to a mayor–city council structure because of the frustration with the commission's inability to allow professional city managers to govern the city. Since the 1970s, now, for more than thirty years, East Cleveland has been governed by African Americans, and every elected official with the exception of two have been Democrats, including those elected to serve East Cleveland in the U.S. Congress and the Ohio House of Representatives and Senate. As Eric Brewer, the current mayor of East Cleveland notes: "African Americans cannot blame whites or the Republicans for their city and school district's fiscal emergencies, jailed elected officials, reduced quality of life, or vacant and abandoned housing."

Today, East Cleveland, a city that some twenty-seven thousand residents still call home, is punctuated with vacant lots. More than two thousand boarded-up homes, many ravaged by fire damage, further mar the grim urban landscape. Vandalism is rampant throughout East Cleveland; condemned housing is left standing, not worth the effort or expense to be torn down. The city's homeless live in abandoned properties, often without electricity, heat, or water. Many apartment buildings that were once fully occupied are now vacant shells.

East Cleveland is a classic inner-city tragedy, demonstrating the welfare state's inability to reverse or solve the problem of inner-city poverty. As we will argue here, East Cleveland can be turned around, but it will require the resolve of honest government officials and the determination of private banks to apply the capital needed to create new jobs and to restore homeownership. A key argument of this book is that we have within our means the ability to get this job done, even in inner-city neighborhoods dominated by poverty, like East Cleveland.

## WHAT HAPPENED TO EAST CLEVELAND?

IN 1994 W. Dennis Keating, professor of law and urban planning as well as associate dean of urban affairs at Cleveland State University, published a book entitled *The Suburban Racial Dilemma: Housing and*

*Neighborhoods* that examined Cleveland's neighborhoods, including a chapter dedicated to East Cleveland.[2] Keating adds an important academic analysis that places the story of East Cleveland in a larger context. Keating's study allows us to see East Cleveland as a case study, identifying inner-city dynamics that are being played as variations on a theme throughout America.

Keating begins by observing, as we noted above, that East Cleveland was one of Cleveland's first and most prestigious suburbs. In 1950 the nonwhite population of Cleveland was less than 1 percent, and it was still only 2 percent in 1960. In the decade 1960–1970, however, East Cleveland went through a "rapid period of racial transition fueled by real estate blockbusting." By 1970, East Cleveland's black population was 67 percent; by 1990, East Cleveland had segregated into a predominately black community with a 94 percent nonwhite population.

The black migration that began out of Cleveland into East Cleveland was barely noticeable in 1960, but by 1970 East Cleveland was rapidly "resegregating," becoming as predominately black as the Cleveland inner-city communities blacks abandoned in the 1960s. By 1994, Keating judged that East Cleveland had "a much poorer population, and its reputation had suffered from political and fiscal scandals."[3] As he explained:

> East Cleveland is a textbook example of the type of "invasion and succession" scenario, described in the study of human ecology, in which racial transition can result in racial resegregation. The suburb's failure to sustain racial diversity stands in contrast to the successful efforts, beginning in the 1960s, of the city of Shaker Heights to prevent black suburbanization from turning into resegregation. East Cleveland's rapid resegregation served as a warning to adjacent Cleveland Heights and to fair housing activists who promoted racial diversity in other Cleveland suburbs.[4]

Clearly, Keating did not believe that East Cleveland's becoming an inner-city black community was inevitable; still, preventing the white flight would have taken active city management to make sure real estate practices remained responsible, not exploitative.

Keating tracks how the migration into East Cleveland began from Glenville, a Cleveland district that borders East Cleveland. Historically, Glenville had been a Jewish community among Cleveland's many ethnically and racially distinct neighborhoods. In the 1950s the Jewish community of Glenville began to migrate to the suburbs, particularly Cleveland Heights and Shaker Heights. In the 1960s Glenville had resegregated into a predominately black community, a precursor of the change that would occur to East Cleveland in the next decade. East Cleveland represented a "pull" to the more-affluent African Americans who could afford to move from Glenville to superior housing opportunities in East Cleveland. At the same time, there was a "push" into East Cleveland as a massive urban-renewal-and-slum-clearance program in Cleveland greatly increased the concentration of the black population in Cleveland communities such as Hough and Glenville. Again, Keating stressed that the transition of East Cleveland's communities was fueled by real estate brokers whose "unscrupulous practices enabled them to reap windfall gains" at a time when steering black buyers to black communities was not illegal or condemned by the real estate industry. As a result, a "filtering" process accelerated, in which "less-expensive housing is occupied successively by lower-income residents."[5]

White flight from East Cleveland was not an immediate process. As Keating noted, the white flight occurred in stages, always with the tantalizing possibility that the community could have become racially integrated:

> The resegregation of East Cleveland occurred in three stages. During the first stage, in the early 1960s, those whites who were uncomfortable with the increasing black presence and who were able to move left the area. During the second stage, in the mid-1960s, those whites who were fearful of economic loss from depreciation of property values fled, spurred by blockbusting and steering practices of some real estate brokers. During the last stage, continuing into the 1970s, those whites who were supportive of racial integration grew discouraged and many left, leaving behind a shrinking white population, except for the largely white Forest Hill enclave.[6]

In 1966 racial tensions in Cleveland escalated with the Hough riots that occurred from July 18–24, resulting in arson and large-scale burning that scarred the community's retail and residential areas. In November 1967, Carl Stokes was elected mayor of Cleveland, becoming the first African American to be elected mayor of a major U.S. city.

Racial violence continued to mark the transformation of East Cleveland, notably with the Glenville riots that occurred the next year, in July 1968. As Keating observed:

> Yet another blow to any hope of maintaining racial integration in East Cleveland was the riot in the city of Cleveland in July 1968. On July 23, armed black nationalists and Cleveland police clashed, and a gun battle ensued. Violence in the Glenville neighborhood continued over the next five days, with sniping and firebombing. Initially, Cleveland's new mayor, Carl Stokes, ordered that only black police officers and civic leaders patrol and enter Glenville. This caused controversy and a backlash by many white police officers and citizens. After trying this strategy, Stokes changed his policy and mostly white National Guard entered Glenville to restore order.
>
> This racially based battle at the doorstep of East Cleveland undoubtedly had an impact on the suburb's remaining white residents, as police and National Guard were sent to guard the border between East Cleveland and Glenville.[7]

By 1986 fully 86 percent of the population of East Cleveland was black, a concentration of a black population "second only to that of impoverished East St. Louis."[8] The black population resegregating into East Cleveland was decidedly less-well-off economically. As a result, the tax base of East Cleveland deteriorated, increasing the city's problems. In Keating's analysis, the fate of East Cleveland serves as "a dire warning of the debilitating effects of allowing black suburbanization to result in the creation of what amounts to a suburban black ghetto next to an urban black ghetto."[9] With the 2000 census, the population of Cleveland declined to fewer than five hundred thousand. Proposals began circulating that Cleveland should annex East Cleveland, with the objective being to add the twenty-seven thousand East Cleveland residents to push Cleveland over the half-million population mark. The thought was that Cleveland was losing political clout as its population dwindled. With a population under a half million, Cleveland was at risk of no longer being ranked among the nation's first rank of cities. Ultimately, the suggestion was rejected, largely because the annexation of East Cleveland would have constituted more of a fiscal drag than an asset to Cleveland.[10]

## THE BLACK UNDERCLASS AND THE URBAN GHETTO

SOCIOLOGISTS Douglas Massey and Nancy Denton published in 1993 a study entitled *American Apartheid: Segregation and the Making of the Underclass*.[11] In this work they applied to the nation as a whole dynamics similar to what we have observed with East Cleveland.

Studying "hypersegregation," Massey and Denton identified the phenomenon of intense racial segregation where poor African Americans end up being concentrated in relatively small urban ghettos. Looking at data from 1980, Massey and Denton concluded that blacks in sixteen U.S. metropolitan areas, including six of the ten largest metropolitan areas in the United States, house 35 percent of the nation's black citizens.[12]

> Thus one-third of all African Americans in the United States live under conditions of intense racial segregation. They are unambiguously among the nation's most spatially isolated and geographically secluded people, suffering extreme segregation across multiple dimensions simultaneously. Black Americans in these metropolitan areas live within large, contiguous settlements of densely inhabited neighborhoods that are packed tightly around the urban core. In plain terms, they live in ghettos.[13]

Massey and Denton examined the process by which hypersegregated urban ghettos concentrate poverty and produce an underclass:

> By building physical decay, crime, and social disorder into the residential structure of black communities, segregation creates a harsh

206

and extremely disadvantaged environment to which ghetto blacks must adapt. In concentrating poverty, moreover, segregation also concentrates conditions such as drug use, joblessness, welfare dependency, teenage childbearing, unwed parenthood, producing a social context where these conditions are not only common but the norm.[14]

In adapting to the social environment of the urban ghetto, Massey and Denton found that "ghetto dwellers evolve a set of behaviors, attitudes, and expectations that are sharply at variance with those common in the rest of American society."[15] Young people in the ghetto were found to experience peer pressure not to succeed in school, with the result that dropout rates increase, dramatically reducing the potential for economic advancement and upward social mobility. Without completing educations and lacking advanced or technological skills, young school dropouts doom themselves to a life of marginal employment and low incomes. The prospect of a difficult economic future in turn increases the likelihood of teenage childbearing and unwed pregnancy, which results in children being raised without fathers, themselves facing a future of educational difficulties and equally grim employment and income prospects.

The downward spiral of poverty entrapment in the African American urban ghetto can be seen in many different aspects. Low incomes mean that individuals living at or near poverty levels can afford only low rents; low rents afford no revenue for maintaining or improving properties. Eventually properties become abandoned, with the result that neighborhood property values decline, resulting in little or no reason for anyone to invest to buy, maintain, or improve the properties. At some point, the deterioration in property values reaches a threshold where the pattern becomes "self-reinforcing and irreversible."[16] The story is familiar from there: the tax base of the community erodes and, as a result, social services in the ghetto also deteriorate. Schools become marginal, so that discipline and safety compete with educational needs for the few available dollars and human resources available.

The concentration of poverty, moreover, sets off a series of ancillary changes in the social and economic composition of neighborhoods.

By concentrating poverty, segregation also concentrates other conditions that are associated with it. Deleterious conditions such as falling retail demand, increasing residential abandonment, rising crime, spreading disorder, increasing welfare dependency, growing family disruption, and rising education failure are all concentrated simultaneously by raising the rate of poverty under a regime of high segregation. They can be produced at any time by a simple rise in black poverty under conditions prevailing in most large U.S. cities, and certainly in the sixteen hypersegregated metropolitan areas we have identified.[17]

A ghetto filled with negative role models ends up creating an environment where "male joblessness, female welfare dependency, crime, drug abuse, teenage childbearing, and single parenthood are common or even normative."[18] Ghetto residents suffer with low self-esteem as a result. Escaping from this environment becomes difficult, if not impossible. "As new generations are born into conditions of increasing deprivation and deepening racial isolation," a culture of ghetto underclass segregation takes over and becomes a trap from which minority individuals rarely emerge, thus the urban underclass risks becoming self-perpetuating as a permanent fixture of our urban environment.[19]

We have to remember that the urban ghetto underclass Massey and Denton document persists after four decades of the War on Poverty and the expenditure of some $10 trillion on government welfare programs. We would argue that the creation of the urban underclass is a direct result of the welfare culture we have built over these years, a culture of blame and guilt that induces anger without generating solutions. We remind readers that African American entrapment in urban poverty ghettos is not an inherent characteristic resulting from race. Any people, regardless of race or ethnic background, placed in a similar situation of joblessness and low incomes from which they are unable to escape can be expected to face the same entrapment of a downward economic and social spiral. We made a serious error as a society to believe that, because we were dealing with a problem of poverty, we could solve the problem with government welfare money. What has always been needed is jobs. With employment and income, families can more reliably be formed so that children will more likely be raised and educated to have brighter futures.

Consistently we have argued that forty years of implementing the same solutions are enough. Despite countless laws and program innovations, the problem of inner-city ghetto poverty remains with us and grows worse as we continue downward on the spiral. What cities like East Cleveland demonstrate is that more is needed than welfare dollars and public-housing programs. Abnormal conditions of concentrated poverty produce the abnormal behavior associated with an economic underclass for any people trapped in this situation. We need to find a way to bring private enterprise back into ghetto inner-city areas so that a culture of jobs and incomes can begin to replace a culture of unemployment and poverty.

This is not simply a problem of Ohio and East Cleveland; chronic urban poverty is a problem across America. We do not mean to suggest that the point of the Blackwell Initiative is to solve the problems of East Cleveland. The Blackwell Initiative is aimed at bringing additional capital into Ohio for economic development of the entire state. Our point is that Ohio's economic development will always be hampered as long as East Cleveland and other areas of urban poverty are allowed to persist, if only because high levels of concentrated poverty increase the welfare-tax burden for all the residents of the state. When problem urban areas are successfully reemployed, the resulting reduction in the burden of welfare payments will provide economic stimulus, especially if state taxes can be reduced as a result. The Blackwell Initiative is meant to be a model that will be applied throughout Ohio. And by successfully implementing the Blackwell Initiative in Ohio, the Buckeye State will be a model for rebuilding America.

## REVERSING THE URBAN GHETTO

ON JANUARY 26, 1966, Martin Luther King Jr.; his wife, Coretta; and their four children moved into a dilapidated third-floor walk-up apartment at 1550 South Hamlin in North Lawndale, a suburb of Chicago. Then known as "Slumdale," North Lawndale had been a middle-class Jewish neighborhood until after World War II, when returning black solders moved into Lawndale, displacing the white residents who lived there. Since 1980 the Chicago affiliate of an influential national nonprofit group, the Local Initiative Support Coalition (LISC), has invested $120 million in Chicago-area inner-city development, a sum that was leveraged into an additional $2.4 billion, which resulted in the construction of twenty-one thousand units of affordable housing and four million square feet of commercial space. Writing in *Newsweek,* journalist Jonathan Alter, who grew up in North Lawndale, commented that LISC demonstrated that "stronger ties between the corporate world and dedicated community leaders are now the proven routes to urban revival."[20] Alter observed LISC also demonstrated how important jobs and financial education are to building the mental skills needed to emerge from poverty:

> Near King's old haunts, I watched ex-convicts sitting at computer screens inside the LISC-backed North Lawndale Employment Network printing résumés and looking for work. Many have problems with bad debt. "A job alone is not the answer—that was my big 'Aha!'" says Brenda Palms Barber, who runs the nonprofit and is teaching entrepreneurship skills to local residents (including placing beehives on empty lots that yield 4,000 pounds of profitable honey). "It's mental health, general health. The missing piece is about financial education." A program in Chicago called First Accounts is focusing on a neglected segment of poor now known as the "unbanked." When they do get accounts, their balances are small, but the vast majority learned to be creditworthy.[21]

Reading the LISC-Chicago newsletter, *Working Assets,* we are struck at how the organization has established the model of making LISC grants and loans to neighborhood community-development organizations, tying in the active involvement of local-area banks. The Winter 2005 issue of *Working Assets* featured an interview with Don Randel, the president of the University of Chicago. He clearly recognized the role the university could play in revitalizing Chicago's inner city:

> Institutions, particularly universities, Randel explained, have a profound effect on local communities. They are employers, pur-

chasers, and community anchors, and depending on their commitment, they can also be powerful change agents, bringing new ideas and the application of those ideas to the task of strengthening neighborhoods.

"We must realize that we all have a responsibility to help improve the communities we share," he said. "We must act in a way that makes it clear we care for our neighbors and all citizens of our country." President Randel called on urban universities to leave the ivory tower behind. "The fact is that universities can no longer afford to be made of ivory," he said. "Everything about the metaphor of the ivory tower suggests something very much at odds with what universities need to be today." Chicago, he said, is the perfect place for a new paradigm of university and community partnership to emerge. "We have an opportunity to make this city an example to the whole country of one applying the energy, imagination and resources it takes to solve big problems."[22]

Inner-city poverty neighborhoods took decades to get to the point of deterioration in which we find them today. We will undoubtedly need to apply decades to reverse this trend. We can start today by taking steps in the right direction. LISC, by combining nonprofit community development with the involvement of local businesses and local banks, is moving in the right direction.

Writing during the 2004 Republican Party's presidential nominating conference in New York City, Jack Kemp, one of the original architects of the idea that private enterprise is the route to curing poverty in America, reflected upon the dysfunctions of the welfare-state mentality:

I cringe when I hear the rhetoric of class warfare, which seems to have become the *raison d'être* of the Democratic Party, whether they are ranting about "the people versus the powerful" or increasing taxes on the "top 2 percent." They just don't get it. The American dream is to become rich, not to punish them.

It's not that Democrats hate the rich—so many of them are rich—or that they care more about the poor; they have little faith in poor people and think the only way the poor can improve their lot in life is for government to take from the rich and redistribute the lucre to them.

Poverty in America is a disgrace and must be addressed through expanding ownership opportunities. It is also, in many cases, more a function of the life cycle than one's station in life. Research shows that as much as 25 percent to 40 percent of Americans move from one income quintile to another in a single year. Today's laborer is tomorrow's investor, owner and job creator. The worker and investor is the same person, just at different stages of his or her life.[23]

We will not advance the poor from the bottom quintile to the top quintiles in one jump. But if we begin the process now, we will be moving in the right direction. The future especially lies with the children.

We solidly believe that many of tomorrow's future millionaires are children living today in the poverty ghettos of our inner cities. Employment, education, and families are the only sure path forward. If we begin today, forty or fifty years from now, we will no longer be lamenting the same problems we are decrying now. Unfortunately, all too many American cities have their own version of East Cleveland's demise. Still, there is no reason why today's inner-city slums cannot become exciting places to live and work in the years just ahead. The downward spiral of abandoned properties and depressed housing values, combined with poverty and substandard education, is not a formula we are bound to repeat in the years ahead. Lives today that are lost in poverty can be brought forward productively if we can apply capital through the private enterprise system to provide jobs that will encourage strong families to educate children with the skills needed for the future.

After decades of trying, we must finally acknowledge that the revitalization in our inner-city landscapes will never happen through more and more government welfare. The welfare state is best capable only of generating massive bureaucracies and welfare dependency, not true advancement out of poverty. Welfare, in the final analysis, is a tax burden we cannot afford to pay, especially since we have no reason to believe that the government welfare system we have created will ever produce the results originally promised—the elimination or even the substantial reduction of poverty. Our goal is to transform inner city poverty areas into tax-generating centers, not the tax-drain sinkholes we see today. Government can play a productive role by structuring the right investment environment to bring the ownership mentality into the heart of the inner-city ghetto we are resolved to transform. As Jack Kemp recommends, we can move "from poverty to prosperity." We end this chapter where we began: Robert Kennedy was right. We will never solve the problem of poverty in America unless we can engage the full creative power of private enterprise in the endeavor.

In 2006, Eric Brewer took over as the new mayor of East Cleveland. Within the first few months, the state of Ohio decided to remove the fiscal emergency designation from the insolvent city, disbanding a state-appointed commission that was established to monitor the city's finances. Brewer took office determined to turn East Cleveland in a positive direction. Coauthor Ken Blackwell expresses confidence that Brewer's leadership is compatible with the vision of jobs and economic development we have expressed in these pages. With a shared emphasis on families and morals, we believe we can work together to implement the Blackwell Initiative in East Cleveland and throughout Ohio. We applaud Eric Brewer's vision for a twenty-first-century East Cleveland transformed from the tragedies of the past fifty years into an economically thriving community of tomorrow.

# CONCLUSION

## Rebuilding America

What you're witnessing today is the beginning of transition into a new era where you're going to get a Republican governor that's a Republican for a change.

—John Kenneth Blackwell, Secretary of State,
Republican Candidate for Governor

THE STORY OF THIS book is about jobs and families. America's strength has traditionally come from within, from the courage and economic self-determination of our citizens. America has succeeded as the world's most successful melting pot because we have opened our borders for generations to legal immigrants who have come here for the opportunity that America represents—the opportunity to work hard, to earn a successful living, to build families, and to grow old securely among one's loved ones. All true Americans cherish this dream. We will only overcome poverty when we stop rejecting and blaming the private-enterprise system. Now is the time that the immigrants who came to America as slaves be given the opportunity to participate fully in the private enterprise system, not the government welfare handout system.

Jobs are central to our ability to redevelop inner-city communities so we can provide the base for homeownership that is needed for healthy families and the productive education of children. In this book we have given a specific plan for applying capital to get private enterprise into the poverty-elimination game. Our call is for less government, not more. We firmly believe that government bureaucracy is no way to run a business.

Successful private enterprise requires marketing savvy and creative energy applied to producing goods and services people want to buy. Bureaucrats are good only at producing forms and writing books of regulations. If a library full of rule books and $10 trillion dollars spent on government welfare programs could have solved the problem of poverty, we would have the solution in place today. The fault is our believing that government dependency of any kind will work to eliminate or even to substantially reduce poverty in America.

We are also dedicated to the proposition that all Americans—including all our complex racial, ethnic, religious, sexual, and age differences—are created equal. Each person has a unique value to contribute to this whole. We credit the War on Poverty and the Great Society initiatives, not with achieving its goal of eliminating poverty, but for occurring at the same time as the civil rights movement and thereby assisting in breaking down the legal barriers to equality in America. In 1950, racial discrimination in employment, housing, education and a host of other areas was a reality; today, discrimination in each of these areas is a crime. This is an important development. Now we must complete the job. Completing the job requires new tools and a mind-set that can engage and involve the private sector.

We have a long way to go before our racial, ethnic, and religious minorities experience equality in results. There is no reason African Americans, or anyone else, should be second-class citizens in the economic sphere. We also reject the idea that special privileges—such as quotas or forced busing to achieve school integration—are necessary for us to reach our goal of equality in reality. No African American child is going to get a better education simply because he or she sits next to a white child in a classroom. No African American needs to be given a job he or she does not deserve in order to experience equality in the job sector. How many Nobel Prize winners or millionaires—or fire fighters, police officers, and schoolteachers—have been lost in the last four decades simply because all we were able to see was a neglected, poor black child—not a creative mind whose contribution we could not afford to lose? Money is never our scarcest resource. Human talent always is. America can never have too much human creativity; our genius is in our people, and our future is in our children, whether we realize it or not.

Our message is simple. Give us all the poor and disadvantaged. We want the talent that lies dormant among people we see as innately talented. Welfare builds a dependency that destroys families. Children are best raised in a loving environment where a father and a mother nurture them and provide educational opportunities for advancement. Quite simply, by encouraging abortion and by destroying families through decades of the welfare-state mentality, we are destroying important human resources that we should be cultivating and growing.

Among America's African American poor in our inner cities are today many great scientists, engineers, educational leaders, artists, athletes, business entrepreneurs, and government visionaries whose talents are squandered because we lack the imagination to engage them productively. The vacant lots and abandoned buildings of today's slums are the breeding grounds of crime, drugs, and violence, but they should be the scenes where creative entrepreneurs can establish the next urban place to be. Restaurants, rehabilitated urban city dwellings, and corporate parks can thrive tomorrow where today we have only chain-link fences and weeds. There is no reason we have to abandon our cities to neglect while our outer suburban areas thrive with parks, schools, and businesses that attract people to buy homes, raise families, and invest in the future.

America cannot afford to waste another generation of its poor. Give us those human resources—regardless of race, ethnicity, religion, sex, or age—and we will resolve to put the people to productive activity that advances us all. America's past was built on employment; we resolve here and now to build America's future on the basis of jobs. Our confidence for the future is focused on employing all of America's human resources, not on a continuing dependence on government bureaucracies or welfare handouts to solve our poverty problems. Rebuilding America, in the final analysis, has everything to do with people, truly our most important and most scarce national resource.

## ELIMINATING POVERTY IS NOT A PUBLIC-WORKS PROJECT

THE INTELLECTUAL foundations for the Great Society's failed War on Poverty can be traced back to the 1958 publication of *The Affluent Society* by Harvard University economist John Kenneth Galbraith.[1] The core argument of Galbraith's book is that a productive capitalist economy inherently produces income inequalities between the rich and the poor as well as a "social imbalance" between an abundance of privately produced consumer goods and scarcity and disrepair among the public goods we depend upon government to provide. Thus, Galbraith argued, we were doomed to have a large and growing class of poor among us as well as deteriorating bridges, roads, and schools—unless government steps in to redistribute income away from the rich to the poor, away from private capital to government spending on infrastructure products.

Galbraith's analysis subtly transitioned the problem of poverty itself into a consideration of "public goods." Writing ultimately about a poverty of public services much as he wrote about income inequality itself, Galbraith laid out his call for action: "We must find a way to remedy the poverty which afflicts us in public services and which is in such increasingly bizarre contrast with our affluence in private goods."[2] He circled the argument back by concluding that unless we took "public goods" issues—such as education—seriously, we would undermine the ability of the private economy to recruit the future talent needed as the entrepreneurs upon whom future economic growth depended. So, too, if we neglected public infrastructure—roads and bridges as well as the "human" public infrastructure of police, hospitals, and sanitation—we would end up undermining economic growth by neglecting the commonly shared public systems upon which business itself depends.

Thus, Galbraith argued:

> To create the demand for new automobiles we must contrive elaborate and functionless changes each year and then subject the consumer to ruthless psychological pressures to persuade him of their importance. Were this process to falter or break down, the consequences would be disturbing. In the meantime there are large ready-made needs for schools, hospitals, slum clearance and urban redevelopment, sanitation, parks, playgrounds, police, and a thousand other things. Of these almost no one must be persuaded. They are unavailable only because, as public officials of all kinds and ranks explain each day with practiced skill, the money to provide them is unavailable. So it has come about that we get growth

218

and increased employment along the dimension of private goods only at the price of increasingly frantic persuasion. We exploit but poorly the opportunity along the dimension of public services. The economy is geared to the least urgent of human wants. It would be far more secure if it were based on the whole range of need.[3]

As Galbraith saw the evolution of the capitalist economy, private goods and services could be sold to individuals; as a result, private goods could be produced and sold by companies for a specific price. Public goods benefited everyone, a technical defect that placed public goods outside the private pricing structure needed for a company to produce the bridge, school, or police system and sell that good or service to someone in particular.

Galbraith had the New Deal enthusiasm for the ability of government bureaucracies to solve social and economic problems: "The solution is a system of taxation which automatically takes a pro rata share of increasing income available to public authorities for public purposes."[4] So a progressive system of taxing individuals and businesses would provide the money for government to restore the "social balance," so schools and roads would no longer be imbalanced, at a disadvantage when compared to the production of abundant automobiles and television sets. Poverty, to Galbraith, was another "social imbalance" that could only be solved through government action resolved to treat it as another public good the private economy would never redress.

Galbraith called for society to provide some sort of minimal income for everyone: "An affluent society, that is also both compassionate and rational, would, no doubt, secure to all who needed it the minimum income essential for decency and comfort."[5] Here began the impulse to provide what later we came to call the welfare "safety net." Galbraith had produced the economic logic for arguing that eliminating poverty was outside the capitalist system of producing consumer goods that could be priced for individual sale. Like roads and bridges, the plight of the poor was outside the "pricing" system of private corporations whose motivation was to "price" and pay for only the minimum number of employees needed for profitable production, not for all those who needed employment. Because private corporations were not welfare agencies, Galbraith could find no logic to explain how or why profit-motivated private companies would ever solve the problem of poverty.

As a senior adviser to presidential candidate John F. Kennedy, and later as Kennedy's ambassador to India from 1961 to 1963, Galbraith had the direct access he needed to influence firsthand New Frontier thinking. After the publication of *The Affluent Society,* solving poverty became a public responsibility expected to be outside the normal activity of private companies. Somehow, on the political Left, the full transition in thought was made to the conclusion that poverty was an inevitable consequence of the capitalist system unless government intervened to redistribute income and restore the proper "social balance" with welfare-system transfer payments.

*John Kenneth* Blackwell's thinking is aimed at reversing *John Kenneth* Galbraith's underlying presumptions that private enterprise causes poverty. By following Galbraith's logic, the welfare state created a governmental bureaucratic transfer-payment solution that did not work. John Kenneth Blackwell has come full circle, arguing that many "public goods" and governmental products and services, such as the Ohio Turnpike, are better off operated by private companies who lease them from the state. We have suggested that a full range of "public services" operated by government—including schools, water systems, and sanitation—might be done better and more profitably if private operators were involved through openly bid contracts. This completely reverses Galbraith's argument that public goods and services cannot be provided within the private sector. We believe government can be downsized, with taxes reduced and substantial public revenue generated, by involving private operators to work in areas that traditionally have been presumed to be the exclusive province of government. Moreover, we have argued that income-redistribution efforts through welfare payments have failed to eliminate or even substantially reduce poverty. Money alone, ironically, will never be the solution to poverty.

### HOW DO WE CREATE A WORK ETHIC AMONG TODAY'S POOR?

FOR YEARS Ken Blackwell has developed the theme of applying capital to the problem of inner-city poverty. Speaking to a luncheon of the Columbus Urban League on June 20, 1994, he addressed the problem of inequality in America:

> The sixty signers of the Declaration of Independence intended to speak for all Americans for all time when they pledged their lives, their fortunes, and their sacred honor to these ideals: "We hold these truths to be self-evident, that all men are created equal, that they are endowed by their Creator with certain unalienable rights, that among these are life, liberty, and the pursuit of happiness."
>
> Throughout our national history, in spite of the clarity of Thomas Jefferson's words, some people have been considered to have been created more equal than other people. Some people have come into the world freer than other people. Some people have found fewer obstacles in their path as they have pursued happiness. For the past forty years we have been engaged in a national effort to right these wrongs—to close the gap between the American dream and performance. We have not sought equality of outcomes. We have sought only equality of opportunity. We have not sought to give more freedom to some citizens than others. We have sought only to make everyone free. And we have not sought a guarantee of happiness. We have sought only the same access to happiness.
>
> We have no quarrel with a society where some people stand on the top rung of the ladder, others stand on the middle rungs, and some stand on the bottom rung. Life is competitive. There are vast differences in individual talents and motivation. What we cannot tolerate is a society where some people are pushed off the ladder as they try to climb it, or, worse yet, are trapped in a cage that keeps them from approaching the first step. We have made progress in recent years in righting these wrongs, but it is time now to reassess the approach we have taken.

The welfare state, as Blackwell described at that luncheon, has been a well-intended failure:

> The federal government in Washington saw poverty and put in place programs with good intentions but unconstructive action.

These programs were built on a lack of faith in the character and the competence of a major segment of our people. The programs constituted a system that nurtured dependency—a program that made sure the poor stayed poor. Having ignored the importance of families, these programs made up a system that rewarded—indeed, that required—the birth of babies out of wedlock, born to women who themselves were not much more than babies. They made up a system that rewarded—indeed, that required—the denial of responsibility of the fathers of these babies for these babies. They made up a system that rewarded—indeed, that required—people to live non-productive lives.

With these well-intentioned but misguided programs, our society went a long way toward restoring all of the human conditions of slavery, with some unbelievably cruel twentieth-century refinements. It is true that government dependency programs do not buy and sell human beings, as slaveholders did; government dependency programs just tell them that they are human beings of no value, that they are worthless. Government dependency programs do not break up families, as slaveholders did; government dependency programs just keep families from forming in the first place. Government dependency programs do not tell people they are not as good as their masters, a lie slave-holders told; government dependency programs just make people tell themselves they are no good by robbing them of their self-respect.

It is time now to move away from the master-slave relationship that has evolved between government and some of its people. It is time now to move into a peer relationship among all our citizens through economic empowerment. It is time to thrash the pacifiers that keep people in the permanent state of dependency as if they were social infants. It is time now to give people something they can get their teeth into, to give them the opportunity to put nourishment into their lives.

The solution Blackwell proposed in 1994 is the same solution we are proposing today: the private enterprise system must become engaged if the problem of poverty is ever to be solved.

It is time to unleash the forces that created the most productive economic system the world has ever known. It is time now to move ahead toward a free enterprise approach to the problems that people with good intentions have tried to solve with demeaning government paternalism.

Thirty years ago all Americans finally were given the right to eat at a public lunch counter. It is time now to make it possible for more of these Americans to own and manage that lunch counter. It is time now for us to replace punitive business taxes and regulations with business tax credits that reward job creation and training. It is time now for us to replace ineffectual governmental expenditures, which encourage joblessness, with economic incentives, which encourage people to take and hold jobs. It is time now to replace public housing projects with tenant ownership and programs that expand homeownership. It is time now to replace government-subsidized ghettos with enterprise zones that create jobs that let people live where they want to live. It is time now to free up the economic strength and creativity of the African American community to deal with the needs of people in the welfare trap.

The black community spends more than $315 billion a year. Ranked among nations, this would make Black America the fourteenth largest economic power in the world. We can find ways to increase investment and reinvestment in our central cities where we find most of the people caught in the welfare trap, to create new businesses and new job opportunities within our inner-city communities where those who live there can also work there. We can stop trying to appease the symptoms of poverty and begin rewarding enterprise in the African American community.

Blackwell encouraged the luncheon attendees to understand that we could reach for the dream of eliminating poverty, not simply reducing poverty.

St. Matthew said, "For ye shall always have the poor with you." This is not an immutable law of nature, to be accepted no matter how regretfully. It is a challenge to humankind to help move people from dependency to self-reliance. America is the country where we have it within our power to meet St. Matthew's challenge. This is the country where we can make it possible for the poor to shed their poverty by allowing them to work.

We have not called for an immediate end to any program in the current welfare system. Our call is for a reversal in direction. Rather than continue down the path of welfare dependency, we want to start putting into place capital and jobs that will revitalize our inner-city urban areas. As people who are poor today learn a productive way out of poverty, the welfare state of tomorrow will be less needed than it is today, not more needed. We have confidence people can emerge from poverty because we have seen countless examples where that is exactly what has happened. America is not a country in which only those who are born into privilege are allowed to advance. Having struggled hard since *Brown v. Board of Education* in 1954, opportunity is available equally to all Americans.

Those who would seek to discriminate are risking their own freedom to pursue the American dream, not the freedom of those they would seek to repress.

We know that a transition will be required. Decades of welfare dependency will not be overcome in the blink of an eye. But today we can resolve to begin, taking steps we know will restore private enterprise to our poverty areas so that tomorrow those areas will no longer be poor. Once we have established a culture in which the poor know they can advance, we will no longer have to face poverty as an inevitability we can do nothing to change. The mentality of the welfare state has become a mentality of failure. We reject that mentality because we know it to be false. Countless poor have advanced from poverty and countless more will do the same. Money alone will not solve the problem of poverty, but a culture of families, jobs, homeownership, and education will get us substantially down the road in the direction we want to travel.

In speaking to a regional conference of the National Association of Urban Bankers, Ohio secretary of state Ken Blackwell emphasized the role banks have to play in the redevelopment of inner-city poverty areas:

I see a potential problem facing our urban areas that have traditionally been denied access to banks, credit, and capital. These are the necessary ingredients to economic growth in a community. It is only fairly recently that pressure from legislators and community groups has given banks the green light to enter these red-lined communities.

Those Bible readers among you might recall Psalm 11:3, which reads, "If the foundations be destroyed, what will the righteous do?" To put this issue in a moral context, those of us who are educated and knowledgeable about finance are the economic equivalent of the righteous. If the foundations be destroyed, if our cities fall into decay, if our people are lost to us, what will we do? We will be held responsible for that failure.

Blackwell reminded the bankers that banks could play a key role in educating the "unbanked," not just in providing the capital needed to bring forth inner-city jobs.

It would be naive to think that communities bereft of wealth-building capital for fifty years would be brought up to speed in ten or even twenty years. These communities are still many years behind in their capital infrastructure—the system of banks, businesses, and mortgages that builds wealth. And yet, what we're talking about today is technology that has much of the banking world looking many years ahead. Just as these communities are catching up to the second wave, there's a real danger of leaving them in the wake of the third.

Some fifty million poor Americans are "unbanked" at this moment. Many of them live in those urban areas where the wealth-building banking infrastructure is underdeveloped. Filling the void is an underground economy, mainly cash-based. Rather than a professional banking office or an ATM, these people must rely on bulletproofed check-cashing operations charging ungodly fees. With the growing technology in America today, my fear is that the temptation will be to turn our attention to distant, accessible markets while turning our back on closer, closed-off communities.

There is a dangerous disconnect when we provide service around the world but not around the corner. There is a price, and it is levied in crime, arson, strife, stress, and general discontent.

Don't wait for collection day. A little investment on the front end pays off big later. Invest in community outreach, in adult and children's education, in small business, in keeping brick and mortar and flesh and blood in the community. The bottom line is that the American government can never provide opportunity like the American market can. Banks serving a community have a vested interest in that community. Isolated communities are on a downward spiral. Ideally, a bank is a community leader that reverses that process. A bank involved in the inner-city community exposes people to opportunity, education, and technology, releasing people from yesterday's routines to take advantage of tomorrow's opportunities.

Economic opportunities await us, not in faraway lands, but right here, at home, within our nation's inner cities. The Blackwell gubernatorial campaign is based on the premise that Ohio can and will attract businesses and jobs by putting capital to work throughout the state. We believe we can work in conjunction with the bank partners who have traditionally stood at the center of America's economic growth and development.

## CONCLUSION

WHERE WILL poverty in America be fifty years or one hundred years from now? Will inner-city African American poverty be a greater or a lesser problem? Will inner-city neighborhoods be more deteriorated or rehabilitated? These are critical questions we must ask ourselves today if we are to have the possibility of advancing in the future.

Americans are committed to the elimination of poverty and racial inequality in principle. The hard test facing us today is whether we can reduce or eliminate poverty and racial inequality in reality. Today, our inner cities are becoming tax holes, with abandoned buildings and vacant lots defining the landscape. Especially in an era of increasing energy costs, our cities should contract back within their earlier borders. The expansion of our major metropolitan areas beyond the original 1960s ring of suburbs into areas once considered rural has been made possible because of cheap fuel and a massive program of building limited-access inner-belt highways. With the price of oil regularly above fifty dollars a barrel, with price spikes to levels of seventy dollars a barrel or higher, we have entered a new plateau of energy costs from which we are unlikely to descend. Today many commuters anticipate one-way travel time between homes and workplaces as long as forty-five minutes or more. Commute times will only continue to increase as our population expands and more cars take to the highways. Inner-city light-rail systems function effectively today in many cities with concentrated populations in and near downtown areas, cities such as Chicago, New York, Philadelphia, and Washington DC. Relatively cheap land for business creation and expansion may today be found more readily in our inner cities, not farther out, beyond our most-distant new suburbs.

What we need is capital and jobs to redevelop America's inner cities, not more government bureaucracy and increased welfare transfer payments. We have argued that today's poor is a talent resource we cannot afford to lose. Rebuilding family structures in poor communities so children can be educated must be one of our highest goals. The waves of European immigrants who came to America in the late 1880s and early 1900s came to escape religious and political oppression and to find greater economic opportunities. Many of the adult immigrants knew that the real opportunity in America would fall to their children. Immigrant families typically made sure children were taught English as a first language and went to school. We must reestablish this work and advancement ethic among today's poor.

Our confidence in the talent that lies dormant in poor children whose education is neglected should drive us forward to the opportunity ahead as surely as those early immigrant families from Europe were driven. We are going to need honest, hardworking talent to fill our inner-city governmental positions. We have learned that simply putting African American politicians in control in African American communities will not alone assure advancement. Additionally, those politicians must be honest and hardworking. At all levels of government, contracts must be openly bid and transparent to public scrutiny to avoid abuse and scandal. Yet these are only the necessary conditions; we must also have access to capital, with banks working as active partners to constitute the sufficient conditions of attracting businesses back to our inner-city communities.

The first decades of the civil rights movement and the War on Poverty have been about establishing equal rights; the next half century must be dedicated to establishing equal results. Our inner cities are lost opportunities, every bit as much as children on welfare are lives lost to poverty. Government must play an important role in continuing to set the rules equally for all and in providing the structures in which private capital can be encouraged to go to work. But we have argued repeatedly that government is truly only good at creating bureaucracies and reams of regulations that tend to go unread, not gainfully applied. We need less government, not more. We need a return to dependence upon ourselves, not dependence upon government to solve our problems. Government, as originally conceptualized by our Founding Fathers, was a minimal institution, not a pervasive intruder into all aspects of our personal, social, and economic lives. We need to return to this perspective if the next fifty years are going to be written any differently than the last fifty on the important questions of poverty in America, racial equality in fact, and the rehabilitation of our inner cities.

We conclude this book on a positive note, believing that we have within our power to apply the creative thought needed to tackle the next phase of the battle on poverty. Rebuilding America is within our means and within our ability. Just as we are calling upon private enterprise to get involved, we are calling on the poor themselves to get involved. Economic advancement begins with the belief that economic advancement is possible. Some of the greatest Americans have emerged from poverty. In every field of endeavor, African Americans have risen to the highest ranks. America today has many of the world's greatest cities; we can expand that horizon even into the poorest inner-city areas where today's neglect can be replaced by tomorrow's accomplishment.

Fifty years from now, let future analysts say we advanced on these issues because we believed advancement was possible and because we applied the capital necessary to get the job done. Let future chapters be written about how gifted government officials at the local and state level partnered with bankers and entrepreneurs to restore business opportunities in our inner cities and to reemploy the poor. These are the goals we must set for ourselves, especially as we resolve to move away from the dependency inherent to the welfare-state mentality. American was built on private initiative, not government bureaucracy. We resolve here and now to get back on the right path to form partnerships between government and business that bring more jobs and educational opportunities to all Americans. In the final analysis, jobs and families remain our formula for rebuilding America.

# ACKNOWLEDGMENTS

# NOTES

# INDEX

# ACKNOWLEDGMENTS

WE WOULD LIKE TO Cleveland attorney Raymond C. Headen for his careful reading of this manuscript and his insightful suggestions for improvement. His expertise in public finance was enormously helpful in providing us guidance.

David Hanson and the Buckeye Institute for Public Policy Solutions, the market-oriented "think tank" in Columbus, Ohio, helped us formulate our ideas on how to most effectively involve private enterprise in our determination to rebuild our inner cities.

Dr. Richard Vetter, Distinguished Professor of Economics at Ohio University, has provided invaluable assistance to us in appreciating the negative effects of tax increases on the economy. Dr. Vetter's trailblazing work on supply-side economics provided guidance to us as we formulated the solutions proposed in these pages.

Community activist Robert L. "Bob" Woodson rightly established himself at the National Urban League in Washington DC as the godfather of the movement to empower neighborhood-based organizations. We thank Bob for sharing with us the experience and wisdom he has gained in a career devoted to helping low-income people transcend their impoverished conditions. Bob's appreciation of microeconomics and neighborhood empowerment establishes him as a light in the public-policy darkness that surrounds big government on the state and federal levels.

Norm Cummings provided the same high level of expert advice in completing this book that has characterized his long-term role as consultant to Ken Blackwell's political career.

Paula Baker provided her always expert research and editing assistance. We thank Paula for her acute sense of idealism.

Cleveland attorney Kenneth F. Seminatore gave the manuscript a careful reading and offered important suggestions that guided our conclusions. Ken Seminatore's involvement in this book completed a circle, harkening back to nearly forty years ago when, as Jerome Corsi's first coauthor, Ken helped pen a book on racial relations that remains relevant today.

Eric J. Brewer, the newly elected mayor of East Cleveland, Ohio, read the manuscript carefully, providing important insights on East Cleveland. We believe that, under Mayor Brewer, East Cleveland can return to the bright days of its former glory.

At *WorldNetDaily.com,* Joseph Farah continues to lead the way with his courage to pursue controversial political issues that shape the future of our families, an issue at the core of this book. Ron Pitkin, the president of Cumberland House Publishing, and Stacie Bauerle, the assistant publisher at Cumberland House, believed in this book and encouraged us from the beginning to make a statement that Ken Blackwell could champion in his 2006 run to be governor of Ohio. Ed Curtis helped us through several rounds of revisions and corrections as we readied this manuscript for publication. As always, we appreciated Ed's intelligent and thoughtful editing.

# NOTES

## PREFACE

1. Louis H. Masotti and Jerome R. Corsi, *Shoot-Out in Cleveland. Black Militants and the Police: July 23, 1968* (Washington DC: U.S. Government Printing Office, 1969). Also known as *A Report to the National Commission on the Causes and Prevention of Violence,* editions were also published in 1969 by Bantam Books and Frederick A. Praeger.
2. John E. O'Neill and Jerome R. Corsi, *Unfit for Command: Swift Boat Veterans Speak Out Against John Kerry* (Washington DC: Regnery, 2004).

## CHAPTER 1: LIVES LOST TO POVERTY

1. Kenneth B. Clark, *Dark Ghetto: Dilemmas of Social Power* (New York: Harper & Row, 1965).
2. Ibid., 25.
3. Ibid., 27.
4. Ibid.
5. Ibid., 34.
6. Ibid., 47.
7. Ibid., 81.
8. Ibid., 139.
9. Ibid., 112.
10. Theodore H. White, *Making of the President 1960* (New York: Atheneum, 1961).
11. Clark, *Dark Ghetto,* 25.
12. The original table appeared in ibid., 24, Table 2A. It is updated here with data drawn from the U.S. Census Bureau, "American Fact Finder," searching the database for each city, available online at http://factfinder.census.gov/home/saff/main.html?_lang=en.
13. See "Population of the 20 Largest U.S. Cities, 1900–2004," at InfoPlease.com, with data drawn from the U.S. Census Bureau, online at http://www.infoplease.com/ipa/A0922422.html and http://www.infoplease.com/ipa/A0763098.html. The statistical data in the next paragraph for Detroit is drawn from the same source.

14. Joel Kurth, "Detroit Falls Behind in Fight Against Blight: City Is Running Out of Time to Tear Down 12,000 Homes Before Super Bowl in 2006," *Detroit News,* March 1, 2005, http://www.detnews.com/2005/metro/0503/01/A01–104173.htm.

15. John D. Kasarda, "Urban Industrial Transition and the Underclass," in *The Ghetto Underclass: Social Science Perspectives,* ed. William Julius Wilson (Newbury Park: Sage Publications, 1993), 43.

16. Clark, *Dark Ghetto,* x.

17. Ibid., 223.

18. The analysis in this section and the quotations come from Economic Research Service (ERS), U.S. Department of Agriculture, "Rural income, poverty, and welfare: high-poverty counties," online at http://www.ers.usda.gov/Briefing/IncomePovertyWelfare/HighPoverty/analysis.htm. The analysis that follows—of Hispanic, Native American, and non-Hispanic white rural poverty counties—is drawn from this source.

19. David K. Shipler, *The Working Poor: Invisible in America* (New York: Knopf, 2004).

20. Michael Harrington, *The Other America* (New York: Macmillan, 1962).

21. Shipler, *The Working Poor,* ix–x.

22. Ibid., 3.

23. Ibid., 11.

24. Bureau of Labor Statistics, U.S. Department of Labor, "Occupations with the Largest Job Growth, 2002–2012," Monthly Labor Review, February 2004, http://www.bls.gov/emp/emptab4.htm.

25. Bureau of Labor Statistics, U.S. Department of Labor, "Employment Gains Among Hispanic Population in 2004," Editor's Desk, Monthly Labor Review, April 26, 2005, http://www.bls.gov/opub/ted/2005/apr/wk4/art02.htm.

26. Paul Hortenstine, "Latino Employment Trend: More Jobs, Less Pay," May 15, 2005, News Service, Hispanic Link Journalism Foundation, Washington DC, http://www.hispaniclink.org/newsservice/columns/4072e.htm.

27. Sharon Hays, *Flat Broke with Children: Women in the Age of Welfare Reform* (New York: Oxford University Press, 2003), 11.

28. Newt Gingrich et al., eds., *Contract with America* (New York: Times Books, 1994), 75.

29. Ibid., 67.

30. Rebecca M. Blank and Lucie Schmidt, "Work, Wages, and Welfare," in *The New World of Welfare,* ed. Rebecca M. Blank and Ron Haskins (Washington DC: Brookings Institution Press, 2001), 70–102.

31. Charles Murray, "Family Formation," in *The New World of Welfare,* ed. Re-

becca M. Blank and Ron Haskins (Washington DC: Brookings Institution Press, 2001), 137–68.

32. Hays, *Flat Broke with Children,* 42.

## CHAPTER 2: THE WAR ON POVERTY FAILS

1. President Lyndon B. Johnson, Annual Message to the Congress on the State of the Union, January 8, 1964, archived on the Web site of the Lyndon Baines Johnson Library and Museum, http://www.lbjlib.utexas.edu/johnson/archives.hom/speeches.hom/640108.asp.

2. President Ronald Reagan, Annual Message to the Congress on the State of the Union, January 25, 1988, archived on the Web site of the Ronald Reagan Presidential Library, National Archives and Records Administration, http://www.reagan.utexas.edu/archives/speeches/1988/012588d.htm.

3. The data on poverty in the United States is drawn largely from the following source: U.S. Census Bureau, *Income, Poverty, and Health Insurance Coverage in the United States: 2004* (Washington DC: U.S. Government Printing Office, 2005), accessible at http://www.census.gov/prod/2005pubs/p60-229.pdf.

4. World Bank data available online at http://devdata.worldbank.org/external/CPProfile.asp?SelectedCountry=USA&CCODE=USA&CNAME=United+States&PTYPE=CP.

5. Bureau of Economic Analysis, U.S. Department of Commerce, *National Economic Accounts,* http://www.bea.gov.

6. U.S. Bureau of Labor Statistics, U.S. Department of Labor Statistics, historical reports on U.S. non-farm employment available at the BLS Web site: http://www.bls.gov.

7. These points were presented by Bill O'Reilly on the Fox News Channel, *The O'Reilly Factor,* in "Talking Points," September 13, 2005, http://www.foxnews.com/printer_friendly_story/0,3566,169347,00.html. The list of welfare programs is also drawn from this source.

8. Gunnar Myrdal, *An American Dilemma: The Negro Problem and Modern Democracy* (New York: Harper & Brothers, 1944), ix.

9. Ibid., vi, from the foreword by F. P. Keppel.

10. Ibid., 205.

11. Ibid., 330.

12. Ibid., 214.

13. Ibid., 1021.

14. *Brown v. Board of Education of Topeka, Kansas,* 347 U.S. 483.

15. Office of Policy Planning and Research, U.S. Department of Labor, *The*

*Negro Family: The Case for National Action* (Washington DC: Government Printing Office, 1965), 5 (hereafter referred to as "Moynihan Report"). The report is published in full in Lee Rainwater and William L. Yancy, *The Moynihan Report and the Politics of Controversy* (Cambridge, MA: MIT Press, 1976), 39–124.

16. Moynihan Report, 5. Page references apply to the original report. The sentence in bold was printed in bold in the original.

17. Ibid., 12.

18. Ibid., 27.

19. Ibid., 29.

20. Ibid., 47.

21. Lyndon B. Johnson, Howard University, June 4, 1965, cited in Rainwater and Yancy, *Moynihan Report and the Politics of Controversy,* 130.

22. Robert Rector, "Illegitimacy Is the Major Cause of Child Poverty," *Intellectual Ammunition,* January 1, 1999, and posted on the Web site of the Heartland Institute, http://www.heartland.org/Article.cfm?artId=403. See also Patrick F. Fagan et al., *The Positive Effects of Marriage: A Book of Charts* (Washington DC: Heritage Foundation, 2005), available at http://www.heritage.org/Research/Features/Marriage/index.cfm.

23. James Farmer, "The Controversial Moynihan Report," *New Amsterdam,* December 18, 1965, reprinted in Rainwater and Yancy, *Moynihan Report and the Politics of Controversy,* 410.

24. Radical socialist organizer Saul Alinsky blatantly advocated ad hominem attacks in his "rules for radicals" when he advocated ridiculing opponents in personal attacks that were designed to polarize issues. See Saul D. Alinsky, *Rules for Radicals: A Pragmatic Primer for Realistic Radicals* (New York: Random House, 1971).

25. Charles Murray, *Losing Ground: American Social Policy 1950–1980* (New York: Basic Books, 1984).

26. Ibid., 58.

27. Ibid., 133.

28. Ibid., 160.

29. Ibid. (italics in original).

30. Ibid., 227–28.

31. Ibid., 228.

32. Ibid., 58.

33. U.S. Census Bureau, "U.S. Interim Projections by Age, Sex, Race, and Hispanic Origin," http://www.census.gov/ipc/www/usinterimproj/.

34. Rakesh Kochhar, Roberto Suro, and Sonya Tafoya, "The New Latino South: The Context and Consequences of Rapid Population Growth," July

26, 2005, ii, http://usconservatives.about.com/gi/dynamic/offsite.htm
?zi=1/XJ&sdn=usconservatives&zu=http%3A%2F%2Fpewhispanic.org.

35. Ibid.

36. The rate of Hispanic births to unmarried mothers is drawn from the U.S. National Center for Health Statistics, *Vital Statistics of the United States,* in the *U.S. Statistical Abstract 2004–2005,* table 71, 60.

37. Federal Reserve Bank of Dallas, "Workers' Remittances to Mexico," Business Frontier, 1 (2004), http://www.dallasfed.org/research/busfront/bus0401.html.

38. Roberto Suro, "Remittance Senders and Receivers: Tracking the Transnational Channels," Pew Hispanic Center, November 24, 2003, http://pewhispanic.org/reports/report.php?ReportID=23.

39. Population Resource Center, "Executive Summary: Status of Children in America," May 2001, available at: http://www.prcdc.org/summaries/children/children.html.

40. Population Resource Center, "Executive Summary: A Demographic Profile of Hispanics in the U.S.," available at http://www.prcdc.org/summaries/hispanics/hispanics.html.

41. Rick Fry, "Work or Study: Different Fortunes of U.S. Latino Generations," Pew Hispanic Center, May 28, 2002, http://pewhispanic.org/reports/report.php?ReportID=9.

42. Newt Gingrich et al., eds., *Contract with America* (New York: Times Books, 1994).

43. The statistics for families on AFDC or TANF assistance are drawn from the U.S. Administration for Children and Families, *Temporary Assistance for Needy Families (TANF)—Families and Recipients: 1980 to 2003,* Table 545, http://www.census.gov/prod/2004pubs/04statab/socinsur.pdf.

44. Office of Family Assistance, TANF, *Fifth Annual Report to Congress,* section 7, "Formation and Maintenance of Two-Parent Families," http://www.acf.hhs.gov/programs/ofa/annualreport5/chap07.htm. The Web site indicates that the document was last modified on September 18, 2005.

45. "Report on the Religious Community Survey Conducted by the National Council of Churches on the Reauthorization of Temporary Assistance to Needy Families and Related Programs," online at: http://www.ncccusa.org/publicwitness/tanfsurvey.html.

46. Ibid.

47. "Welfare Reform: Issues in Brief," posted on the Web site of the Heritage Foundation at http://www.heritage.org/research/features/issues2004/welfare.cfm#FF.

## CHAPTER 3: THE POLITICS OF GUILT, RAGE, AND VIOLENCE

1. Gordon W. Allport, *The Nature of Prejudice* (Boston: Beacon Press, 1954), 233.
2. *Brown v. Board of Education of Topeka, Kansas,* 347 U.S. 483 (1954).
3. The discussion of the civil rights movement in this section is largely drawn from an earlier work coauthored by Jerome Corsi. See Louis H. Masotti, Jeffrey K. Hadden, and Kenneth F. Seminatore, *A Time to Burn? An Evaluation of the Present Crisis in Race Relations* (Chicago: Rand McNally, 1969).
4. Richard Wright, *Native Son* (New York: Harper & Brothers, 1940).
5. Masotti, Hadden, and Seminatore, *A Time to Burn?* 35–36.
6. *Report of the National Advisory Commission on Civil Disorders* (New York: New York Times, 1968), 1. Referred to hereafter as the Kerner Commission.
7. Ibid., 2.
8. Ibid., 13.
9. Ibid., 29.
10. Louis H. Masotti and Jerome R. Corsi, *Shoot-Out in Cleveland: Black Militants and the Police: July 23, 1968,* Task Force Report to the National Commission on the Causes and Prevention of Violence (Washington DC: U.S. Government Printing Office, 1969).
11. Richard Leiby, "Cosby, Saying the Darndest Things," *Washington Post,* May 19, 2004, http://www.washingtonpost.com/wp-dyn/articles/A37869–2004 May18.html.
12. Matt Rosenberg, "Bill Cosby & the Blogosphere," *National Review OnLine,* June 3, 2004, http://www.nationalreview.com/comment/rosenberg2004 06030907.asp.
13. Ta-Nehisi Coates, "Ebonics! Weird Names! $500 Shoes! Shrill Bill Cosby and the Speech That Shocked the Black World," *Village Voice,* May 26–June 1, 2004, http://www.villagevoice.com/news/0421,coates,53761,1.html.
14. Ibid.
15. "Statement from the Brokaw Company: Bill Cosby Responds to Media Criticism," PR Newswire, May 22, 2004, http://www.prnewswire.com/cgi-bin/stories.pl?ACCT=109&STORY=/www/story/05–22–2004/0002179697&EDATE=.
16. Ibid.
17. Bob Lewis, "Cosby Delivers Tough Talk to Richmond's Black Teens," *Washington Times,* October 12, 2004, http://www.washtimes.com/metro/20041011–115330–3793r.htm.

18. Brotherhood Organization of a New Destiny, BOND, http://www.bondinfo.org/.
19. Jesse Lee Peterson, "Dr. King and the Dream Today," WorldNetDaily.com, January 15, 2005, http://www.worldnetdaily.com/news/article.asp?ARTICLE_ID=42416.
20. Jesse Lee Peterson, *Scam: How the Black Leadership Exploits Black America* (Nashville: WND Books, 2003), xi.
21. Ibid., xii.
22. Charles Murray, *Losing Ground: American Social Policy, 1950–1980* (New York: Basic Books, 1984).
23. Richard J. Herrnstein and Charles Murray, *The Bell Curve: Intelligence and Class Structure in American Life* (New York: Free Press, 1994).
24. See, for instance, Steve Fraser, ed., *The Bell Curve Wars: Race, Intelligence, and the Future of America* (New York: Basic Books, 1995).

## CHAPTER 4: THE ATTACK ON THE BLACK FAMILY

1. Martin Luther King, Jr. *Where Do We Go from Here: Chaos or Community?* (New York: Harper & Row, 1967), 107.
2. *Roe v. Wade*, 410 US 113 (1973).
3. Many of the statistics in this chapter are drawn from Center for Disease Control and Prevention, U.S. Department of Health and Human Services, "HIV/AIDS Among African Americans," http://www.cdc.gov/hiv/topics/aa/resources/factsheets/aa.htm. Referred to hereafter as "CDC Data."
4. Quoted in Tanya L. Green, "The Negro Project: Margaret Sanger's Eugenic Plan for Black Americans," Concerned Women for America, http://www.cwfa.org/articledisplay.asp?id=1466&department=CWA&categoryid=life. Sanger's letter to Gamble was dated December 10, 1939, and is archived in the Margaret Sanger Collection in the Library of Congress.
5. The statistics in this paragraph are drawn from LEARN, the Life Education and Resource Network, as posted on the organization's Web site, http://blackgenocide.org/.
6. U.S. National Center for Health Statistics, *Vital Statistics of the United States,* Table no. 72, "Births and Birth Rates by Race, Sex, and Age: 1980 to 2002," U. S. Census Bureau, *Statistical Abstract of the United States: 2004–2005,* 61.
7. David Kupelian, *The Marketing of Evil: How Radicals, Elitists and Pseudo-Experts Sell Us Corruption Designed as Freedom* (Nashville: WND Books, 2005), 187.
8. Ibid.

9. Steven D. Levitt and Stephen J. Dubner, *Freakonomics: A Rogue Economist Explores the Hidden Side of Everything* (New York: Morrow, 2005), 139.

10. Transcript printed on the *Freakonomics* Web site, September 30, 2005, http://www.freakonomics.com/2005/09/bill-bennett-and-freakonomics .html. In November 2005 a search found that this Web page had been removed. The reference could only be found by a search of Bennett's name on the authors' blog section of the Web site, see http://www.freakonomics.com/blog/index.php?s=Bill+Bennett&submit=Search.

11. CNN, "Bennett Under Fire for Remarks on Blacks, Crime," September 30, 2005, http://www.cnn.com/2005/POLITICS/09/30/bennett.comments/.

12. Fox News, "Bill Bennett Explains His Controversial Remarks," September 30, 2005, http://www.foxnews.com/story/0,2933,170880,00.html.

13. *Freakonomics* Web site.

14. William J. Bennett, *The Book of Virtues: A Treasury of Great Moral Stories* (New York: Simon & Schuster, 1993).

15. Larry L. Eastland, "The Empty Cradle Will Rock: How Abortion Is Costing the Democrats Voters—Literally," *Wall Street Journal* Online, June 28, 2004, http://www.opinionjournal.com/extra/?id=110005277.

16. *CDC Data.*

17. Jacob Levenson, *The Secret Epidemic: The Story of AIDS and Black America* (New York: Pantheon Books, 2004), 270.

18. Cathy J. Cohen, Alexandra Bell, and Mosi Ifatunji, "Reclaiming Our Future: The State of AIDS Among Black Youth in America." See Black AIDS Institute, September 2005, 6, http://www.blackaids.org/ShowArticle.aspx? pagename=ShowArticle&articletype=RESOURCE&articleid=139& pagenumber=1.

19. Ibid. The quotation and the next sentence are both drawn from this source.

20. Paige M. Harrison and Allen J. Beck, "Prisons in 2004," U.S. Department of Justice, Bureau of Justice Statistics (BJS), BJS Bulletin NCJ 210677, October 2005, 8, http://www.ojp.usdoj.gov/bjs/pub/pdf/p04.pdf.

21. *CDC Data.*

22. Ibid.

23. Kai Wright, "The Time Is Now! The State of AIDS in Black America," Black AIDS Institute, February 2005, 5–6, http://216.247.26.28/05%20 time%20now%201-1.pdf.

24. Cohen, Bell, and Ifatunji, "Reclaiming Our Future," 7–8.

25. L. M. Bogart and S. Thorburn, "Are HIV/AIDS Conspiracy Beliefs a Barrier to HIV Prevention Among African Americans?" *Journal of Acquired Immune Deficiency Syndromes*, vol. 38, no. 2 (February 2005),

http://www.rand.org/health/feature/hiv/bogart_050125.html. The quotation at the end of the paragraph is drawn from this source.

26. Greg J. Duncan and Saul D. Hoffman, "Teenage Underclass Behavior and Subsequent Poverty: Have the Rules Changed?" in *The Urban Underclass,* ed. Christopher Jenks and Paul E. Peterson (Washington DC: Brookings Institution, 1991), 155. Much of this section follows the logic of this article.

27. Ibid.

28. Charles Murray, "According to Age: Longitudinal Profiles of AFDC Recipients and the Poor by Age Group," Working Seminar on the Family and American Welfare Policy, 1986, cited by ibid., 155.

29. William Julius Wilson, *The Truly Disadvantaged: The Inner City, the Underclass, and Public Policy* (Chicago: University of Chicago Press, 1987), 49.

30. Ibid., 57.

31. Ibid.

## CHAPTER 5: VICTORY IN THE COURTS

1. Justice Antonin Scalia, concurring in part and concurring in the judgment, *Adarand Constructors, Inc. v. Pena,* 515 U.S. 200 (1995).

2. *Brown v. Board of Education,* 347 US 483 (1954).

3. Matthew Richer, "Busing's Boston Massacre," Hoover Institution, *Policy Review,* November–December 1998, http://www.policyreview.org/nov98/busing.html.

4. Ibid.

5. Greg Toppo, "Young Rioter Recalls Seething in Southie," *USA Today,* May 17, 2004, http://www.usatoday.com/life/people/2004–05–16-busing-riots-usat_x.htm.

6. Richer, "Busing's Boston Massacre."

7. *Board of Education of Oklahoma City v. Dowell,* 498 U.S. 237 (1991).

8. Jonathan Kozol, "Still Separate, Still Unequal: America's Educational Apartheid," *Harper's Magazine,* September 1, 2005, http://www.mindfully.org/Reform/2005/American-Apartheid-Education1sep05.htm.

9. Gary Orfield and Chungmei Lee, "*Brown* at 50: King's Dream or *Plessy's* Nightmare?" Harvard Civil Rights Project, January 2004, 21–22, http://www.civilrightsproject.harvard.edu/research/reseg04/brown50.pdf.

10. Thomas Sowell, "Half a Century After Brown: Part II," TownHall.com, May 13, 2004, http://www.townhall.com/opinion/columns/thomassowell/2004/05/13/11677.html.

11. The Web site, entitled "The State of Public School Integration," is part of

the American Communities Project at Brown University, http://www.s4
.brown.edu/schoolsegregation/index.htm.

12. Jerome R. Corsi, *Judicial Politics: An Introduction* (Englewood Cliffs, N.J.:
Prentice-Hall, 1984), 25–28.

13. *University of California Regents v. Bakke,* 438 U.S. 265 (1978).

14. *Richmond v. J. A. Croson Co.,* 488 U.S. 469 (1989).

15. *Grutter v. Bollinger,* 539 U.S. 306 (2003).

16. *Gratz v. Bollinger,* 539 U.S. 244 (2003).

17. Kevin A. Ring, ed., *Scalia Dissents: Writings of the Supreme Court's Wittiest,
Most Outspoken Justice* (Washington DC: Regnery, 2004), 97–102.

18. *Plessy v. Ferguson,* 163 U.S. 537 (1896).

19. Richard H. Sander, "A Systemic Analysis of Affirmative Action in American Law Schools," *Stanford Law Review,* vol. 57 (November 2004):
367–483.

20. Ibid., 426.

21. Ibid., 429.

22. Ibid., 441.

23. Ibid., 445.

24. Ibid., 481–82.

25. David L. Chambers, Richard O. Lempert, and Terry K. Adams, "The Careers of Minority and White Graduates of the University of Michigan Law
School, 1970–1996," published by the University of Michigan Law
School, December 3, 2005, http://www.law.umich.edu/NewsAndInfo/
lawsuit/survey.htm.

26. Ibid.

27. Ibid.

28. See, for instance, Commission on Racial and Ethnic Diversity in the Pro-
fession, "Executive Summary," American Bar Association, http://www
.abanet.org/minorities/publications/milesummary.html.

29. "Ending affirmative action would devastate most minority college admissions," news release, Princeton University, December 3, 2005, http://
www.princeton.edu/main/news/archive/S11/80/78Q19/index.xml?section
=newsreleases.

30. U.S. Department of Housing and Urban Development, *Discrimination in
Metropolitan Housing Markets: National Results from Phase 1, Phase 2, and
Phase 3 of the Housing Discrimination Study (HDS),* http://www.huduser
.org/publications/hsgfin/hds.html

31. Ibid., Phase 1 Final Report, November 2002, Executive Summary, iii–iv.

32. Ibid., Phase 1 Final Report, Section 6, Conclusion, 16.

33. Gregory D. Squires, "Race, Poverty and Homeowner Insurance," *Poverty*

& *Race,* November–December 2002, http://www.prrac.org/full_text.php?
text_id=773&item_id=7802&newsletter_id=65&header=Housing.

34. Jane Manning Thomas, "Race, Racism, and Race Relations: Linkage with
Urban and Regional Planning Literature," Association for Collegiate
Schools of Planning Diversity Committee, American Sociological Association's Response to the White House Request for Race Literature, December
15, 1997, http://www.acsp.org/Documents/Race_LitReview.pdf.

35. *Hills v. Gautreaux,* 425 U.S. 284 (1976).

36. Business and Professional People for the Public Interest (BPI), a public-
interest law and policy center headquartered in Chicago, "What Is
Gautreaux?" on the Public Housing Transformation section of the BPI
Web site, http://www.bpichicago.org/pht/gautreaux.html.

37. David Rusk, "Inclusionary Zoning—Gautreaux by Another Pathway,"
*Poverty & Race,* January–February 2005, http://www.prrac.org/full_text
.php?text_id=1021&item_id=9347&newsletter_id=79&header=Housing.

38. U.S. Commission on Civil Rights, "Findings and Recommendations Over-
view: "Voting Irregularities in Florida During the 2000 Presidential Election," June 2001, http://www.usccr.gov/pubs/vote2000/report/ch9.htm.

39. Letter from Ralph F. Boyd Jr., assistant attorney general, U.S. Department
of Justice, Civil Rights Division, addressed to Senator Patrick Leahy, chair-
man of the Senate Committee on the Judiciary, June 7, 2002, http://www
.gwu.edu/~action/dojf1060702.html.

40. Ibid.

41. Peter Kirsanow, "Florida Forever: The Political Urban Legend That Facts
Won't Kill," *National Review OnLine,* March 9, 2004, http://www.
nationalreview.com/comment/kirsanow200403090858.asp.

42. The Conyers Report on the 2004 Presidential Election, published as *What
Went Wrong in Ohio?* (Chicago: Academy Chicago Publishers, 2005). Also
available on the Internet at http://www.house.gov/judiciary_democrats/
ohiostatusrept1505.pdf.

43. Paul M. Weyrich, "Ken Blackwell: An Extraordinary Individual," February
8, 2005, posted on the Web site of the Free Congress Foundation,
http://www.freecongress.org/commentaries/2005/050208.asp.

44. John Fund, *Stealing Elections: How Voter Fraud Threatens Our Democracy*
(San Francisco: Encounter Books, 2004), 152.

45. Kirsanow quoted in ibid., 29.

46. Susannah Rosenblatt and James Rainey, "Katrina Takes a Toll on Truth,
News Accuracy," *Los Angeles Times,* September 27, 2005, http://www.la-
times.com/news/nationworld/nation/la-na-rumors27sep27,0,5492806,
full.story?coll=la-home-headlines.

47. Mark Tapscott, "When Will Mainstream Media Apologize for Katrina Goofs," TownHall.com, October 15, 2005, http://www.townhall.com/opinion/columns/marktapscott/2005/10/15/171465.html.

48. Dinesh D'Souza, *The End of Racism: Principles for a Multiracial Society* (New York: Free Press, 1995), 24.

49. Ibid., 551.

50. Jesse Lee Peterson with Brad Stetson, *From Rage to Responsibility: Black Conservative Jesse Lee Peterson and America Today* (St. Paul, Minnesota: Paragon House, 2000), 17–18.

51. Stan Faryna, Brad Stetson, and Joseph G. Conti, eds. *Black and Right: The Bold New Voice of Black Conservatives in America* (Westport, CT: Praeger, 1997), xiii.

52. Ibid.

## CHAPTER 6: THE BLACKWELL INITIATIVE

1. "Regional Update: Is Privatization Coming to a Toll Road Near You?" Princeton University, Policy Research Institute, Woodrow Wilson School of Public and International Affairs, http://region.princeton.edu/issue_61 .html.

2. To get a sense of the many different approaches that have been taken to community development over the past decades, see Julia Sass Rubin and Gregory M. Stankiewicz, "Evaluating the Impact of Federal Community Economic Development Policies on Targeted Populations: The Case of the New Markets Initiatives of 2000," July 2003, Federal Reserve System Community Affairs Research Conference, Washington DC, March 27–28, 2003. The article is particularly good at highlighting the tension between the pursuit of economic growth and a more targeted aim to alleviate poverty in the many community economic-development programs launched by the federal government over the past four decades.

3. To appreciate the wide scope of community development investment programs made by bank holding companies and state-chartered banks, see Board of Governors of the Federal Reserve System, *Community Development Investments: Bank Holding Companies and State Member Banks, 2002 Directory* (Washington DC: Federal Reserve Board, 2002).

4. For a description of the Community Reinvestment Act, see Federal Reserve Board, "Community Reinvestment Act," http://www.federalreserve .gov/dcca/cra/.

## CHAPTER 7: STRENGTHENING FAMILIES AND BUILDING WEALTH

1. Quoted in John Herbers, "Moynihan Hopeful U.S. Will Adopt a Policy of Promoting Family Stability," *New York Times*, December 12, 1965, http://www.nytimes.com/books/98/10/04/specials/moynihan-stability.html.
2. Robert Rector, "Understanding Poverty and Economic Inequality in the United States," Backgrounder #1746, September 15, 2004, http://www.heritage.org/Research/Welfare/bg1796.cfm. The analysis and statistics for this section are drawn on this source.
3. Ibid.
4. Here we pay homage to a classic book on the subject: Darrell Huff, *How to Lie with Statistics* (New York: Norton, 1954).
5. Rector, "Understanding Poverty and Economic Inequality in the United States."
6. Ibid.
7. Ibid.
8. Eloise Anderson, "The Great Divide: Why Conservatives Fail to Persuade Blacks," unpublished.
9. Howard Husock, *America's Trillion-Dollar Housing Mistake: The Failure of American Housing Policy* (Chicago: Ivan R. Dee, 2003), 5.
10. Ibid., 23.
11. Ibid., 13.
12. Ibid., 15–16.
13. Ibid., 18.
14. Ibid., 30.
15. Ibid., 96.
16. Alan Maass, "Working Poor in Bush's America," *Socialist Worker OnLine*, June 4, 2002, http://www.socialistworker.org/2004–1/502/502_02_WorkingPoor.shtml.
17. Ibid.
18. Brian W. Jones, "Two Visions of Black Leadership," in *Black and Right: The Bold New Voice of Black Conservatives in America,* ed. Stan Faryna, Brad Stetson, and Joseph G. Conti (Westport, CT: Praeger, 1997), 39.
19. Thomas Sowell, "The 'Working Poor' Scam," *TownHall.com,* June 1, 2004, http://www.townhall.com/opinion/columns/thomassowell/2004/06/01/11875.html.
20. U.S. Census Bureau, *Statistical Abstract of the United States: 2004–2005* (Washington DC: Government Printing Office, 2005), 443. Table 665: "Money, Income of Households—Percent Distribution by Income Level, Race, and Hispanic Origin, in Constant (2002) Dollars: 1980 to 2002."

21. Joseph H. Brown, "The Moral Vacuum in Black America Must Be Filled," in *Black and Right: The Bold New Voice of Black Conservatives in America,* ed. Stan Faryna, Brad Stetson, and Joseph G. Conti (Westport, CT: Praeger, 1997), 95.

22. Diann Ellen Cameron, "The Black Family and Parental Licensure," in *Black and Right: The Bold New Voice of Black Conservatives in America,* ed. Stan Faryna, Brad Stetson, and Joseph G. Conti (Westport, CT: Praeger, 1997), 101.

23. Ibid.

24. George Barna and Harry R. Jackson Jr., *High Impact African-American Churches: Leadership Concepts from Some of Today's Most Effective Churches* (Ventura, CA: Regal Books, 2004), 75.

25. Ibid., 147.

## CHAPTER 8: REVITALIZING THE URBAN LANDSCAPE

1. James F. Sweeney, "Carrying a City's Hope," *Cleveland Plain Dealer,* February 20, 2005, http://www.cleveland.com/chiefs/plaindealer/index.ssf?/chiefs /more/1108906201148550.html.

2. W. Dennis Keating, *The Suburban Racial Dilemma: Housing and Neighborhoods* (Philadelphia: Temple University Press, 1994).

3. Ibid., 77.

4. Ibid., 77–78.

5. Ibid., 81.

6. Ibid., 84.

7. Ibid., 89. See also Louis H. Masotti and Jerome R. Corsi, *Shoot-Out in Cleveland. Black Militants and the Police: July 23, 1968,* National Commission on the Causes and Prevention of Violence (Washington DC: U.S. Government Printing Office, 1969).

8. Keating, *Suburban Racial Dilemma,* 92.

9. Ibid., 95.

10. Thomas Ott and Jesse Tinsley, "Is Annexation the Solution for Troubled E. Cleveland?" *Cleveland Plain Dealer,* September 29, 2003.

11. Douglas S. Massey and Nancy A. Denton. *American Apartheid: Segregation and the Making of the Underclass* (Cambridge, MA: Harvard University Press, 1993).

12. Ibid., 74–78.

13. Ibid., 77.

14. Ibid., 13.

15. Ibid.

16. Ibid., 131–32.
17. Ibid., 146.
18. Ibid., 184.
19. Ibid., 184–85.
20. Jonathan Alter, "King's Final Years," *Newsweek,* January 9, 2006, http://www.msnbc.msn.com/id/10654677/site/newsweek/.
21. Ibid.
22. LISC-Chicago, "Beyond the 'Ivory Tower,'" in *Working Assets: The Newsletter of the Chicago Program of Local Initiatives Support Coalition,* Winter 2005.
23. Jack Kemp, "From Poverty to Prosperity," *TownHall.com,* August 30, 2004, http://www.townhall.com/opinion/columns/jackkemp/2004/08/30/12842.html.

## CONCLUSION: REBUILDING AMERICA

1. John Kenneth Galbraith, *The Affluent Society* (New York: Houghton Mifflin, 1958).
2. Ibid., chap. 22, "The Redress of the Balance," pt. 1.
3. Ibid.
4. Ibid, pt. 3.
5. Ibid, chap. 23, "The New Position of Poverty," pt. 5.

# INDEX